Daily Life SERIES 19

DAILY LIFE OF FRENCH ARTISTS
IN THE NINETEENTH CENTURY

Only the following titles in this series
are available from Praeger Publishers:

DAILY LIFE IN SPAIN IN THE GOLDEN AGE
DAILY LIFE IN JAPAN AT THE TIME OF THE SAMURAI
DAILY LIFE IN VENICE IN THE TIME OF CASANOVA
DAILY LIFE OF FRENCH ARTISTS IN THE 19TH CENTURY

Artists transporting their work to the Salon (*frontispiece*)

JACQUES LETHÈVE

DAILY LIFE OF FRENCH ARTISTS IN THE NINETEENTH CENTURY

Translated by Hilary E. Paddon

PRAEGER PUBLISHERS

New York · Washington

BOOKS THAT MATTER

Published in the United States of America in 1972 by
Praeger Publishers, Inc., 111 Fourth Avenue, New York,
N.Y. 10003

© 1968 by Hachette
Translation © 1972 by George Allen & Unwin Ltd.
Library of Congress Catalog Card Number: 70–134526

Printed in Great Britain

CONTENTS

ILLUSTRATIONS

Source of Illustrations, Bibliothèque Nationale, Paris

INTRODUCTION

It would seem paradoxical to claim that French nineteenth-century artists were not well known. After all, their works are represented in museums the world over and collectors bid against each other at auctions, often fantastic sums, for those remaining in private hands. Not just historians, but novelists and film-makers have retold the lives of Toulouse-Lautrec and Gauguin for the benefit of the public at large.

And yet, apart from such exceptional cases, there is general ignorance of the conditions under which the authors of so many masterpieces lived and worked. For this reason our aim is not to recount unusual anecdotes concerning a handful of geniuses or to describe their special characteristics; it is rather to conjure up a picture of an entire social class, one far bigger than is commonly realized. In 1801 258 artists exhibited at the Salon; in 1831 there were 1,280 and in 1880 3,190. And there were many others who never managed to become accepted at official exhibitions yet made a living from painting or sculpture. The *Bottin* street and trade directory for 1899 names almost 2,500 persons professionally engaged in the fine arts in Paris alone.

What sort of training did these artists have? What opportunities and material difficulties did they encounter, and what contact did they have with the society of their day? These are some of the things we have tried to discover. From our point of view, honest journeyman painters and those who enjoyed success in their day but are now forgotten are as significant as the great masters. We are just as interested in Horace Vernet and Gigoux as in Delacroix or Renoir; and from those who barely scratched a living at least we learn the pitfalls their more fortunate colleagues escaped. It was a highly diverse world in which genius rubbed shoulders with mediocrity. But unfortunately we are unable to discern all aspects of it. If painters appear more often than sculptors it is because we have less information about the latter. As for architects, their careers were subject to contingencies peculiar to them and they make only an occasional appearance. Finally, we have left out the provincial artists and given the lion's share to Paris – too large a share no doubt, but Paris was at the time the goal of the ambitious and the crucible of all the talents.

Henri Focillon commented that the artist in the nineteenth century filled the role which the humanist, the *honnête homme* and the *philosophe* respectively had played in the preceding centuries. In a society undergoing far-reaching changes the artist became very much more than the skilled craftsman that the Ancien Régime had all-too-often reduced him to being. The Romantic movement went further – it made of him one inspired, a prophet; and the nineteenth-century public, dominated as it was by middle-class values, did not know whether to admire or to fear the artist's power of imagination. In the end the artist came to represent an ideal, although it was his life-style rather than his works that was imitated by the aesthetes of the 'nineties.

When we open the doors of the studios we do not often find demigods or princes – most of the artists are quite ordinary men. All, however, share the same high conception of their art in spite of the difference in their talents. And although we cannot hope to discover the secrets of genius and artistic creation, we can at least come to a better understanding of the conditions in which so many works of painting and sculpture were produced, some of which rank today among the finest of any age.

CHAPTER ONE

MASTERS AND APPRENTICES

The 'artist's life' was a mirage which attracted young men and alarmed their families. The young grocer's assistant would dream of this 'hectic, untrammelled, completely idle existence'[1] described by a reporter in 1885. For the average man in the street in the nineteenth century an artist's life was a glorious succession of pleasures and gratification, devoid of moral or physical constraint.

Even the most courageous and most determined to succeed in an artistic career sometimes allowed themselves to be carried away by this dream. Reality was harsher and the road to success and honours harder even for the most gifted. Before the young artist could assert himself in the eyes of others, he had to learn the first principles of a difficult calling, become accepted himself by the established masters, succeed in the competitions and get the better of his many rivals.

The artist's life began on the day when a young man who was determined to become a painter or a sculptor decided to devote the greater part of his time in future to the study of his art and entered the studio of a recognized master. It would often happen, if he was from the provinces, that he found himself in the capital for the first time in his life, obliged to depend on himself for his future. He would be sixteen or eighteen years old, seldom older, and rich only in the letter of recommendation which he carried and in his confidence as an artist.

Who can say how an artistic vocation was born? It might happen that a fancy for successfully catching the likeness of a teacher or fellow pupil, or for sketching and putting down on paper his recollections of a landscape he had seen or of some scene he had witnessed, attracted the attention of the child's family or of one of his teachers. Whether he was congratulated or taken to task he would become aware of his gift and, if he was even moderately successful in his studies, would acquire a feeling of superiority, sooner or later to be encouraged by a drawing master or a friend of the family.

In other cases the ambition to become an artist grew after the young man had seen some masterpiece in a museum or in the house of a patron of the arts. Manet never forgot his Sunday visits to the Louvre with one of his uncles. Delacroix used to claim that it was his obsession with the brilliantly successful details observed in famous paintings, like the orange hood hanging down the back of the servant standing on the left in the *Marriage at Cana*, or the drops of water trickling down over the hips of the water nymphs in the *Arrival of Maria de Medici at Marseilles*, which made him become a painter. Rude was a child in Dijon when he attended the prize-giving at Devosge's drawing school and came away convinced by the speeches he had heard of the importance of the teaching of art. And Carpeaux was only seven when he witnessed in Valenciennes the apotheosis of his cousin, the sculptor Lemaire, who had recently been appointed to the Legion of Honour. Dazzled by it all he decided: 'I want to be a sculptor!'[2]

It was rare for these often precocious childish revelations to be encouraged by the parents. 'As poor as a painter' was a popular saying. Well-to-do families feared the poverty and loss of status signified by the social position of the artist. Manet's parents made him sit the examinations for the Naval College several times; Bazille's only allowed him to take up painting on condition that he did not give up the study of medicine. Corot's father, a wealthy merchant, gave his son a choice: 100,000 francs to set himself up as a draper or an allowance of 2,000 francs if he really wanted to paint; painting won.

To poor families a career in the fine arts seemed too uncertain and not sufficiently serious. And many great artists came from very humble homes: Prud'hon was the son of a stone mason; Rude was the son of a metal worker; Millet was a peasant's son and Renoir the son of a tailor. Few indeed were the young men who were encouraged by their families to follow the arts: for every Detaille or Albert Besnard, who had the good fortune, there were many who met with suspicion if not downright disapproval. It is hardly surprising if they in turn developed a certain hostility both towards the family and towards society as a whole.

Yet society, provincial society in particular, did not always prove ungrateful to the youngster who showed promise. Local authorities were often more open-minded as regards artistic matters than one might have expected: 'One local council I could name sends a budding Raphael or Michelangelo to Paris every year.'[3] A gifted young man, star pupil at one of the many art schools or schools of drawing (France under Louis-Philippe had fifty-five) might leave for the capital with the first month's instalment of his allowance in his pocket – an allowance he would continue to receive for three or four years as long as he remembered to send one of his early works to the museum in the capital city of the department or to one of the chapels of the cathedral.

The department of Maine-et-Loire gave Maindron a scholarship of 500 francs a year to become a sculptor; Chapu received 200 francs a year from Seine-et-Loire, a sum which increased to 1,000 francs the year he won the Prix de Rome. Baudry had 400 francs from the department of La Vendée and a few years later this sum too was increased to 1,200 francs.

David d'Angers, however, had only forty francs in his pocket when he left his home town, and these were a loan from his drawing master. But he set out for Paris with a self-confidence which made him say: 'In three years' time I shall have won the Prix de Rome!'[4] He was as good as his word.

The young artist sometimes arrived on foot. More often he stepped down from the stage coach or, during the second half of the century, from the train. And he hastened to enter the studio of the master to whom he had been recommended. If he had no letter of recommendation he could still show examples of his work. Except for the very rare artist who was self-taught, they all began their training in this way. Attendance at the studio of one of the masters was the only way to prepare for the various competitions of the Ecole des Beaux-Arts: a difficult road which led to the famous Prix de Rome, gateway to glory. And though the beginner could not be unaware that other artists had succeeded in making names for themselves without following the traditional academic path, before the end of the nineteenth century very few of them attempted to dispense with the prestige attaching to the official institutions at the outset of their careers.

What primitive tribes would have recognized as initiation rites were practised in most schools and studios, and these ceremonies – which might be either futile 'rags' or an essential part of the training – were consistently imposed on newcomers to the world of the fine arts. Most artists retained very vivid memories of their entry into the studio where they began their career and would recount the reception accorded the newcomer with a wealth of detail in which one may detect indulgence towards youthful memories embellished in maturity. Most of these rags were in very poor taste and great indulgence would be needed to find them amusing.

In each case the reception facing the newcomer followed a basic pattern, with such variations as the imagination of the *massier*, the senior student in charge in the studio and the ringleader, might suggest. One of the traditional 'ordeals' was a speech described in a caricature of 1843.

'The newcomer shall recount the history of his life and the circumstances which decided him to follow a career in the fine arts; then, in a less elevated style, he shall tell the story of his earliest love affairs.'[5]

Another compulsory ordeal was one liable to offend the modesty of the novice. Stark naked, he was obliged to sing some sort of song, to perform successfully various balancing exercises, and to endure jibes of all kinds from his fellows with as good a grace as he could manage. If they considered him badly built or too clumsy he would be daubed with Prussian blue on different parts of the body. Sometimes the *massier* would pretend to be the master of the studio, the better to test the new student, and would get him into embarrassing situations. When the caricaturist Cham was *massier* of Delaroche's studio he was considered a dab-hand at these farcical interrogations. He crushed a newcomer who admitted eating sardines in oil with the remark: 'In oil! Unhappy boy, fish oil never dries: there's nothing worse for painting!'[6]

Unlucky the newcomer whose timidity or over-confidence annoyed his fellows. The jokes could turn into brutal ragging; the most common procedure was to hang the victim upside down from the rungs of a ladder for several hours. Those living near the Ecole des Beaux-Arts often rescued young men who had been abandoned in this position against a wall. It sometimes happened that these ordeals ended in broken limbs. A still more tragic case occurred in 1843 when a novice who was overcome by fear died during the night of a heart attack. It is easy to understand why Ingres should have forbidden ragging in his studio, but it required all his exceptional authority to interrupt a tradition which still continues.

Joining a studio also represented a charge on the newcomer's purse; the custom of standing his seniors a drink can be taken for granted, but he also had to pay a sum of from fifteen to twenty-five francs which was called *la bienvenue* (the welcome). Nor did the expense end there: every month in a painter's studio he had to contribute twelve to twenty-five francs to the common fund or *masse* (sculptors paid a little less). This was the money used to pay the teachers and models and to cover minor expenses like the soft soap used to wash the brushes. It sometimes seemed a lot to a beginner and the case of Granet is often cited; Granet had to leave David's studio after a few months becase he was unable to keep up his regular contributions to the *masse*.

The *massier* was in charge of the studio finances (i.e. of the *masse*) and enjoyed considerable authority. He was chosen from among the most popular seniors and was usually a gay and dynamic personality. He acted as his comrades' spokesman in their dealings with the master while at the same time enjoying the latter's confidence. He kept the register of models, organized the studio entertainments, checked the materials used, and saw to it that broken windows were paid for.

Until another novice appeared to replace him, the newcomer occupied the most junior position in the hierarchy, that of *rapin*. The origins of this expression are obscure; it came into general use during the first three decades of the century and by extension was applied to all budding artists and finally to all unsuccessful artists. But its principal meaning was to describe the newcomer to the studio and the tasks he performed. The *rapin* was a sort of studio servant. He had to arrive early to air the room in summer and light the stove in winter – which meant being there before six in the summer and before eight when the days grew shorter. He was supposed to keep the place clean, fill the water-jugs, grind the colours; and occasionally run errands for his comrades who sent him out with letters or to buy bread or tobacco.

The studio was a large rectangular room with a much higher ceiling than an ordinary room. It was lit by a row of high windows along one side or else by a skylight which let in the cold northern light; the sun had to be kept out to prevent reflections and patches of sunlight. In the summer a light awning might be hung across the glass as protection against the heat.

There would be a few plaster casts of busts and bas-reliefs collecting dust on the bare walls. But sometimes these would be hung with canvases, abandoned sketches for pictures which were never painted or copies by the master or his pupils. There would be scribbled messages in chalk or charcoal on the walls, reminders of dates to be remembered or purchases to be made, or the addresses of models or dealers, perhaps a rapid sketch caricaturing one of the students or a member of the Institut des Beaux-Arts and, pretty well everywhere, palette scrapings and crude daubings. New canvases stacked facing the wall displaying the dealer's name on the stretcher in large black letters and various accessories jumbled alongside: vases, weapons, clothes or wigs.

The activity of the studio took place in the centre of the room in the free space where the light was best. Right in the middle, or possibly against one of the walls, was a platform for the models. The model, who might be either a man or a woman, was usually naked, but might perhaps be draped and would be seated on a stool or reclining on a divan, unless he or she was standing in a fixed pose, when ropes from the ceiling or a bar along the wall, or heel rests for supporting the foot which was not resting on the ground, would be used to help the model keep the pose.

The students sat with their drawing boards resting on their knees or else worked standing up at their easels. However, they drew more often than they painted, using grease crayons, the lead pencil invented by Conté in 1795, charcoal or chalk. And as they judged the proportions of the model through half-closed eyes, carefully stumped in the half-tones, made erasures, indicated shadows by hatching or cross-hatching, and whether they did these things quickly or slowly, confidently or hesitantly according to the dictates of skill or temperament, they repeated gestures unchanged since men have known how to draw. Yet it is doubtful whether any age has taken such pains to trace the exact outlines, to so model the contours, to obtain shadows falling with such mechanical precision.

The newcomers found themselves banished to dark corners where the model could only be seen from an awkward angle and with their comrades obstructing the view. They envied their seniors who occupied the best places. In some studios places were allocated weekly or monthly according to position in class; at Louis David's studio lots were drawn at the beginning of each week.

These youngsters were boisterous and ripe for any mischief. Sometimes a student would relax for a while and entertain the others by playing the guitar. Some serious-minded groups organized poetry readings, and in this way romantic literature captured the imagination of the young. Some teachers – Chapu was one – had works on aesthetics read aloud, or the sayings of great artists. All too often, though, the students would burst into song, stupid choruses as a rule and usually obscene. These sessions would often end in uproar and the studio furniture rarely escaped undamaged.

Artists' memories of the time spent in these studios are contradictory. There are those who appear to have experienced a serene, studious atmosphere surrounded by youthful geniuses who thought only of their ideals. Others, on the contrary, stress the futile conversations and the coarse manners. Willette goes so far as to describe his fellow students at Cabanel's studio round 1875 as riff-raff of the worst type, bullying their younger comrades and raiding the *masse* to pay for their drinking. Raffaëlli, who studied at Gérôme's studio a little later in the century, has left this grim description of it: 'Not once in this gathering of men called to be artists did I hear art discussed or any serious ideas. Nothing but crude and stupid joking all the time, nothing but filth.[7]

There was a complete change when the teacher appeared. But although the master, the 'patron', directed the teaching, he only really came into contact with his pupils once or twice a week. Those who came every day, like Rude, were few. The teacher's visit was a crucial moment in the life of the studio; everybody concentrated and the hubbub subsided. The students, who were concerned about a judgment which could be decisive for the future of their work, behaved deferentially towards the master. So it was bad luck when a bucket of water placed above a door fell over Guérin as he entered his studio; the water had been intended for one of Géricault's comrades, but Géricault was dismissed.

The nature of the corrections to the pupils' work and the way they were done varied from one teacher to the other. Some – Delaroche was one – liked to raise their voices so that the community as a whole could profit from remarks addressed to individuals; others, like Gleyre, preferred on the contrary to make any necessary comments as discreetly as possible. Jules Lefebvre used to put on working clothes when he arrived at the studio, the better to become part of it, whereas Gustave Moreau used to keep his gloves on to avoid the temptation to retouch the work before him. One of

Girodet's pupils has left us a sketch of the master correcting pupils' work: he wears a top hat and carries a walking stick.[8] Ingres, on the other hand, never hesitated to intervene. Balze tells us: 'He used to correct our drawings with his thumbnail, so surely and with such force that he often cut right through the paper, thus combining theory and practice.'[9]

Ingres was considered merciless: there was only one way to see things, and that was his way. More than one gifted but independent student was discouraged by a teacher of this type. Gentle Odilon Redon was a rebel in the eyes of Gérôme: 'He so obviously tried to inculcate in me his own way of seeing and either to make me his disciple or disgust me with art altogether.'[10]

It was unusual for a successful artist of repute not to think of taking pupils; he sought nothing better than to pass on the principles of his art and the tricks of the trade that had been handed down to him by a distinguished master.

Traditional apprenticeship, still used for training craftsmen, was becoming rarer in the nineteenth century. Chapu had learnt sculpture in this way in Pradier's studio, getting his work ready for him and receiving useful advice at the same time. But he ran into difficulties when he tried this method himself; in 1887 he complained to a friend that pupils at the Ecole des Beaux-Arts who had come to him for training were 'too much the fine gentlemen to stoop to the lowly tasks of a studio'.[11] Delacroix had apprentices about him after 1838, but he was mainly concerned to train the assistants who were essential to him in carrying out his great decorative works.

Artists who opened a separate teaching studio away from their place of work often did so to replace an ageing colleague or at the request of young admirers. At the end of 1843 Gleyre took over the studio of Delaroche – Delaroche himself had succeeded Gros and Gros had replaced David – and we see here the line of succession in a very famous studio which had once had the good fortune to be lodged within the walls of the Louvre itself.

Gleyre hesitated, however, and yielded only to the entreaties of his young followers; in twenty-seven years he was to see between five and six hundred painters pass through his hands and was to train not only pupils following in the purest academic tradition but also 'independents' like Bazille, Sisley, Renoir and Monet. In the same way Ingres agreed to the request of a group headed by

Amaury-Duval, whose father, an official in the administration of the Ecole des Beaux-Arts, had done him some service. The pupils of David d'Angers, who was constantly away travelling, asked Rude to be their teacher when David finally abandoned them.[12]

It was the success of a single picture that caused Couture to be sought after as a teacher. His *Romans of the Decadence* was the sensation of the Salon of 1847. Couture, who had a very high opinion of himself, published a small book, *Méthode et entretiens d'atelier*, in which he summarized his own highly debatable principles of art. Yet both Puvis de Chavannes and Manet, among others, passed through his studio. And Manet, who was a rebellious student, spent eight or nine years with Couture, in spite of the fact that the latter once told him it was better to leave a master if one did not agree with his teaching. The models were often put out by young Manet's comments when he criticized their lack of naturalness, and one day Dubosc, who was by way of being a celebrity among models, took exception to his remarks:

‘ "Monsieur Manet," he said, "Monsieur Delaroche never had anything but praise for me, and it's hard to be misunderstood by a young man like you."

‘ "I'm not asking you Monsieur Delaroche's opinion, I'm giving you mine."

‘ "Monsieur Manet," said Dubosc in a slow voice choked with emotion, "many a one has gone to Rome thanks to me."

‘ "We're not in Rome and don't want to go there. We're in Paris, so let's stay here." ’[13]

It is hardly surprising that when Manet himself was achieving hard-won and increasing fame he refused to teach. Yet he was asked to do so by the students of Lehmann, who was in charge of a studio at the Ecole des Beaux-Arts from 1873 inwards. Lehmann's students used to sing, in protest against his sterile authoritarianism:[14]

> *'Courbet, Manet, tous ceux qu'ont du génie*
> *N'ont pas la croix, ça dégoute de la vie. . . .'**

Painters of lesser importance often proved excellent teachers. It is very striking how many of the heads of the most important studios towards the end of the century were artists whose work is today

* Those who like Courbet and Manet have genius do not have the cross of the Legion of Honour – it's enough to disgust you with life.

considered mediocre; yet their influence was beneficial where they were able to show an understanding of original talent. For thirty-nine years Gérôme imposed the same concept of style on all his pupils; but Cormon, who specialized in laboriously-composed scenes from prehistory, was able to encourage the development of Toulouse-Lautrec, Anquetin and Emile Bernard, and we know that in 1886 he was prepared to accept Vincent van Gogh in his studio when the latter was still no more than an odd Dutchman of thirty-three who had just arrived in Paris.

Gustave Moreau, who painted *Salome* and *Oedipus and the Sphinx*, was still more unusual. His own works were wrapped in a complex symbolism, but he knew how to arouse artistic vocations and he regarded as a sacred trust his responsibilities towards the young artists who had asked for his appointment to the Ecole des Beaux-Arts in 1892 in place of Delaunay. He spend more than two hours with his pupils in the studio, went to the Louvre to meet the students he had sent there to make copies, and invited some of them back with him. Moreau was an excellent teacher and those he taught included men who followed paths as different as those of Matisse, Rouault and Marquet.[15]

The young artist did not have to begin from scratch when he entered the studio of a master. He had already shown what he could do and had produced work by which he could be judged. He was no longer at an elementary stage of the drawing school, learning to trace eyes and mouths and noses carefully. But there could be no question of allowing him to paint until he was completely sure of his draughtsmanship. One of Ingres' pupils, Balze, has described how the master proceeded with a newcomer:

'Monsieur Ingres would set the young man *au cadre*, that is among the prints or drawings after old masters that he was to copy – usually works after Raphael, for whom Ingres professed the deepest admiration, and the new arrival would often spend five or six months in this way before he was allowed to progress to working from reliefs.'[16]

In Girodet's studio it was Aubry-Lecomte's lithographs of the master's own works which the students had to copy.[17]

Whatever branch of painting the student eventually adopted, his training consisted of learning to represent the human face and the human body. He studied them from engravings (drawing 'from the flat') from plaster casts (drawing 'from the cast') and finally from the living model. He began by copying over and over again from collections of model drawings, those sets of crayon engravings (a technique giving an effect similar to that of a chalk drawing) published by Lebarbier which became popular at the end of the eighteenth century. Books such as these, with their insipid easy-to-copy style, became still more widely used after the invention of lithography in the nineteenth century. One of Gros's pupils, Bernard Julien, made a living after 1840 by issuing numerous collections of this kind: *Etudes académiques, Fantaisies par divers artistes,* and so on, all of them so many variations on the idea of fragments from famous pictures. One even finds in the studios collections called *Cours progressifs de paysage,* intended to teach the students how to draw groups of trees, rustic gates and bridges over streams.[18]

The student then reached the next stage when he was promoted to drawing from the round: he practised from casts, architectural motifs, busts, bas-reliefs, and finally from statues after the antique, like *The Dying Gladiator* or *Laocoon.* For moral and aesthetic reasons the antique alone was considered noble, and the artist was supposed to try to imitate the idealizations of the great masters he was copying. At the same time, to improve his knowledge he was referred to Pierre Chompré's classic work *Dictionnaire abrégé de la fable pour l'intelligence des poètes et la connoissance des tableaux et des statues dont les sujets sont tirés de la fable.* First published in 1727, this book had reached its twenty-eighth edition by 1855 and continued to be republished until the end of the century. It was a mine of allegorical and mythological information which not only helped in understanding classic works of art but also nourished the inspiration of those who sought to imitate them.

And while awaiting the still distant day when he could allow his inspiration free rein, the good student acquired knowledge of a set of techniques and conventions from which all personal feeling was banished. In addition, the concept of the work of art in its entirety was lost in a welter of detail. As Charles Blanc said: 'They taught us how to finish our paintings before we learned how to construct them.'[19]

It was just the same when the student progressed to the next stage, the study of the living model, which was held to be the alpha and omega of the artist's training. The nude model had to be made to conform to the standards of antiquity which nature herself could seldom match. And woe betide those who tried to paint what they saw! Monet has left us this account of how Gleyre used to reproach him:

> 'You've a dumpy little man there, and that's how you've gone and painted him! He's got big feet, so you give him big feet! It's very ugly all that sort of thing. Just remember this, young man: when you do a figure study, always have the antique in mind.'[20]

We know already about Manet's disputes with the models, and this is how he complained in Couture's studio:

> 'I don't know why I come here; everything that meets the eye is ridiculous. The light is wrong, the shadows are wrong. When I arrive here I feel as if I were entering a tomb. I am perfectly aware you can't undress a model in the street. But there's always the country; in summer at least one could do studies from life in the fields, since the nude it seems is the beginning and end of art.'[21]

The primary importance of drawing was another dogma of this type of instruction. Ingres claimed: 'Drawing is seven-eighths of painting.' Here, we certainly find an indirect echo of the polemics which raged between Delacroix and the painter of the *Apotheosis of Homer*. But colour was long considered – it is not quite clear why – as being somehow revolutionary. Gleyre too warned his pupils: 'Beware of that demon colour, it will go to your heads.'[22]

However, one had to come to it in the end and learn how to cover the canvas. But for those who upheld the traditions of David and Ingres the tints must be sober; certain colours, among them emerald green, Indian yellow and Smyrna lake, were regarded as suspect. Later the excessive use of bitumen, which drowned the colours, was mistakenly advised. Once again, in order to learn to paint, the exercise most advised was copying the masters. But at this stage reproductions were not enough: it was necessary to work from the originals, and this is why we shall be finding so many artists working at their easels in the galleries of the Louvre, each armed with a permit and a letter from his teacher.

This kind of teaching, which was set in its ways and dominated by the servile copying of existing works, acted as a brake on the development of the personality. Had it not been for the shock-stimulus supplied by a few independent artists it might have been forgotten that, in the words of Leonardo da Vinci, painting was *cosa mentale*, and that only when the mind revealed itself and came into play could art be said to have begun. Today we are more aware of the contribution made to traditional art teaching by a few original minds; it was they, far more than their colleagues, who contributed to the development of French art.

Lecoq de Boisbaudran was a humble man, but his pupils were very ready to express their gratitude to him. He was first a teacher at, and then from 1841 to 1869 director of what was known as the '*petite école*', the Ecole Royale de Dessin et de Mathématiques, founded during the reign of Louis XV to train craftsmen and especially designers of ornaments. Lecoq was to make the institution famous. It might have seemed no different from others scattered throughout the capital whose students seldom became anything more than amateurs or rose above the level of utilitarian drawing, but for artists like Régamey, Fantin-Latour, Alphonse Legros, Carpeaux, Dalou and Rodin, who emerged from its upper school. The basis of Lecoq de Boisbaudran's method consisted in drawing from memory instead of copying directly from models. His pupils acquired great facility of expression and more character in their rendering of form and colour.[23]

Courbet also attempted an orginal sort of teaching, though it proved a short-lived experiment. He only undertook to direct a teaching studio after much hesitation, as he was anxious for everyone to enjoy complete freedom. In his desire for realism he extended the choice of models to include animals as well as people; and horses, oxen and deer could be seen at his premises at 83 rue Notre-Dame-des-Champs. It does not seem to have occurred to Courbet that it might have been more 'realistic' to go and study these animals in their natural surroundings. The studio opened in December 1861; on February 2, 1862, the landlord asked for the lease to be terminated on account of the damage sustained by the property. Courbet took no more pupils.[24]

Another way of respecting the personality of the future artist was to allow him to practise on his own, without criticism or compulsion – something very well understood by a former model of David's. When the Bourbon monarchy was restored in 1815 Suisse, as he was called, collected together a group of models, both men and

25

women, and let students work from them away from the supervision of their teachers for seven (and later ten) francs a month. His premises were in the Quai des Orfevres on the corner of the Boulevard du Palais, and many of the most famous artists of the nineteenth century attended, among them Ingres, Préault, Courbet, Manet and Cézanne. The names in themselves are enough to indicate the part played by the Académie Suisse in the training of artists, even if it only offered supplementary training.[25]

There is yet another nursery of art which needs to be mentioned both because of the great number of painters who passed through it and also because it was run on original lines. Julian's studio, also known as the Académie Julian, prepared students for the Ecole des Beaux-Arts as other studios did; but some aspiring artists found a substitute for official instruction in the greater flexibility of the teaching. Rodolphe Julian was only a mediocre painter himself, but he was astute enough to have had the idea of providing potential candidates for the Ecole des Beaux-Arts – and also those who had already tried and been rejected – with a place where they could work freely without restriction. In spite of a difficult start in an old dance hall in the passage des Panoramas, the early members of the Académie Julian were to proclaim its advantages and to bring in others. One of the main advantages was that the studio was open every day of the week except Sunday from eight o'clock in the morning to nightfall, whereas the other studios, including those in the Ecole des Beaux-Arts itself, were closed in the afternoon. Another advantage was that students were accepted at any age and prize-winners who already had places at the Beaux-Arts often came back again.

Julian was not able to undertake all the teaching himself, but he was able to attract well-known artists, even members of the Academy. Names like Gustave Boulenger, Bouguereau, Chapu, Flameng and Carrier-Belleuse rule out any idea of a break with academic tradition. Indeed, by the end of the century the Académie Julian was accused of promoting a sort of Mafia: the teachers and some of their students would back each other in the elections to the jury of the Salon and in the distribution of prizes.

By 1889 Julian had some 600 students and needed to open further studios: three of them in the rue de Berri were for women only. The principal studio for men was in the rue Saint-Denis until a new one was opened on the left bank in the rue du Dragon. Paul

Sérusier was *massier* at the former for a while; he was there when he met Gauguin and told his younger comrades, Maurice Denis, Bonnard and Vuillard, about the ideas of the man from Pont-Aven.

The Nabis were not the only group to be formed at the Académie Julian. There was no obligation to enter the monthly competitions or to attend when the teachers made their rounds and corrected pupils' work; only to contribute to the *masse*. A young man of independent outlook would derive more profit from the advice of a comrade whose ideas he shared and would be quite ready to turn his canvas to the wall when the teacher came along and this kind of impertinence was quite generally accepted. So it was that an atmosphere of freedom was born which found echoes as far away as London and Munich. Foreigners like George Moore, Lovis Corinth, William Rothenstein, whom discriminatory measures excluded from the Ecole des Beaux-Arts, came straight to the Académie Julian to enroll. They brought with them a breath of fresh air and took back to their own countries a knowledge of French art.[26]

However debatable its teaching of the fine arts might have been from some points of view, it was Paris that artists the world over dreamed of visiting to gather up the fruits of a tried-and-tested tradition and at the same time to experience a spirit of free creativity.

CHAPTER TWO

FROM THE ECOLE DES BEAUX-ARTS
TO THE VILLA MEDICI

What a young artist most wanted when he joined a studio was to develop his natural gifts and to learn the first principles of his art. But however little a conformist he might be, he could hardly be unaware that he must also lay the foundation for his career: how could he become known, when would he be accepted by the Salon, who would get him commissions from art lovers?

He needed the support of an influential patron and still more perhaps to acquire qualifications which retained their prestige in the eyes of the public. To graduate from the Ecole des Beaux-Arts, to win the Prix de Rome: these were trump cards which no assertions of original talent could replace. It is easy to understand why, apart from a few self-taught artists and a few others of particularly independent character who were to become more numerous towards the end of the century, everyone dreamt of starting out on the royal road to success by entering the Ecole des Beaux-Arts.

Throughout the greater part of the century it was not particularly difficult to enter the Ecole; it was enough to have achieved some success at any well-known studio and the recommendation of a generally respected master – if he was also a member of the Institut all the better—sufficed to open all doors. Once he had enrolled the young artist was allowed to work at the Ecole des Beaux-Arts and to profit from the teachers' correction of his work, but he was not entitled officially to call himself a student of the Ecole until he had won a medal in the series of competitions open to him. It was only in 1883 that a proper entrance examination, consisting of two sets of papers, one practical and one theoretical, was instituted.

The obligation to take part in competitions was the main one imposed by the Ecole. Some of these had originated back in the eighteenth century and their effect was to keep the students in a state of permanent rivalry. Among the subjects taken were figure drawing, figures modelled after the antique and from life, studies of heads, and historical composition. Most of these competitions were compulsory and they formed a long series of rungs to be scaled before the summit, the famous Prix de Rome, was reached, success in the earlier stages giving partial exemption from the preliminary examinations for the Prix de Rome itself.

For the rest there was complete freedom; the students were allowed to paint or sculpt from the model for two hours a day under the nominal guidance of the teachers. Until 1863 these were chosen by the Institut des Beaux-Arts from among its own members, but each of the twelve chosen was only responsible for the teaching for one month, so that even though the academic tradition was the only one recognized or taught the continual change of teachers meant that there could be no real continuity.

In 1863 there was a great to-do about the reform of the Ecole des Beaux-Arts which had been decided by Imperial decree without consultation with the Institut, and the Institut protested against this slight to its prestige. One of the merits of the reform was, however, to set up a fixed number of studios headed by a single teacher. But the teachers, though appointed by the Minister, continued to be chosen from among the ranks of the Academicians and the change therefore affected the structure of the teaching rather than its spirit. Henceforth there were to be three studios for painting – Gérôme remained at the head of one of them for thirty-nine years until 1903 – and three for sculpture, plus two additional studios, one for copper-plate engraving and the other for engraving on semi-precious stones, another innovation. A compulsory syllabus comprising anatomy, perspective, history of art, archaeology and aesthetics replaced a few vague theoretical classes. The nomination of a Director completed this reorganization, but for another twenty years the teachers themselves retained control of the admission of students, even allowing some students to attend free on their own initiative. The anarchic state of affairs prevailing at the Ecole des Beaux-Arts was in fact the result of an awkward compromise between the traditions inherited from the Ancien Régime and the attempt to break with this official concept of art. From the beginning, teaching had been one of the functions of the former Académies (Lebrun had founded the earlier academy for painting and sculpture and that for Architecture dated from 1694). By suppressing them the Revolution would have broken the tradition whereby the masters passed on their

29

experience to younger men; but fortunately a few devoted artists had been prepared to carry on under difficult conditions. After the Institut des Beaux-Arts was founded in 1793 and the Académies were reorganized to form part of it, it seemed only natural for the Institut to undertake the official teaching of art. It was this privilege that was questioned and came under attack from the reform of 1863. But the Académie des Beaux-Arts retained control of the Prix de Rome and the Académie de France at Rome; therefore decisions concerning the richest prizes remained in its power. And since recruitment to the Institut des Beaux-Arts was by co-option, thus ensuring a continuity of ideas, it is easy to understand how the Institut managed to keep official art teaching on the straight and narrow path – or, as a few innovators would have it, in a rut.[1]

The studios of the earlier Académie were in the Louvre itself; when they had to leave, in 1807, they moved to the other side of the Seine and joined the Institut des Beaux-Arts in the former Collège des Quatre-Nations where until 1830 they occupied a number of uncomfortable rooms, two of which had been given up by the sculptor Houdon, who made the 'sacrifice for the fatherland'.[2]

The transfer of the Ecole des Beaux-Arts to the former Augustinian convent had been envisaged ever since 1816, but the conversion of the buildings to their new purpose took some forty years. The architects for the new building were first Debret, then Duban, and its design was quite unusual. Not only did what was left of the old convent have to be incorporated into buildings intended for teaching, administration and exhibitions, but a number of 'relics' saved from destruction by the Revolutionaries and placed within the convent walls through the zeal of Alexandre Lenoir, had also to be accommodated; they included such large fragments as the portico of the Château d'Anet and the Arc de Gaillon. Another building was erected in 1858 on the Quai Malaquais and the seventeenth-century Hôtel de Chimay was incorporated in 1884, making the appearance of the whole still more incongruous.

The great central hall, the *palais des études*, used for lectures and ceremonial occasions, became known as the Salle de l'Hémicycle, and famous for the long fresco by Paul Delaroche, which when newly completed was considered one of the greatest achievements in painting of all time. More useful from the teaching point of view were the reproductions, copies and casts of great masterpieces:

architectural fragments and famous statues, usually taken from antiquity, rubbed shoulders with copies of paintings by former pupils of the Ecole des Beaux-Arts. The convent chapel received Michelangelo's *Last Judgement*, copied from the Sistine Chapel by Sigalon in 1883. The hall next to it, the so-called Salle Melpomène, was crammed with a bewildering variety of copies of works of art of every epoch – a strange sight to greet the newcomer. The dusty plaster casts gave a very poor idea of what Greek marbles were like and the paintings which had been copied by skilful apprentices without the spark of genius were still further removed from the originals. Those who did not have the good luck to discover the authentic works of art in the course of their travels must have acquired a completely false conception of them.

The general atmosphere of the Ecole des Beaux-Arts thus encouraged academic copying and eclecticism, both of which the nineteenth-century artists long held in honour, but it must be acknowledged that they found the atmosphere to their taste and contemporary artists frequently praised its charm.[3] The reform of 1863, however, brought about changes. For example, new studios not included in the original plan had to be created. This was done by partitioning off disused exhibition galleries. But sound travelled from one room to another so much that when a teacher paid a visit to one of the studios the students there had to warn their comrades in adjoining studios to make less noise. The conversion of the Hôtel de Chimay in 1890 provided studios of this sort with better working conditions.

The many competitions that were held, including the supreme contest each year to select the award-winners of the Prix de Rome, took place in a separate wing divided into a number of small rooms to the left of the central courtyard, the *bâtiment des loges*.[4]

In theory, any Frenchman aged over fifteen and under thirty was eligible to sit the examination for the Prix de Rome, without having to be a student of the Ecole des Beaux-Arts. But preliminary trials from which medal-winners at the Ecole were partially exempt reduced the number of candidates where painting was concerned to twenty, then to ten, and those for sculpture and architecture to eight each. These competitions required the candidates to produce a sketch within a single day. The final test, the competition for the Prix de Rome itself, called for greater stamina: the competitors had two months in which to produce a finished work, the painters a size 80 canvas, i.e. 1·5 m × 1·2 m, the sculptors either a bas-relief 1·55 m × 1·15 m or else a free-standing figure one metre high and in proportion.

The theme, chosen by members of the Institut des Beaux-Arts, was drawn by lot on the morning of the examination itself to prevent any leaks occurring. A member of the Académie nominated by his colleagues, or sometimes the Secretary of the Ecole, would read it out to the candidates on the steps of the *bâtiment des loges*; he was heard in silence, followed by uproar as the young men rushed upstairs to take possession of their cells.

The gentlemen of the Institut took subjects from ancient history or from the Bible, selecting episodes capable of suggesting dramatic scenes. The future holders of the Prix de Rome were asked to imagine the return of young Tobias, the meeting of Ulysses and Nausicaa, or Saint Peter curing a lame man. They needed to be sufficiently well acquainted with the great figures of antiquity to be able to illustrate from imagination alone one of those conventional scenes which were nevertheless rich in erudite allusions and were held to be the quintessence of great art

Candidates had thirty-six hours in which to prepare a detailed sketch, indicating the main lines of the composition with sufficient clarity so that nothing could be changed in the final painting. A tracing of this sketch was placed in a sealed portfolio and did not see light of day again until the judging, when the sketch was compared with the completed work. For the competitor was not supposed to modify his original inspiration under the influence of advice or models from outside. The system stressed the construction of the work and the choice of protagonists, as the candidate's inspiration had to settle these from the very beginning and he was quite unable to alter anything.

During these thirty-six hours he lived the life of a prisoner. He ate nothing at all or else had his meals brought in from a cheap restaurant by one of the attendants or supplied by the owner of a neighbouring wine-shop. He slept in his cell on an old mattress or in an armchair. He was allowed out for fresh air in the courtyard only twice a day, was not permitted to communicate with anyone whatsoever, and was watched all the time by the attendants.

Once the sketches had been handed over, seventy days were left for the final work. During these two months the regime was naturally

1   The Bonnat studio at the Ecole de Beaux-Arts

2   Advice from the master

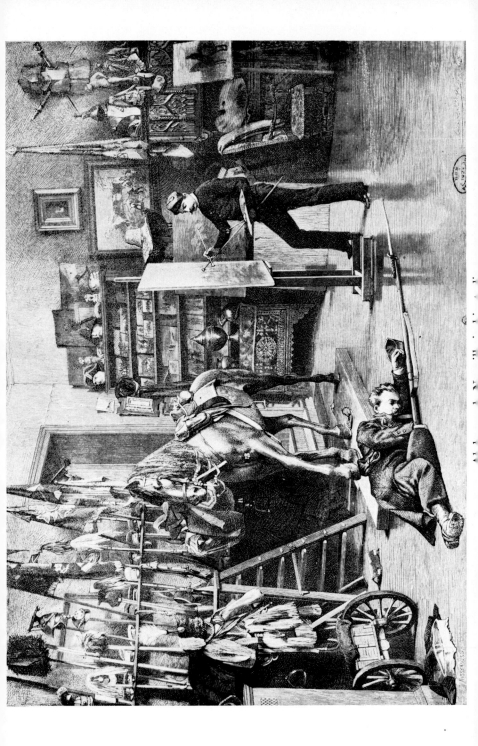

much freer. The competitors were no longer obliged to sleep on the premises and could come and go as they pleased. But no one except the Director and Inspector of the Ecole and the official models, both men and women, was allowed to go into the cells – and this included other competitors. Nor was it permitted to bring in models, tracings, drawings or engravings from outside; photographs were added to the list of prohibited articles at the end of the century. The candidate had the right to seek verification for his inspiration from outside, but not to bring back any document.

Excitement mounted as the final weeks of the contest approached. Friends laid bets on the winners on the basis of the news which filtered through. Towards the end of the last day (the *salopage*, as it was called) the doors were flung wide open and the competitors were allowed to visit each other, their hopes rising or their discouragement increasing at the sight of their neighbours' work. At six o'clock the cells were finally abandoned and the doors were sealed by a member of the jury.

There followed a period of purgatory for the competitors, seemingly interminable. Then the pictures were varnished and exhibited in public for three days, and judgment was given. Whereas the other competitions were the concern of the painting or the sculpture sections of the Académie, as the case might be, the Prix de Rome was awarded by the entire Académie des Beaux-Arts; consequently architects were judging painters and sculptors were judging architects, and even the musicians had their voice in the ballot.

The official announcement of the results took place in the great central hall, the Salle de l'Hémicycle, and each major prize-winner, 'a pupil of Monsieur X', was warmly congratulated and applauded. All that was left for the winners to do was to celebrate their success, often at a dinner to which their teachers were invited, and await their departure for the Eternal City, dreaming the while of the glory which henceforth could not fail to smile upon them.

And yet, how often was the Prix de Rome held by artists whose importance posterity has had no hesitation in recognizing? So many names little known today appear in this annual roll of honour and many of those whom we now admire are absent. Neither Delacroix, nor Géricault, nor Corot, nor any painter of the Barbizon School is there; nor, one may be sure, are Courbet, Manet, Degas or any of the Impressionists. Ingres, who won the Prix de Rome in 1801, is virtually the only 'big name' among the painters of the nineteenth century; others – Flandrin, Hébert, Bouguereau – have seen their glory sadly faded.

More important artists are to be found among the sculptors: David d'Angers, Rude, Pradier, Carpeaux and Falguière head the list which, however, does not include either Rodin or Maillot. And although the principal architects of France were winners of the Prix de Rome – Labrouste, Vaudoyer, Baltard, Garnier – none of them, with the possible exception of Garnier, achieved any great renown in the world.[5]

Winning the Prix de Rome was no guarantee of genius; nevertheless it helped launch the young artist in his chosen career. The morning after his victory his future appeared to him in a completely different perspective. At first his feelings were of relief following his exertions; then he realized that he was about to start on a marvellous holiday. French artists had always been fascinated by Italy, and ever since the Renaissance they looked towards the land where the great masterpieces of the ancient world and of its direct heirs were to be discovered. When Colbert founded the Académie de France at Rome in 1666, he wished to give members of the French Académie the means of developing their art in a direction influenced by the Italian tradition. The winner of the Grand Prix de Rome was highly privileged: his success enabled him to realize the dream of so many artists and in the most favourable circumstances. He was assured of a very pleasant life for four or five years in a Roman Palace and of considerable freedom as regards his work. Even when the Prix de Rome had lost much of its prestige in the public eye at the end of the century there were many young men who were unable to resist the advantages it offered them.

Rome, it is true, was a long way from France and the journey was still a difficult one: to leave one's native land and one's family, with little hope of returning before a number of years had passed, might give rise to anxiety, but the interest of a new life and the spell of a delightful country soon banished the regrets of the least carefree.

The journey itself to Central Italy was the first revelation. Simart wrote as much to his parents in Lyons in 1833: 'The prize is worth it for the journey from Lyons to Rome alone.' The prize-winners usually travelled by coach and were supposed to be in Rome by January. Although not the pleasantest time of year for travelling, at least there was the marked contrast in climate for the traveller who, having crossed Mont Cenis in the snow, would discover the plain of Lombardy bathed in sunlight below. Some preferred to travel round by the coastal route which avoided the difficulties of crossing the Alps and which even allowed one to go part of the way by boat. In 1859 Henner set sail from Leghorn after visiting Florence and Genoa and reached Rome via Civitavecchia. In either case the slowness of the means of transport customary at the time made it possible to enjoy the landscape to the full and to make close contact with the country on the way.

Discoveries were easier still for those on foot. The 1823 prize-winners, Bouchot, Duban and Dumont, were able to vist most of Central Italy at their leisure: they had an arrangement with a carter in the rue Gît-le-Coeur, who undertook the journey regularly and provided food and lodging, but they had no hesitation in following the cart on foot for long distances.

The railway made the whole journey simpler and quicker in the second half of the century but at the same time robbed it of much of its attraction. Nevertheless, the prize-winners would still break their journey in order to get to know the works of art to be found at each stop. Those of 1866 made a detour via Venice, which did not prevent them wishing to visit all the small towns between Florence and Rome as well. Henri Regnault travelled out with Hébert, who was on his way to take up his post of Director of the Villa Medici in 1867. The two of them took the train from Paris to Nice, the stage coach from Nice to La Spezzia, and then train again to Florence, where they spent two and a half days, and finally reached Rome by train; the journey had taken from March 4th to 15th.

Usually all the prize-winners in one year travelled out together, announcing their arrival in advance. But in 1868 the architect arrived alone – a break with tradition which annoyed the seniors already in residence who looked forward to greeting the newcomers. They used to go out to meet them north of Rome and the encounter was the occasion for a certain amount of horseplay.[6]

Once the newcomers had joined their seniors at the Villa Medici they were not slow in appreciating its charm. They must have been grateful to Napoleon for making it the home of the Académie de France in Rome by negotiating with the papal authorities the exchange with the Palazzo Mancini on the Corso, which had been the home of the Académie before the Revolution. The Villa Medici was fortunately sited on one of the hills of Rome, and though it no longer contained the treasures collected by Ferdinand Duke of Tuscany at the end of the sixteenth century it was still splendid. It was impossible not to be moved by the harmony of the garden façade, decorated or rather inlaid, with the arms of the Medici and with fragments of antique sculpture set between the windows; or indeed to the charm of the loggia with its six columns, open the whole length of the main wing. The view towards the city stretched away as far as the light grey dome of St Peter's. The sunsets seen from the terrace, dominated by its two square campaniles, were magnificent. A fresh breeze from the hills stirred in the trees of the Pincio gardens. It is not hard to understand the enthusiasm expressed by the residents of the Villa Medici; when Flandrin, for example, came to daydream before this landscape he used first to dip his fingers in the basin of the long fountain beneath the evergreen oaks and cross himself. [7]

The shade on the garden side was all the more precious since shade was hard to find in that city of stones and ruins; and the pines of the Villa Borghese extended further the area of silence and greenery. When the weather was fine, dinner was taken on the terrace and followed by a stroll in the *bosco*, a sort of artificial hill or belvedere, its walks lined with hedges of severely clipped and pruned trees, giving a view of the blue-tinged Sabine hills in the distance. The chirping of crickets accompanied games of bowls among the clumps of box and oleander. Other residents preferred *ruzzica*, a kind of quoits. The residents' rooms were light and airy, situated on the upper floors or in the wing of the Villa, but the studios were scattered among the shrubberies or built against the old Aurelian Wall like the pavilion of San Gaetano, which contained two rooms and five studios, one of them used by Ingres.

People have sometimes contrasted the charm of the surroundings with the ordinariness of daily existence in the Villa. Much depended on the temperament of its residents and on the authority of the Director. Around 1850 each of the *pensionnaires*, as they were called, received a grant of 100 francs a month, 25 francs of which were deducted to provide them with a lump sum gratuity at the end of their stay. They paid for lighting and heating themselves.

The rooms on the upper storey or in the wing of the Villa were plain, but they were large, light and airy. Food was abundant, if we are to judge from a letter by the Director in 1807, Pâris, addressed to the French Ambassador, in which he summarizes the instructions he had received:

'Herewith, in accordance with Your Excellency's instructions, an account of the food provided for *Messieurs les pensionnaires*.
Breakfast: Two rolls of bread and a glass of wine each.
Dinner: Boiled beef, roast veal or poultry, etc. According to the season, a salad, a side dish and sometimes small meat patties on Sunday. Choice of two desserts.
Supper: A roast. Sometimes fish, depending on the weather, two dishes of vegetables, dessert as at dinner.[8]

What irked some over-independent spirits about this comfortable existence was the need to live in a community. They were sorry at finding themselves thrown together with some fifteen other young men, whose conversation was not always on the highest level and whose jokes were often rather coarse, in a somewhat bleak dining-room waited on by half-trained Italian servants. And yet, this mixing of talents and of different artistic callings created a situation in which a painter could catch sight of the architects' drawings, or the sculptor discover the musician, and in spite of the triviality and even stupidity of some conversations, all might derive great benefit from the exchange of theories and from the confrontation of different concepts of art. It is hard to believe that nothing worth while emerged from such exchanges of views as might have occurred between young architects like Duban, Duc and Vaudoyer, between men like Berlioz and Hébert, or Denys Puech and Debussy. Even the least sentimental 'ex-Roman' used to recall these privileged moments nostalgically.

Not everyone appreciated the social obligations which filled up the evenings. Here the role of the Director was crucial. Those like Guérin, Lenepveu or Cabat who were too deeply occupied in their own work, kept their *pensionnaires* at a distance and lived apart from Roman society. In 1827 Leon Vaudoyer complained of the dreary receptions held by Guérin every Thursday: 'Only men present and one hardly dares talk to them.'[9] Other directors, for example Horace Vernet and Hébert, gave very lively parties and, ever zealous for French prestige, turned the Villa Medici into a sort of annexe of the Embassy.

Ingres, who was a quiet retiring man, liked to have his *pensionnaires* about him, and his wife watched over their needs like a mother.

He himself played the violin (who has not heard of the famous Ingres violin?) and used to hold musical evenings, accompanied on the piano by students like Gounod and Ambroise Thomas; and the great Liszt himself willingly participated in these gatherings when he passed through Rome.

Before Ingres' time Horace Vernet had given parties at the Villa Medici which shone with a different kind of lustre. A prolific painter himself, Vernet liked to invite foreign artists working in Rome and his Directorate was notable for the presence at the Villa of Overbeck, Thorwalsen and Mickiewicz. As for the *pensionnaires*, they only had eyes for his charming daughter, who played the tambourine when the company danced the *saltarello*. Dancing was very popular at certain periods. Even the austere Schnetz organized masked balls. He used to like to come across groups of his students disguised as *contadini* posing in *tableaux vivants* reminiscent of his own paintings. Schnetz even felt obliged to watch the carnival on the Corso amongst all the confetti and applaud his students' chariot.

The Villa Medici as an artistic centre was fully in touch with Roman society, at certain periods in its history at least, and also with influential members of the French colony in Rome: diplomats, soldiers, ecclesiastics and artists. Such an atmosphere could not fail to make an indelible impression on the young *pensionnaires*. The very title earned them prestige, reflected in the honourable rank they occupied in the ceremonial life of papal Rome. Many of these young men came from very humble homes and profited from such opportunities which helped them to make their way in society.

However, the principal reason for the presence of these young artists in Rome, where they were to spend five years (four years after 1863), was to improve their knowledge of art through contact with surroundings exceptionally rich in models from the past. Each of them would have interpreted this clause in his own way had it not been for the regulations. So in return for their stay at the Villa Medici these young men owed a number of rigidly specified works. When Louis XIV founded the Académie de France he had dreamed of embellishing his palaces and his spirit still lived on: the residents at the Villa were expected to supply original works or copies to decorate public buildings.

Here, for example, is what the regulations required of a painter in 1868 – they differ but little from the requirements of previous years. In his first year he had to complete a figure from life, a drawing after a painting by an old master, including at least two figures, and finally a drawing from a bas-relief or statue of either the Renaissance or antiquity. In the second year he had to do a painted sketch; a portfolio of drawings after old masters; and studies from nature, figures, monuments, landscapes. The third year had to be devoted to copying a painting by an old master; and it was only in his fourth year that the student was allowed to do original work and, in accordance with the academic hierarchy of the different genres of painting, this had to be a history painting.

One is struck by the unimaginativeness of this programme and the strict control exercised over the artist's work; and the Directors of the Académie de France were continually coming into conflict with their students over it. It was not only the lazy ones who resisted what Henner called 'the sword of Damocles of the *envois*'. Those who were lazy preferred drinking the local wines in the taverns along the Via Appia or galloping on horseback across the Roman Campagna. Regnault, who was an enthusiast for such outings, justified himself by saying: 'I prefer to look and understand rather than get down to work straightaway.'[10] But the rebels tried in vain to shake off the yoke. Their resistance was the more prolonged in that the choice of subjects, and even of works to be copied, had to be submitted to the Director. Guérin in 1828 insisted on the copying of the Vatican Raphaels; at the back of his mind was the idea of keeping his students away from the romantic temptations which were beginning to attract them. Four years later the critic Planche wrote ironically in *L'Artiste* on the narrow range of choice allowed:

'That Paolo Veronese is a dangerous fellow – you can't be too careful with him. It's unfortunately true that his *Marriage at Cana* is there, occupying far too much space in the Salon carré of the Louvre, but you've got to take it at its true worth. It's a concession made to the depraved taste of visitors and the Académie ought to protest against the conclusions that might be drawn from it.'[11]

The subject of the original work was equally hedged about with restrictions: scenes had to be taken from ancient history, mythology or religion. While Horace Vernet was Director, a student had the unusual idea of depicting 'the plague in Rome during the pontificate of Nicholas V'. Perturbed, the painter of numerous Napoleonic scenes hastened to disclaim responsibility, writing to the Institut:

'Monsieur Larivière, in his fifth year, has just begun work on his picture. He has chosen a subject from the fifteenth century. The only observation I felt it my duty to make to him was that the Académie might perhaps disapprove of this innovation. . . .'[12]

The architects were the first to rebel openly against the rigidity of the system imposed on them. The project of restoring an ancient monument certainly allowed them to look at the ruins of southern Italy or Sicily, but contact with architecture inspired by the Greeks made them anxious to study the Greek genius at its source. In 1845 they won their case and from then on the architectural Prix de Rome included a visit to Greece in addition to the stay in Rome. Better still, this decision marked the beginning of fruitful exchanges between Athens and Rome. Sainte-Beuve had been one of those who urged the creation of the Ecole française d'Athènes, which was in fact set up in 1845–6 and provided the young architects with a second home, while the archaeologists sent to Greece, who were nearly all university-trained, enjoyed in their turn the hospitality of the Villa Medici. In Rome they made worthwhile contacts, paid leisurely visits to painters' studios and enjoyed the comradeship of the artists. At the same time the restoration of Greek monuments could figure among the architects' *envois de Rome*.[13]

These *envois*, the works of art sent back by the students which aroused so much curiosity among the Paris public interested in the fine arts, were strictly controlled by the Institut. In the judgments it passed the Académie never failed to recall the principles of great art to those who were tempted to stray from them. When, for example, the musician Halévy (a strange choice of *rapporteur*) criticized Carpeaux's *Napolitan fisherboy* on the grounds that the young sculptor should try to 'elevate his style by working on noble subjects',[14] one can see the kind of attitudinal sclerosis such judgments entailed and also how it discouraged the young artists. To the victims of this sermonizing the Villa Medici appeared that day like 'an academic barracks'.

The disappointments and restrictions did not prevent the painter Henner from regarding his stay in Rome as a paradise: 'To think there are only two years of such happiness left!' The sculptor Chapu wrote: 'Every day I think I have only ten months more.'[15] With a few exceptions most of the 'Romans' thus dreaded their departure.

One soon came under the spell of Rome. The daily life of the town in the nineteenth century was a blend of pomp and ceremony and rural charm. Even without the great works of the past, the spectacle of the streets was an unending source of entertainment and distraction: the papal train, with the carriages of the cardinals and the variegated robes of church dignitaries of every rank, the noisy fervour of religious ceremonies, the seething crowd itself, afforded an inexhaustible flow of subjects for the artist. Many of them liked to visit the working-class districts of the city, the lively Trastevere first and foremost. And again these young Frenchmen marvelled at the beauty and freshness of the Italian women. Crowds full of feeling for everything to do with art contained so many faces recalling Titian or Botticelli. Like many others Henner rhapsodized about the opportunities Italian women presented to the painter:

> 'The most picturesque among them – and they know well they are picturesque – will come up to you when they see you with your box of colours and say: "*Signor, volete intratarmi*", that is: "Do you want to paint my portrait?" They themselves ask nothing better and when you draw houses or monuments they deliberately stand beside them, so beautiful and in such graceful poses that you almost forget that the government has sent you here to do history painting'.[16]

It is hardly surprising that the young artists were easily tempted by the girls of Rome as well as by the wines. Some of these girls used to visit the Villa as models. It was a perfectly respectable occupation and one especially popular among the peasant women of the Roman Campagna, who were known as *Ciociare* (or *Chauchardes* the French artists called them) and wore a particularly attractive traditional costume, Their morals were strict and they were often accompanied by a father or brother when they went to the Villa. In any case, the regulations which were generally respected and were enforced by the gate-keeper as well as the Director were against their lingering on the premises outside the studios, and of course still more against their spending the night at the Villa. None the less there was more than one romance between these dark-eyed girls and the artists. Some of them became very attached to a painter or sculptor and were like widows when they left three or four years later – widows who were sometimes consoled by a successor.

The episode in which Carpeaux figured as hero was particularly touching. The peasant girl whom he immortalized under the name given her in her village of La Palombella was obliged to marry a man of her own class, although Carpeaux had promised marriage; she died of sorrow soon after.[17] Carpeaux could not in any case have kept his promise until after he had left Rome. Here too the rules were inflexible; the residents had to be bachelors and lost their grants if they married.

Throughout the century this clause was a source of difficulty for directors as well as students. A blind eye was turned to the first cases which occurred as long as the students fulfilled their other obligations. The situation was more delicate when the 1831 competition honoured two artists who were already married, the painter Schopin and the musician Eugène Prévost. Their cases, like others in succeeding years – for example the architects Baltard and Léveil in 1833 – were decided variously and with varying degrees of equity. Schopin and Baltard were given permission to work in Rome on condition they lived outside the city. Léveil's marriage, which actually took place in Italy, greatly perturbed the then Director, Horace Vernet. Without mincing matters he wrote to warn the Minister, who was his friend Thiers:

'I am convinced that if the matter is not settled properly all that will be left to my successor at the Academy to do will be to direct wet nurses and nursery maids and I think that a midwife would serve in place of a painter.'[18]

Léveil's situation was eventually regularized, however, in the same way as that of his predecessors. Some of their comrades, on the other hand, preferred to renounce all their rights at the time of marrying to avoid complications. After 1845 the regulations stated that only single men could compete for the Prix de Rome. And when Xavier Leroux, who was already in residence at the Villa, returned to Paris in 1886 to marry, he was forced to resign, and what was worse he was then caught for five years' military service from which the 'Romans', by virtue of a law of 1807, were exempt.

Another matter for discussion questioned the very principle of residence in Rome. This was the ban on travel, which seemed all the harsher with the improvement in communications in the second half of the century. The basis of the contract was the opportunity to reside at the Villa Medici for four or five years, but did this mean that the right was also an obligation? Certainly the students were able to visit the small towns of Central Italy; they were sometimes to be seen in Naples, less often in Florence. And the architects had soon acquired the right to travel as far as Sicily, even before they were allowed to spend part of their term in Athens. But the painters and sculptors would also have liked to enjoy the same opportunities.

It is also interesting to observe how the question of travel was linked with attacks upon the Académie de France itself. It was those who supported a breach with tradition who wanted to offer young artists horizons other than those of the Roman Campagna, and other works of art than those of the Forum or the Vatican. Why should contact with the great Flemish or the great Dutch painters, for example, be deemed to possess fewer virtues?

The reform of 1863 introduced a certain flexibility and required residence in Rome during the first and last years only; during the two middle years the students were not only permitted but encouraged to travel. A few, like Henri Regnault, visited Spain or even Morocco. But one country remained forbidden, and that paradoxically was France itself. Only death in the family could justify a return to France. The increasing speed of transport added to the temptation. There was a scandal in 1880, when it was discovered that several students had returned secretly to Paris with the complicity of the secretary of the Académie, an ex-*zouave** called Brandois.

France was not just family and friends; France was the Salon, the exhibitions where candidates who had failed the Prix de Rome were perhaps beginning to make a name for themselves while the winners were lingering in the shade of the Villa Medici. Paris and France represented new developments in living art and not all of them had their origin in imitation of Antiquity. In spite of the advantages of the Prix de Rome, the prestige of the title and four years spent perfecting one's art at government expense, the real problems were those when the winner returned home. He had then to establish himself and become known to the public at large.

---

* The *zouaves* were a tough infantry regiment originally recruited from among the Algerians but later consisting of Frenchmen.

CHAPTER THREE

LODGINGS AND STUDIOS

A poet can write in an attic by the light of a candle, or on a café table, but a painter needs space and light; even more does a sculptor. So their most urgent task at the outset of their careers was to find a studio. The studio was the artist's workplace and to some extent his laboratory; sometimes he lived, ate and slept there as well when the nature of the room or of the adjoining rooms made it possible for him to live on the spot. The studio therefore is the best place to study his daily life.

The fortunate ones had studios acquired through official commissions or official protection. Favours of this kind were common currency under the Ancien Régime, but by the nineteenth century there were only a few survivals of the custom unequally shared among artists. Still important in the lives of certain artists, they became less frequent with the years.

Letters patent granted by Henri IV in 1608 and confirmed by Louis XIV in 1673 permitted painters and sculptors under the King's protection to live within the walls of the Louvre itself. The troubles of the Revolution, far from putting an end to this favour, caused a veritable invasion of the private apartments. However, the Consulate used the dual pretext of the re-establishment of the learned societies, traditionally housed in the Louvre, and the need to find room for the exhibition of works of art brought back from Italy, to clear the place. A decree of 3 Fructidor year IX (August 20, 1801) expelled those living in and around the courtyard and other occupants realized they had only been granted a reprieve. When the Emperor decided suddenly to empty the building the inhabitants of the Louvre had to leave within a fortnight and by May 18, 1806, all was over. They received in exchange an annual pension of between 500 and 1,000 francs according to the size of their families.[1]

44

Many artists were affected by this measure. David had a studio in the rue de Seine, but he also had sole use of three studios in the Colonnade. One of them was for his own work, called the '*Atelier des Horaces*' because it was there he had painted his famous picture, the *Oath of the Horatii*, in 1784. It was high up in the building, lit by a skylight about ten feet long in the roof and facing Saint Germain-l'Auxerrois. His teaching studio was directly underneath and he had acquired yet another in order to work on his *Sabine Women* on the side overlooking the river. Vestier, Gérard and Redouté, on the top floor of the Pavillion de l'Horloge also had to move.

The most crowded part of the Louvre was a series of apartments overlooking the Seine above the Galerie du Bord de l'Eau. Twenty-six rooms that opened on to a noisy corridor where children played harboured a mixed bunch of tenants, including a mathematician and examiner at the Ecole Polytechnique. Fifteen of them however, had been reserved for artists. At the time of the exodus their number included some who, like Greuze, Fragonard and Pajou, had either just died or else had only a few years left to live. Vien had taken his uncle Pigalle's place in 1801; and he and Regnault, Isabey and Moitte all had to reorganize their lives elsewhere. So did Carle Vernet whose son Horace had been born within the walls of the Louvre. The painter Vincent was the only one rehoused by the state in the Collège des Quatre-Nations. Most of the others moved into houses on the Left Bank with the aid of the annual pension they received as compensation.

Henceforth the Louvre was to house artists' works instead of the artists themselves. Some exceptions were made, particularly during the reign of Louis-Philippe, in favour of artists engaged on official work such as the decoration of Versailles. The sculptor Triqueti was also given a studio when he was asked to prepare the chapel of the Duke of Orleans; and Pradier complained bitterly at not receiving the same privilege, even though he too was engaged on a state commission.[2]

In spite of having forced the artists out of the Louvre the Empire did not abandon the royal tradition of helping the arts by the grant of studios or even lodgings to artists. Two buildings in particular which the Revolution had secularized were used for this purpose: the Collège des Quatre-Nations and the Sorbonne. The former was given the provisional title of Palais des Beaux-Arts in 1805 and

45

was allocated to the Institut, which as we have already seen had been made responsible for the teaching of art. A number of artists lived there: Vincent, a 'refugee' from the Louvre, and Gérard in apartments near the dome. The painter Lethière and the sculptors Lemot, Houdon and Bosio had their studios there. Other studios in the same building came directly under the Ecole des Beaux-Arts, awaiting transfer to the rue des Petits-Augustins. Thus it was that David's pupils, who had been housed for a while in the Collège du Plessis, rue Saint-Jacques, moved in 1811 into a room which had been left vacant on the death of Moitte. It was there that first Gros then Delaroche succeeded David, teaching there until the mid-century.

The sculptor Chaudet, replacing the painter Regnault, had his studio in the rue Mazarine, the self-same that young Brideau wanders into by accident at the beginning of Balzac's *La Rabouilleuse*. Drolling, Picot, Pradier, Horace Vernet and Robert Fleury also occupied rooms in the Institut building, even after the studios had been transferred to the Ecole des Beaux-Arts. As late as 1863 the sculptor Dumont was to be seen moving in to take Pradier's place after he had had to leave the East Pavilion on account of the expansion of the Mazarine Library.[3]

David's departure from the Louvre coincided with the preparatory stages of his great painting of the Emperor's coronation which he had begun at the end of 1804. It therefore comes as no surprise to learn that a place was reserved for him to paint this great canvas, nearly thirty feet long, in which the Emperor took a special interest. The Minister of the Interior lent the old church of the College de Cluny in the Place de la Sorbonne, which was demolished a few years later. Here it was that one fine day the Emperor's first painter saw Napoleon and Josephine arrive with a train of followers curious to discover how the picture was progressing.

Other former ecclesiastical buildings which the revolution had secularized served the same purpose. A few years earlier David had painted his *Oath of the Tennis Court* in the former church of the Feuillants which he had to abandon later when the rue de Rivoli was extended. The convent of the Petits-Augustins was to become the nucleus of the Ecole des Beaux-Arts and the Carmelite and the Capuchin convents in their turn harboured various groups of painters. The Capuchin cloister, which has given its name to a boulevard and a street, was a very active centre of art during the first years of the century. Girodet, Gros, Ingres and Delécluze, the future historian of David's pupils, all had their studios in the austere cells of the convent whose gloomy corridors Granet loved to paint.[4]

When David established himself in the Place de la Sorbonne he became neighbour of yet another centre where the Empire gave shelter to favoured artists. Just as the Collège des Quatre-Nations had become the Palais des Beaux-Arts so the ex-theology faculty of the University of Paris, the Sorbonne, was to become in its turn a palace of the arts.

Napoleon had the architect Moreau build fifty-three apartments there: twenty were for scholars, twenty-one for painters, and twelve for sculptors. The church itself, with the tomb of Richelieu removed, was divided up by partitions and nine artists were able to move in Some thirty households in all found suitable accommodation in this building. And the inevitable rivalry between successful and less successful neighbours did not prevent painters like Prud'hon and Charles Meynier – who was then by far the more celebrated of the two – draughtsmen like Dutertre and Constant Bourgeois, engravers like Tardieu and sculptors like Roland and Cartellier from living side by side in a fraternal community.

In spite of the depredations of a flower painter called Van Dael seeking further models for his paintings, all the families used to meet in the garden on summer evenings and musical entertainments were organized in the large hall which Prud'hon's pupils normally occupied. But twenty years later the Palais des Arts was to change its function yet again when the King decided in 1821 to return the Sorbonne to the University, and a terrible tragedy darkened the last weeks of this artistic retreat. For many years Constance Mayer, Prud'hon's beloved disciple, had taken the place of his worthless wife both for the painter and for his children. Her studio was separate from his but next to it. Prud'hon had been unable to soften the blow for her and the prospect of the change led her to cut her throat on May 27, 1821.[5]

The custom of giving artists official studios gradually fell into disuse, but a few survivals of the custom made it possible for certain artists to benefit from studios in the Louvre under Louis-Philippe and from those at the Institut right up to the Second Empire. However, the quarters allocated to certain artists in the Marble Depot towards the end of the century should be mentioned. The

Marble Depot was founded by Colbert to store blocks of marble of various sizes which would be handed over to artists who had received official commissions; and statues which had ceased to find favour, usually for political reasons, would be relegated there rather than destroyed.

The Marble Depot was originally built in the seventeenth century on the Ile aux Vaches, which later acquired the more poetic name of Ile des Cygnes. By the beginning of the nineteenth century the island, whether of cows or swans, was an island no longer and the Marble Depot was to be found by the Champ-de-Mars, next to the Garde-Meuble and facing the Palais de Chaillot.

The district was light and airy and a number of studios were built in a central pavilion. Here Pils painted the *Surrender of Algeria* and Carolus-Duran a ceiling for the Louvre. In 1899 Jean-Paul Laurens was still working there on decorations intended for the Capitol at Toulouse. But the most famous tenant of all was Rodin, who occupied two adjoining cells lit by a large north-facing window after 1889.[6]

The run-of-the-mill artist who had no official studio had to shift for himself to find one, or at least something which could be converted to meet his requirements. At a time when very large pictures were the rule, space was essential and the place had to be easy of access. Light was essential too, but the room had to be lit from above as far as possible and direct sunlight excluded.

Sheds, ex-gymnasia, former fencing schools, all were turned into studios. Perhaps the most attractive were the studios which occupied the top floor of a house, and the trend towards easel painting at the end of the century allowed a number of painters to work in one of the rooms of their apartments.

But though a painter might be satisfied perched up under the roof, a sculptor had to take other requirements into account; the weight of his sculptures and difficulties of transport obliged him to live on the ground floor.

The artist was often noisy, bringing with him a constant coming and going of friends and models; he needed freedom and elbow room. Also he was suspect as a tenant since the irregularity of his income often left him short of funds. Both the landlord, and even more the concierge – a new arrival upon the scene and one whose importance grew with the years – regarded him with mistrust.

'Ah! So the gentleman is an artist! I'm afraid my room is already let!' Such, according to a caricaturist of 1850, was the reaction of these formidable guardians.[7]

Although the conditions an artist needed might be found in almost any part of the capital, the difficulties encountered by many of them explain why they should have preferred to settle in new districts only just beginning to take shape, where not much building had been done and where flimsy temporary constructions of various kinds were more common than solidly built houses.

It is impossible to give all the addresses even of well-known artists, but a map of Paris marking the position of the principal studios throughout the century would show both how widely they were scattered through the town and also their tendency to concentrate in a few districts in particular.

Starting from the south, the first of these clusters is concentrated in the area between the Jardin du Luxembourg and the outer boulevards. Until 1860 the wall of the *fermiers-généraux* (built in 1780 to facilitate the collection of taxes by the *fermiers-généraux* as the tax farmers were called) followed the line of the outer boulevards, and constituted the boundary of Paris. The Montparnasse district was empty then and still rural in many respects. The middle class seldom had occasion to go there and it was already a centre of artistic activity. Félix Pyat, in his *Nouveau Tableau de Paris*, even described it in 1834 as being 'the favourite district of the artist'.[8] The most popular roads were the rue de Fleurus and the rue Notre Dame-des-Champs, the rue de l'Ouest, which later became a prolongation of the rue d'Assas, and the rue de l'Est, which joined it below the Luxembourg Gardens before it became part of the boulevard Saint-Michel.

Eugène Deveria was working in the rue de l'Est around 1825, sharing a studio with Louis Boulanger in the same house as the sculptor Cartellier, who had been forced to leave the Sorbonne. Henri Regnault moved in after Deveria's death. But Deveria actually lived in the rue Notre-Dame-des-Champs near Victor Hugo, who was a close friend. Jehan du Seigneur's studio in the rue de Vaugirard was yet another centre for friendly gatherings during the Romantic era. This studio was an old greengrocers' shop and owes its fame at the present time not so much to its owner's works as to the meetings of the *Cénacle* which took place there – gatherings where poets rubbed shoulders with artists. During the same period the landscapist Paul

49

Huet was working a little further north in 27 rue Madame. He moved into the rue de l'Ouest after 1857. Degas also lived in rue Madame after his return from Italy in 1858.

In 1830 Rude had found a studio in the courtyard of an ordinary working-class house, 66 rue d'Enfer, not far from where David had lived for a short while in 1815. Rude later had larger studios, still in the same road, first at number 65 then at number 61.

Artists were particularly numerous in the rue Notre Dame-des-Champs during the latter half of the century, among them Laurens, Chapu and Français. In particular there was the artistic coterie which formed at the house which Toulmouche senior had built, known as The 'Tea Caddy' because of the paintings of two Chinese on one of the walls; across the gardens there was an alley which led to a series of studios, demolished after 1886, where Toulmouche, Brion, Gérôme, Lecomte de Noüy and Paul Baudry worked.[9] These academic painters might well have come across the society portraitist Carolus-Duran, who established himself in the passage Stanislas which led into the rue Bréa in 1875. During the same period another block of tenement houses in the rue d'Assas gave a roof to less well-known painters like Signol and Monginot and to the sculptor Mathieu.

Towards 1870 there was another hotbed of young sculptors at 68 rue d'Assas in studios built round a cul-de-sac: Préault, Falguière, Paul Dubois, Saint-Marceau.[10] It was quite near where David d'Angers had worked for a long time in a house on the corner of the rue de Vaugirard which was later occupied by the animal painter Rosa Bonheur.

If we leave this district and move north we come to another district dear to artists on the fringes of Saint-Germain-des-Prés. This central district, between the church of Saint Germain and the Seine, contained two natural poles of attraction for artists, the Ecole des Beaux-Arts and the Institut. Under the Empire many of the artists who had to leave the Louvre took refuge here: Carle Vernet, for example, at 34 rue de Lille, and Bervic in rue de Grenelle. Delacroix was very fond of this corner of Paris: in the course of his many moves between 1823 and 1828 we find him first at 20 rue Jacob with the English water-colourist Fielding* and then at 46 rue de la Université. Between 1829 and 1835 he occupied a sixth-floor studio

* This was Thales Fielding who invited Delacroix to England in 1824, one of four brothers, Theodore, Copley, Thales and Newton Fielding, all artists.

at 15 quai Voltaire, which curiously enough had also belonged to his great rival Ingres and to Edouard Bertin. He also lived in rue des Marais-Saint-Germain, now rue Visconti, a narrow street famous for Balzac's printing works. Ingres also had both his own studio which Paul Chenavard took over and his teaching studio in the rue Visconti, the latter having another entrance in the rue des Beaux-Arts. Fantin-Latour worked at number 8 in this self-same street at the back of a courtyard, and Bazille lived there with Renoir during 1866–7. Delacroix's last studio still survives, now a museum. The painter had it built in rue de Furstemberg in December 1858 and he died there in 1863. Two years later Bazille and Monet spent a few months in the house opposite.[11]

Still in the same district, but closer to the Latin Quarter, is where Courbet settled towards 1848 in number 32 rue Hautefeuille. His studio was on the first floor in what was the apse of the former chapel of the Premonstrant College. On the ground floor was the Café de la Rotonde.

Continuing towards the east we need to make a detour to the Ile-Saint-Louis, which was then a quiet corner little frequented by the middle classes and one which had harboured a small colony of artists ever since the July Monarchy (i.e. after 1830). Zola situated the first studio of Charles Lantier, hero of *L'oeuvre*, in this district. Banville has described this period in his memoirs:

'They silently took over the Ile-Saint-Louis as it belonged to no one, and it was not unusual to see artists like Moine and Feuchère, the Benevenuto Cellini of a new Renaissance, visiting each other without bothering to change their working clothes. They could walk casually dressed along the quai Bourbon and the quai d'Anjou without offending the gaze of the absent crowd. . . .'

The liveliest centre was the Hôtel Lauzun, which was then called Pimodan, 13 quai d'Anjou, where the first floor was let to the painter Ferdinand Boissard de Boisdenier and painters and poets used to meet. Daubigny also lived here, next door to the sculptor Geoffroy-Dechaume, and at the end of the century his studio was occupied by Guillaumin. Daumier lived quite near in 9 quai d'Anjou in an enormous room with a bay window at the top of the house, which could only be reached up a very steep and narrow staircase.[12]

The central districts of the Right Bank were less congenial to artists, particularly those of limited means. You had to be Auguste Biard to possess an enormous studio on the top floor in the Place Vendôme; Biard was a painter who knew how to profit from popular success and the favours of the court.[13]

Balzac made Schinner, hero of his novel *La Bourse*, live in the rue de Surène near the Madeleine, but the novelist is careful to tell us that the painter's fame had brought him sufficient means so that he no longer had need to work 'in one of those inexpensive studios near the *barrières* [gates in the city walls] on the outskirts of the city'. So it is that we find Eugène Giraud, the friend of the Princess Mathilda, in rue des Ecuries-d'Artois near Saint-Philippe-du-Roule and Henri Lehmann in the rue Balzac after 1870 towards the end of his career.

The avenue Montaigne at this time was a more remote district. Where the painter Jacquet lived in 1875 was still semi-rural. Close by was the rue Bayard where Gustave Doré had a gymnasium converted into a studio in order to paint his enormous but mediocre canvases, through which he hoped to achieve a success even greater than that which he had already undeniably won for himself as an illustrator.

On the way up from the centre of the town towards the north one soon comes to the first of the roads leading up the slope to the hill of Montmartre. We have now reached the second major pole of attraction of artistic life. Montmartre, like its southern twin Montparnasse, was a rapidly growing district and did not become densely built up until the end of the century. It did not spread beyond the external wall and the famous *barrières* until these were demolished under the Second Empire. Until then the district of Montmartre, sometimes called 'the second Athens', stretched from the rue Saint-Lazare to Pigalle with the rue des Martyrs forming its central axis.

Philippe Burty could still write about the district in 1860:

'A new district, a quiet district if ever there was one, and a district favourable to the arts. Little noise or bustle. Mysterious little hotels are dotted about on either side of the roads; the only shops which have been opened are those selling essential food-stuffs; cabs never risk struggling up the steep slopes unless they have to; the colour merchant and dealer in artists' materials can peddle his packets of brushes and his stacks of canvases without let or hindrance; and the model is sure to find her time fully employed.'[14]

Corot's studio was on the fringe of this district, in the rue de Paradis. Henri Regnault settled in the rue Lafayette in 1865 before he left for Rome, and it was in this self-same rue Lafayette that the Goncourt brothers made Anatole, the Bohemian painter of *Manette Salomon*, live.

Granet, Isabey and Horace Vernet had lived in the district ever since the First Empire, when it was hardly built up at all, and Ary Scheffer and Delaroche were soon to move in to the rue Tour-des-Dames. In 1828 Gavarni lived in 27 rue Saint-Lazare in a house which the Goncourt brothers described as a *phalanstère d'art* (an artistic commune) and where a miniaturist, a young sculptor and a painter of decorative scenes on clocks also lived. In the same road in 1839 we find yet another 'republic' of artists grouped about two courtyards, whose outstanding figures were the sculptor Dantan and the landscape artist Léon Fleury.[15] And Fantin-Latour lived in 79 rue Saint-Lazare in 1864.

Troyon, and later Carrier-Belleuse, lived in the rue de La-Tour-d'Auvergne, and Couture and Gavarni in the rue Fontaine in 1837 where later Leopold Flameng was to reside. Géricault lived and died in 23 rue des Martyrs. Fromentin worked in the rue La-Rochefoucauld where Gustave Moreau succeeded him. His studio is unchanged and now a museum.

Delacroix was faithless to the Left Bank for more than ten years when he lived at 54 rue Notre-Dame-de-Lorette from 1845 to 1857 in the studio the public got to know about in *L'Illustration* in 1852. Chassériau never left the district but had various addresses in twenty years: 18 rue Saint-Georges, 26 rue de La-Tour-d'Auverge and then, in 1844, 34 rue Frochot which had formerly belonged to De Dreux, the painter of horses. At that time this studio was on the very edge of the town and as it overlooked the rampart walk around the city wall its windows were heavily barred. In 1847 he was still living quite close in the rue Laval; he died ten years later in rue Fléchier in the shadow of the new church of Notre-Dame-de-Lorette, built in 1823. This was the church which gave its name to the *lorettes*, the young women of easy virtue who haunted the district.

The landscape painter Boudin, too, for a few years during the

Second Empire was moving from one studio to another: 66 rue Pigalle, 27 rue Trudaine, then 21 rue Fontaine; in 1864 he ventured as far as the heights of Montmartre (la Butte) and spent a short while at 15 rue Durandin. After 1870 he went to live further west on what is now the place Adolphe-Max, where Bonnard was to settle in 1875.

Once he had made a bit of money, Renoir finally managed to find a large studio at 35 rue Saint-Georges, where he stayed ten years. Degas, on the other hand, moved frequently: first he lived in rue Blanche, then in rue de Laval, rue Lepic, and rue Notre-Dame-de-Lorette; then he returned to rue de Laval, which had become in the meantime the rue Victor-Massé, and finally the boulevard de Clichy.

The constant moving does not only reveal the instability of some artists, and in the case of others the need to flee unpaid rent; it also shows the great number of buildings suited to artists which were available to them in such districts, and to artists of every class, not only the important ones. Studios congregated around the place Pigalle; the dubious reputation which this square acquired abroad should not lead us to forget that it was named in honour of an eighteenth-century sculptor. In 1840 Théodore Rousseau and Jules Dupré were already occupying a building in rue Frochot with two studios while Clésinger, Fontallard and the two Pils were living on the ground floor. Puvis de Chavannes moved in to place Pigalle in 1852 in order to undertake the direction of a teaching studio jointly with other painters, among them Bida and Ricard; he preferred, however, to do his own work in a distant studio at Neuilly. Henner and Boldini rented the same house which was separated from the road by a small garden in 1875. And Bonnard and Vuillard shared a studio in 1890 at the beginning of the rue Pigalle.

The Goncourt brothers chose the rue Frochot, which they described as 'gay and full of studios belonging to wealthy artists' for the home of their society painter Garnotelle in 1860. Ten or twenty years later studios belonging to wealthy artists were going up along the boulevard de Clichy: for example, the splendid Hôtel de Gérôme, with its stables belonging to Antoine Vollon, or that other studio, the whim of the amateur sculptor Sarah Bernhardt. A little further along was the studio of Ernest Hébert on the boulevard Rochechouart.

But the most luxurious district till then settled by artists was to be found further west. After 1860 the Plaine Monceau, which had formerly been given over to market gardening, was covered with elegant town residences and blocks of flats. Manet lived at 81 rue Guyot on the edge of this zone, next to the village of Batignolles; and it is common knowledge that at one time malicious critics used what they regarded as the unflattering name of 'Batignolles School' to describe Manet and his friends. Those who built themselves elegant studios on the Plaine Monceau after 1870 were, on the contrary, painters respected by the critics, and the money they had earned made them seem worthy of honour in the eyes of the public.

Cabanel had already 'arrived' as an artist when he moved into the rue Alfred-Vigny. So had Roll, whose studio stood on the corner of the rue Brémontier and the boulevard Bertier. Still more successful were Lecomte du Noüy who lived on the boulevard Flandrin and Edouard Detaille; and Detaille's disciple, Alphonse de Neuville, whose reconstructions of military scenes were almost as highly valued as his master's, lived in his residence on the rue Legendre about 1875.

But the most typical of them all was certainly Meissonier. He lived for years in the outer suburbs at Poissy, but after the Franco-Prussian War in 1870 he built himself a mock-Renaissance villa on the place Malesherbes with a spiral staircase and an inner courtyard. Zola may have had Meissonier in mind when he made Fagerolles, the only one of the painters in *L'oeuvre* to win official recognition, live in a similar residence in the avenue de Villiers which he described as a 'darling little house'.

During the same period De Nittis raised the roof of the building he had just bought in the avenue Bois de Boulogne so that he could have his studio on the top floor. And, even though the district was comparatively inexpensive then, the newspapers were full of admiring comments when the caricaturist Forain bought a plot of land near the Porte Dauphine in 1897 to have a private residence built there.

The contrast is very sharp in every respect between the wealthy artists who installed themselves in style in the fashionable districts and the ever-increasing numbers who flocked to the heights of Montmartre during the same years. Certainly it was not just those who were poverty-stricken who preferred these still semi-rural districts where a certain freedom prevailed and where the concept of art did not necessarily conform to the traditional norms.

Ziem, one of those who pioneered the Montmartre district, was

55

a case apart, as he left the quai Malaquais around 1855 and built himself a sort of fortress in the rue de l'Empereur, the future rue Lepic.[16] But most of the artists of Montmartre worked in a much freer atmosphere.

Forain, for example, settled on the corner of the rue Tourlaque and the rue Lepic in 1875, long before he gained admission to elegant society, and Renoir lived in a charming old house in the rue Cortot where the painter Henri Rivière would as often as not find him in the garden when he called. And there was that small group of cruel, ironical illustrators of contemporary life: Willette in rue Véron, Toulouse-Lautrec in rue Tourlaque, and Steinlen in rue Caulaincourt. So that by the end of the century a tradition had been established at least as strong as that of the fashionable painters which was to make Montmartre one of the holy places of French art in the eyes of the world.

> 'Savez-vous ce que c'est que l'atelier d'un peintre,
> Lecteur bourgeois? . . .
> . . . C'est un monde;
> Un univers à part qui ne ressemble en rien,
> A notre monde à nous.*

Gautier is describing[17] the studio of a Flemish painter in the Middle Ages but addressing readers of 1831; he introduces that provocative note expected of a Romantic artist, stirring up a fairly general curiosity. The bourgeois in fact imagined that in such a diabolically wicked place he could catch a whiff of adventure, of unbridled freedom, even debauchery. Those who were motivated by a more rational curiosity supposed that by entering the artist's studio they could surprise that mysterious process of transmutation which transformed base matter, be it clay or pigment, into a work of art.

The reality was usually much more prosaic. Many studios differed little from the uncomfortable workshops where artisans carried out heavy work requiring much space. Their appearance varied of course according to the type of work produced by the artist and still more according to his temperament. But many of them were quite unprepossessing. Often the artists who worked there enjoyed very limited resources. Ready as they were to take in the essentials of line at a glance or the unusual harmony of some special

---

* Do you know what a painter's studio is like, bourgeois reader? . . . It is a world in itself, a universe apart, resembling our world in nothing.

tints, they were also able to hold themselves aloof from mere appearances.

Closer than one might think to the poet or the musician, the painter and the sculptor carried a whole world within them; and even if they almost always needed to refer to models (whether living models or objects) in carrying out their works, yet in the last resort they used them in order to transform them. They might turn a poor girl hired for five francs an hour into a Queen of the East or immortalize a basket of apples or a pewter jug.

Their working surroundings mattered little to them so long as they felt at their ease. Many studios resembled that described by Gleyre's biographers:[18] a great barn where the wind came in through every crack, lit by two enormous windows, one vertical facing north into a courtyard and the other sloping in the roof; a minimum of furniture – a model stand, a high stool, two broken chairs, an old armchair, a chest of drawers which held drawings, a table with a basin and some soft soap for washing brushes, a plank supporting a few plaster casts, two or three easels and portfolios leaning up against the walls, and a coal house for storing fuel. Gleyre would not allow anyone to sweep up because dust was bad for paintings, and he used for a long time to sleep in the room on a camp bed and so caught rheumatism. Yet it was here that he painted the *Apocalypse of Saint John* and the *Dance of the Bacchantes*.

There is little that needs to be added to the above description except to say that a painter required light and some warmth; the stove, with its great thick pipe bent at right angles, figures prominently in pictures of studios. The easel supporting his current work was the centre of the painter's existence; nearby, somewhere within reach, was a table covered with a collection of bottles of oil, paraffin, varnish and siccative, brushes and materials for cleaning them and also all those other 'nameless objects which might one day come in useful' that Paul Valéry has described in Degas's studio.[19] Sometimes it all went on a small trolley with a number of compartments. And this was all it took to paint great masterpieces or mere daubs: the difference being a matter of the artist's genius.

There were usually additional canvases to be found in the studio; these might be other paintings the artist was currently working on, or unfinished or abandoned works, or works which had failed to find a purchaser. When the correspondent of *Le Figaro* had the audacity to venture into Manet's studio in 1875 he discovered there paintings rejected by the public and now known the world over: *Olympia, Lunch on the Grass, The Balcony. . . .*[20] Some painters liked to have by them works they admired. Fantin-Latour kept the many copies he did in the Louvre, while Degas had a sketch by Delacroix, some drawings by Ingres and a nude by Puvis de Chavannes on his walls – but only the most rudimentary furniture.

For the rest, studios were often crowded with items used by the artist as models in his paintings, their nature varying according the artist's usual subjects. The disorder which was so common among artists was partly a reflection of their scorn for bourgeois refinement, partly sheer necessity. Degas's studio contained a bath tub, a cot, a chest of drawers with one drawer missing and a lectern; yet Degas used to say: 'I like order.' Manet kept the bar where the girl in blue in the *Bar at the Folies-Bergères* had stood, the table where the young couple sat who posed for *At Père Lathuile's*, and the mirror used by *Nana*.[21]

The flower painter only required a few vases; but Rosa Bonheur the animal painter had a whole stable, only separated from her studio by a light dividing wall, where she kept not just horses but goats and sheep.

The landscape painter who mostly worked out of doors only had his sketches, but the history painter, who was the most demanding and the most respected because he occupied the highest position in the hierarchy of genres, and his modern disciple the military painter, could never have enough weapons and accessories and costumes belonging to all periods.

Decamps had accumulated a veritable arsenal and the catalogue of his sale in April 1853 mentions twenty-five different kinds of rifles, carbines, pistols and arquebuses, including types from Kabylia and Albania. At Biard's, thousands of different objects brought back from his travels were piled about a divan beneath a royal canopy: oriental vases, feather headdresses and an eskimo kayak, all of which appear in his paintings. Others required jewels, costumes, armour, carpets to reconstruct the scenes they imagined, which soon led to the accumulation of collections of bric-à-brac.

Contemporary opinion held that the painter of battle scenes should undertake the most painstaking reconstructions. Alphonse de Neuville, who painted the Franco-Prussian War, owned what was virtually a museum of military headgear and contemporary weapons. A contemporary writer comments that he had:

'. . . a very special way of decorating the room where he worked. Faithful historian of the dramas of war that he was, he had surrounded himself with picturesque horrors: broken cannon wheels, bloodstained mattresses, muddy straw – these were the curios that lined his walls in place of shelves'.[22]

It was this chaos of heterogeneous objects piled pell-mell together, partly out of necessity, partly out of carelessness, which went to create the image of the typical artist's studio that society men and women were to imitate for their own use at the very end of the century.

A counter-influence caused painters whose success with a wealthy public had brought them riches to try to live up to what was expected of them. They shunned the artisan-type studio and also the messier aspects of their work. To make their places of work resemble elegant and comfortable drawing-rooms was to raise themselves in the social hierarchy and at the same time place themselves, or attempt to place themselves, on the level of the society people whose favours they hoped to win. Even under the Empire Gros had a studio which was sumptuously adorned with priceless materials and armour, while Isabey's studio in the Louvre was decorated by Percier and Fontaine.

The Goncourt brothers placed Garnotelle, the successful painter in their novel *Manette Salomon*, in this type of surroundings:

'The furniture was upholstered in grey rep that toned in well and discreetly with the colour of the studio. Two apothecary's jars with handles like twisted serpents stood on top of a glass-fronted cabinet which held the gilt-edged bound volumes of Garnotelle's studies and sketches. On one corner there was a fig plant with large shiny leaves; in another a banana plant in a copper pot next to an open upright piano. Everything was clean, tidy and spotless; even the plants looked as if they had just been scrubbed. Nothing, not a sketch, not a plaster cast, not a copy nor a brush, had been left lying around.'[23]

Meissonier's enormous studio in his Renaissance villa on the Plaine Monceau, with draperies and tapestries hanging from the carved beams and mullioned windows with their locks covered in finely wrought gold, came very close to this description.[24]

Some well-to-do painters, however, preferred to keep their

59

collections and their work apart. Both Albert Besnard and Lecomte de Noüy were highly cultivated collectors, but their studios were traditionally simple. Léon Bonnat extended his by adding a gallery. Here could be seen the admirable works of art collected by a mediocre painter who yet had excellent taste, a collection which he bequeathed to his native city of Bayonne.

The sculptor was still more likely to separate his place of work from the place where he kept his collection of valuable objects or received lovers of art. For his studio was subject to still more stringent physical requirements. Apart from the exceptions who produced statuettes and curios, the weight of the stone, marble or clay, and the difficulties encountered in transporting bulky objects out of the building, made it impossible for the sculptor to work anywhere but on the ground floor. The studios of even the most fastidious were always dirty; chips of stone, crumbling plaster and clay created dust and mud; while the damp cloths used to protect unfinished work made the atmosphere as humid as that of a laundry. The heat emitted by the stove was hardly adequate, particularly as the floor often consisted of beaten earth, as it did in Rude's studio.

Sculptors, even more than painters, kept plaster casts they used as models, and it was hard to prevent them getting covered with dust without large cupboards, as Duret had in his studio in the Institut to protect his casts of antique bronzes. Nearly everyone had fragments of the Parthenon frieze hanging on his walls.

The wealthier and more fastidious divided their studios into two parts, a 'practical room' where the blocks of stone or marble were rough-hewn, the plaster mixed and the preparatory work carried out by aides and assistants for the most part, and a second room where the master himself worked, where only the fine work was done and the sketches or preparatory drawings were made. In Dantan's studio in the Beaujon district in the 1850s – as in many another later – it was this room that housed the fine works of art and there 'the lovely ladies who came to visit the master at least knew where to place feet shod in satin boots'.[25]

Truth to tell none of these arrangements for pleasing visitors were of much use to the sculptor, any more than to the painter. The work of art had no need of such refinements, either for its conception or its execution.

CHAPTER FOUR

SUBJECTS, INSPIRATION AND MODELS

In the studio he had chosen the artist formulated his work. To discover what motivated him, to follow him during his preparations and then through each stage of the genesis of a picture or a statue, this would truly be to relive his daily life. But here, unfortunately, we come up against the mysteries of artistic creation and only outward appearances are within our grasp. But at least, thanks to the confidence of the artists themselves and the testimony of their friends, it is possible for us to catch a glimpse of them as they go about their work.

Everything began with the choice of subject. Here we must distinguish between commissions and free inspiration. We shall return to the reasons for an artist accepting the former; it was sometimes sheer necessity or a last resource for an artist in need. But it was unusual for the work commissioned to have no connection with an earlier success, and since the same subject could be treated in many different ways the artist retained a considerable degree of freedom in the organizing of his composition. Even a portrait presented opportunities for variations, in attitude and expression and in the handling of the background, which were not solely determined by the demands of the sitter.

If a work proved popular the artist would be encouraged to try to repeat the success or it might bring him commissions for other similar works. The sculptor who had once modelled a bull or a lion found himself for ever classed as an animal sculptor. The artist who had succeeded with a religious painting was henceforth in demand for the decoration of churches. The shrewder ones shamelessly exploited a successful vein, but those whose standards were more exacting suffered from being confined within a formula by the public. Fromentin, who was famous for his North African scenes had difficulties of this kind:

'Whatever he suggested he would get the reply, "No, do us one of your Algerian things. You know, one of those little horses with glossy coats you're so good at!" So he would curse and for the hundredth time begin to paint the little white horse, the little blue sky, the little silvery river, the little tree unknown to botanical science and the little Arab boy with bare arms.'[1]

Even when working for himself alone the artist was subject to more limitations than he realized. He was still influenced by his teachers, particularly in the early stages of his career. David's pupils had a hard time freeing themselves from the Greco-Roman subjects he had introduced them to for life.

It was also difficult to escape the influence of fashion and of the atmosphere of the times, which affected the way pictures were painted as well as the subject. And it was fashion which led the most traditionally-minded artists to imitate the innovators they had formerly opposed. We shall see members of the Institut using a lighter palette towards the end of the century, thus coming closer to the same Impressionists they had denounced as dangerous revolutionaries twenty-five years earlier.

Who, apart from a few solitaries, could completely escape the demands of the century? There is more than a grain of truth in Taine's famous dictum when he claimed somewhat over-dogmatically, around 1865, that the artist was the product of his time and his background. It was hardly possible for the nineteenth-century artist not to accept the then sacrosanct principle of the hierarchy of genres. For the critics and the public, and consequently for the artists themselves, the subject matter of a painting automatically indicated the importance and value of a work. Now, when the very concept of subject matter has almost disappeared and when a a still life, a few apples on a table, maybe painted by an artist like Cézanne, ranks higher than a great historical, decorative painting of the type of Paul Delaroche's Hémicycle of the Ecole des Beaux-Arts – to say nothing of the work of non-figurative artists – it is hard for us to understand these once formidable imperatives. But the following conversation between young Ary Scheffer and his teacher Guérin which took place in about 1820 should help us to reach a better appreciation of their importance.

The young painter had just finished *The Soldier's Widow* and brought it to show his master. Guérin burst out: 'Ah! Scheffer, is it possible that you would abandon great painting in this fashion? Have you renounced in advance all the success I predicted for you?' The future painter of *Saint Augustine* replied: 'Sir, I love my mother and I need money, both for her and for myself. Do not be concerned if I now take a different direction. When I have made a name and my position is secure I shall return and then perhaps I shall do my teacher greater honour than he seems to expect from me now.'[2]

For at that time the true artist, the only one who could be compared with the great masters of the past, was the history painter. History painting meant paintings in the grand style which took their subjects from mythology as well as from history and which had gods and heroes as their protagonists in preference to kings. For the pre-eminence of subjects from antiquity was unquestioned. Even the painter of religious subjects occupied a slightly lower position. As for the landscape painter, he was only worthy of consideration if he subordinated his art to the genre of 'historic landscape', that is if he painted setpieces where a stylized landscape served only as a background. Jean-Baptiste Deperthes' *Théorie du paysage* published in 1818 advised as to the choice of subjects: the painter should select a scene which would inspire the spectator with noble sentiments and take only his raw material from nature, eliminating everything which conflicted with ideal beauty.

Where history was concerned all periods did not rank equally. The more exacting disapproved of the battle scenes Napoleon got Gros or Gérard to paint under the direction of Vivant-Denon. Thirty years later Ingres was to judge his contemporaries, Delacroix in particular, as follows:

'Modern painters call themselves history painters: it is essential to destroy this claim. A history painter is one who represents heroic deeds, and such deeds are only to be found in the history of the Greeks and the Romans; and it is through them that the artist can display his skill in painting nudes and draperies; all other periods only yield *genre paintings* because the costume conceals the body. It is because of costume that so-called Romantic painters are able to construct their pictures so easily without having learned the first thing about the structure of the human body.'[3]

'Genre painting' – this was the label often scornfully attached to subjects taken from contemporary history or contemporary life, or to those story paintings which nevertheless became increasingly popular with painters, as they flattered the curiosity of the bourgeois public. Portraits ranked no higher unless they were official portraits. Pure landscape had a hard struggle to become accepted; a man like Corot seldom refrained from adding at least a few figures in silhouette to his splendid views of Italy or the Ile-de-France.

When the realists wished to renew what was after all also an honourable tradition, that of the minor Dutch masters, and paint scenes from the life of their times, even its sordid aspects, they provoked either laughter or scandal. Take for example Couture's reply to young Manet when he was about to enter his *Absinthe-Drinker* for the Salon of 1859 (it was in fact rejected): 'An absinthe-drinker! How can you paint anything so abominable? My poor friend, you are the absinthe-drinker, you are the one who has lost his moral sense.'[4]

Choice of a subject in the grand style presupposed knowledge derived from reading. But the artist worthy of the name had to be able to visualize the scene in plastic form, taking the written text as his point of departure.

In 1804 Prud'hon was dining with Frochot, Prefect of the Seine, when someone mentioned the picture which had been suggested to decorate the assize court and during the course of the conversation Frochot quoted these lines from Horace:

> '*Raro antecedentem sceler atum*
> *Deseruit poena. . . .*'

These few words by the poet were enough to awaken Prud'hon's imagination and there and then he sketched out a dramatic allegory. Such was the origin of his famous painting *Divine Vengeance and Justice pursuing Crime*, which is now in the Louvre.[5]

When Delacroix was trying to find a subject to decorate the library of the Luxembourg his friend Villot, who had been reading Dante, showed him the passage where Dante meets Homer and the other poets of antiquity at the entrance to Hell. At once the artist's imagination set to work.[6]

Gérôme's *The Century of Augustus*, an enormous canvas ten yards by seven, was inspired by a page from Bossuet whom he followed in the greatest detail when depicting the protagonists. The public loved these *grandes machines*, as this type of painting was called, and

4 Bouguereau's studio

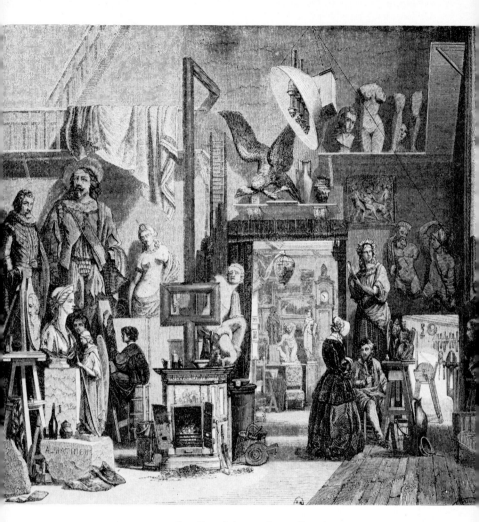

5   Studio of the sculptor Dantan

liked to find in them echoes of what they had learned at school, but one can understand how other artists came to attack this conception of painting, dismissing it with the phrase (whose authorship is disputed): *'Défense de déposer de la littérature le long des beaux-arts'* (leave no 'litter-ature' in the fine arts).

Yet it was from their readings that many artists of the romantic era found themes far removed from the Greco-Roman tradition. Endless examples could be quoted: Louis Boulanger's *La Ronde du Sabbat* was inspired by Victor Hugo; a text from Chateaubriand inspired the sculptor Maindron to create *Velléda*, and Delacroix found subjects in Shakespeare, Goethe and Byron which shocked his contemporaries by their novelty, while delighting the younger generation.

Spontaneous and unacknowledged recollections of their predecessors' work also inspired artists. Visits to museums had an important part to play in what was a more or less sub-conscious process. The opening of the Muséum des Arts, later the Musée du Louvre, gave nineteenth-century artists opportunities not available to those in earlier years. Of course, only very unscrupulous artists set about constructing a picture in the way Balzac's Pierre Grassou did; the novelist describes his *Toilette de Chouan** as follows:

'Quite simply he took his inspiration from Gerald Dow's masterpiece: he turned the group in the *Woman with Dropsy* to face the window instead of facing front, replaced the dying woman by the condemned man – the same pallor, same stare, same appeal to God; instead of the Flemish doctor the cold official figure of the *greffier* dressed in black. . . .'

When Didier Boguet exhibited his Italian landscapes in 1836 the accusation was made, not without some justification, that they were a pastiche of Van der Meulen.

Borrowing from well-known works of art was more common than is generally realized, but it was usually less obvious than in Boguet's case. When Manet's *Lunch on the Grass* caused a scandal at the Salon of 1861 nobody seems to have recognized the engraving by Marc Antonio Raimondi after Raphael, where the figures are grouped in exactly the same way, nor to have remembered Giorgione's *Pastoral*

---

* *Chouan* was the name given to the Breton peasants who rose against the Revolutionary government in support of the king and Catholic religion.

Symphony, which uses the same combination of dressed male and nude female figures.

Girodet was inspired by a bas-relief in the Villa Borghese for his *Endymion*, and David by an antique medallion for his *Sabine Women*. We know from Delacroix's *Journal* that the artist liked to look at Andrea del Sarto's *Charity* in the Louvre, so it is hardly surprising to find the pyramidical composition of this picture and the group of young children dominated by a woman's torso in the *Medea* which Delacroix painted in 1838.

Nor can it be denied that the subject might be purely and simply copied from an existing picture when we know that Cézanne could reproduce illustrations from the *Magasin pittoresque* or from fashion magazines lent him by his sister when he ran out of ideas.

Even the greatest painters sometimes went as far as to model details on pictures in museums. Louis de Planet, who collaborated with Delacroix in his great decorative paintings, confides in his notes:

'Use Giorgione's *Pastoral Symphony* for the clouds, copy them exactly; and for the trees study how the trees in Giorgione's picture stand out sharply against the clouds and less sharply against the blue of the sky. Also use Salvator Rosa's *Battle* for the blue of the sky, just the right tone for my picture. . . . Use also the old tree in Swanewelt's landscape. . . .'[8]

Since sculptors were less tied than painters to the requirements of the background, they had greater freedom in choosing their subjects. They would often carve a nude or a draped figure, naming it afterwards as occasion or fashion suggested, Eve, Venus or Silence. When Perraud was asked in 1872 what his idea was in sculpting a *Galatea* he replied: 'Ideas, I never bother about them. I wanted to do a beautiful woman, that's all.'[9] A raised arm, a gesture which had attracted Pradier, inspired his statue of *Nyssia*; his *Cassandra* originated with a fine torso.

'Even his *Sappho*, the only one of his statues which expressed an idea or which tried to depict a character, was inspired by the position which a model had adopted spontaneously with both arms resting on the knees.'[10]

According to tradition, which may be no more than a legend, Rude's *Napolitan Fisherboy* who is crouching playing with a tortoise, arose out of the sculptor's wish to use a triangular block of Parian marble.

It sometimes happened that circumstances caused a work of art to change its name. Etex wanted to submit a figure he had called *Poland in Chains* to the Salon of 1859, but on learning that it was likely to be refused for political reasons, he had it accepted, and even purchased for the state, under the name of *Olympia*. When a statue was to be raised to the Republic in 1878, Clésinger had no hesitation in putting forward the one he had carved in honour of Imperial France![11]

Though in many cases the origin of the subject is to be explained by chance, in others it corresponds to the deepest feelings of the artist. Both *Massacre at Chios* and *Liberty Leading the People* were painted under the shock of tragic events or out of strongly held principles. Other works are the expression of a recognized or an unacknowledged obsession on the part of the artist; such is the explanation of the sensuality of *The Death of Sardanapalus* as imagined by Delacroix or of *The Turkish Bath* painted by Ingres at the age of eighty. Gustave Moreau's mythological reconstructions and Odilon Redon's visions reflect the wish to make the kingdom of the gods or the infinite world of dreams accessible to others but first of all to oneself. Psychoanalysis has since come to explain or justify these creations in the service of the invisible world, but the artists did not wait to enter and take us with them.

The first idea was not enough by itself; it was necessary to give body to the theme; it might take a long time to come to fruition or might result from a sudden flash of inspiration, depending on circumstances and the temperament of the artist. Said Detaille:

'I compose a picture in my head, like a musician composing without a piano; but to bring it to maturity I need walks, solitude, the open air. One picture may require whole months of inner reflection; and there are others which have been germinating inside my head for years. It is only when I can see my vision with the inner eye that I commit it to paper; it is then complete and I seldom change anything.'[12]

With other artists the germination process took place at night or while they were asleep. Gustave Moreau always had a sketchbook

67

on his bedside table to enter the ideas that had come to him as he lay awake the following day.

But daily practice made the creative faculty more supple for both painter and sculptor; they kept up their skill, like the virtuoso musician practising scales, through exercises, sketching possible subjects and trying to improve their style. Their sketchbooks afterwards provided them with a stock of forms. According to Théodore Silvestre, Delacroix had accumulated 'mountains of drawings, in ink and in pencil, both from life and from memory'.[13]

They improved their knowledge of anatomy by the study of corpses. Gleyre in his youth haunted the mortuary. Géricault and Delacroix gained entry to the dissecting rooms to study the insertion of the muscles and how they functioned. But it was also necessary to catch attitudes from life which models did not assume so spontaneously: this was the reason for those sketches in the street, on the omnibuses, on the café terrace and in the theatre. The most skilful preferred to observe closely and to draw afterwards from memory.

Animals required lengthy studies, hardly possible at the Ecole. Accordingly, artists could be seen witnessing the departure of the stage coach, or at horse markets, or at the races. Delacroix noted in his *Journal* for 1823 that he ought to visit a stable every morning. Many studies could be made in the Jardin des Plantes of the animals in the menagerie there while the nearby museum contained skeletons and stuffed animals. Frémiet, Gérôme and Rodin all spent much time here. Barye, who was to become the great animal sculptor of the century, has left us copious notes, including a list of the different breeds of dog, with even the animals' measurements noted on his sketches.

But they all copied the old masters, an exercise which had formed the basis of their formal art training; many in fact enjoyed doing so and some even overdid it. Long after they had left behind them the age for entering competitions, painters continued to make copies. Manet reproduced canvases by Titian, Tintoretto and Velazquez when he was already over twenty-five. Ingres as an old man still subjected himself to this discipline, claiming that he always had something to learn.

It should be remembered that it was much more difficult to get to know works of art in museums, particularly museums abroad, than it is now. The ex-'Romans' could recall the museums of Italy; the lucky ones had stacks of sketches in their notebooks of the works of art they had come across during their travels. But for others – the mediocre copies and casts, such as those of the Ecole des Beaux-Arts apart – their studies had to be based on engravings: pale shadows of the great originals, often rough approximations in line-engraving or lithograph by interpreters themselves without talent.

Nevertheless, engravings were very important and many artists visited the Print Room of the Bibliothèque Nationale (or Royale or Imperiale according to the regime in power) to study them. During the early years of the century they were allowed to take part of the collection home with them. As late as 1822 Gérard, engaged on a royal commission, was authorized to enjoy this privilege. But usually they studied in the Print Room itself; some had had their names put down when barely more than children – Isabey's son for example was only thirteen and Alexandre Hesse fourteen. Delacroix was only eighteen when he paid his first visit in 1816 and Daubigny was the same age when he came for the first time in 1833. But many came back gladly. David d'Angers might be seen next to Bourguereau, and Corot next to Raffet in the hall in the rue de Richelieu. In 1833 alone 476 cards were issued to artists. Degas's name appears in 1853, Rodin's in 1856, Renoir's in 1861, Detaille's in 1868, and Vuillard's in 1887.[14]

Engravings were easier to collect and less expensive than paintings. Until photography was invented they were the only way the individual could build up his 'imaginary museum'. No painter's or sculptor's studio was complete without boxes of prints of his favourite pictures. In order to 'fix the shapes in the memory', Fantin-Latour often used to finish the evening tracing the outlines of famous paintings by lamplight. Delacroix, on the contrary, studied his collection in the morning, spending most time on Rubens and copying details. Charles Blanc used to say of him that he 'took Rubens like other people take coffee'. And Bergeret wrote maliciously about the painter of the *Apotheosis of Homer*: 'Take away M. Ingres' casts, his prints, his works of art and we shall see just what emerges from his difficult and painful labour!'[15]

Engravings not only got the artist's imagination working, they were an inexhaustible source of documentation. Here were to be found details of costume, the exact lines of a ship, the silhouette of a momument, the attributes of a god or a hero. Once the subject had been decided and the composition of the painting fixed, and its broad lines sketched in, then actual models not memories were to be used for its execution. Both sculptor and painter – but particularly the painter – needed documentary source materials; they had now to compose the elements of the scene they had imagined, using real objects, and their figures had to be drawn from living models capable of reproducing the poses and the gestures required.

We possess a certain amount of information about the way David worked on his great picture of the coronation of the Emperor Napoleon. The painter had obtained a place in the stands on the day of the ceremony and had been able to make valuable observations. But as he was only given the commission after the event he took his inspiration from engravings of the coronation of Louis XIV at Rheims and from Rubens' *Coronation of Maria de Medici* which was then in the Luxembourg (now in the Louvre). He was able to make portraits of most of the main figures, including several of the Pope. The moment selected was chosen by agreement with the Emperor to whom David had made various suggestions: it shows Napoleon himself crowning the Empress Josephine. David then constructed a model of the choir of Notre Dame lit from above, using dolls to study the attitudes adopted by the protagonists and the effects of light. The picture itself was prepared by his pupil Rouget before David himself took up work on it again and finished the figures and the main details of the scene. It took three years' work in all.[16]

The Raft of the Medusa, which made such an impression on visitors to the Salon of 1819, caused Géricault special problems. He had a carpenter make a replica of the famous raft, haunted the hospital of Beaujon to observe the dead and the dying and, quite undeterred by decay and putrefaction, even had corpses and severed limbs brought to his studio.

The artist's choice of subject did not always confront him with such disagreeable experiences, but the need for authenticity often compelled him to seek information from the most diverse sources. When Delacroix, who had never visited the East, wanted to depict the massacres on the Greek island of Chios in 1823, he had to interrogate witnesses and borrow oriental costumes from his friend M. Auguste.

Puvis de Chavannes did not have to follow history so closely when he painted the life of Saint Geneviève in the Pantheon, but he adapted contemporary sources, cleverly transposed; he made use of scenes he had observed at Les Halles and the quai Saint-Bernard, took the face of Saint Germain from a church dignitary he had seen one day, and was inspired by the landscapes along the banks of the Seine and in the plain of Nanterre.

When Paul Baudry undertook the decoration of the great foyer of the Opera he engaged in many more preparations. He travelled all over Europe for six years seeking or revisiting models for his inspiration. He copied Michelangelo in the Sistine Chapel for eight months; then went to London to study Raphael's tapestry cartoons in the Victoria and Albert Museum at South Kensington; in Madrid he studied Velazquez; in Venice Titian and Tintoretto.[17]

The spirit of the times favoured recreating scenes from history and romanticism stressed the importance of local colour. But the search for documentation exact enough to satisfy the historians led down the dangerous path of archaeological reconstruction. Taine in 1867 criticized artists who deviated from their proper role, saying:

'In order to acquire local colour many of our artists have turned themselves into antiquaries, or tourists, or dealers in second-hand clothes; they have become Greeks, Egyptians, Etruscans and men of the Middle Ages. Their pictures are instructive but terrifying; such concern for authentic detail turns the work into a scientific document and should make its author eligible for the Académie des Inscriptions.'[18]

When Paul Baudry, who was always very conscientious, was called upon to paint episodes from the life of Joan of Arc for the chapels of the Pantheon, he died before he had finished his researches; he worked on manuscripts in the Bibliothèque Nationale and in the library of the Arsenal, visited Lille and Brussels to consult others which had belonged to the Dukes of Burgundy, and went personally to study sites at Orleans, Amboise, Chinon and other places. A historian said of Baudry that no one knew the first half of the fifteenth century as he did.

Military painters were among the most conscientious, whether they produced enormous frescoes like Horace Vernet, Detaille and Alphonse de Neuville, or small pictures full of minute detail like Meissonier. Painting contemporary scenes or scenes from the recent past increased the burden of reconstruction.

So Meissonier, who had spent fourteen years on his famous *1807*, was overcome by scruples just as he was about to send it to the

Salon of 1880; realizing that he had made a mistake in the regi-
mental numbers of the dragoons, he repainted them all. Many other
examples could be quoted of Meissonier's mania for accumulating
documentary materials. After his death his collection was left to the
Musée de l'Armée. He bought old carriages in order to draw them;
he got his wife to follow old patterns and early engravings and make
up costumes he could dress his models in out of pieces of material
and old uniforms. In order to be sure of depicting the Emperor with
the bearing he wanted him to have, he dressed himself up in
specially made clothes and was to be seen in the garden of his house
at Poissy astride a construction representing a horse: 'He had a
board in one hand covered with a sheet of white paper and copied
his reflection in the great upright mirror in front of him, using
watercolours.'

The absurdity of such proceedings became patently obvious when
he dressed a model in hussar's uniform, made him pose motionless
as a statue for several hours – and only painted the carbine hanging
from his belt! In order to paint the ground for the retreat from
Russia he had to wait until it snowed, get his servants to trample
the snow underfoot and have a cart rolled over it to create ruts.
Then he sat down to paint in the open, regardless of the cold.

These methods were adopted by other painters of the time, like
Roll, Neuville and Jean-Paul Laurens, and won them the admiration of 'connoisseurs' and unbounded success with the public. They
also gave rise to a number of jokes like this story told by Duranty
about Meissonier's famous *Cavalry Charge*. If we are to believe
Duranty, the painter first had a troop of cavalry charging in his
park, but the horses disappeared out of sight before he could catch
their movements. Whereupon the artist did not hesitate to employ
still more grandiose methods; he had a railway track built so that
he could follow the whirling horses in a truck.[19]

Pure landscape and still life were considered minor genres: a picture
worthy of the name included people. However, it was more difficult
to invent an attitude than it was to invent the shape of an object.
Apart from the rare cases when existing drawings could be used, a
model had to be posed, using exactly the gestures required for the
scene. Study of the living model then represented an important
stage in the execution of a painting or a statute.

Some artists used, instead of real people of flesh and blood, articulated mannequins bought from specialist shops which gave an approximate silhouette. Gustave Moreau used his skill in modelling to fashion wooden lay figures covered with paper-mâché on which he arranged his draperies. The discovery of photography led some artists to believe they could dispense with living models. Delacroix who, let it be noted, was one of the first members of the Société Française de Photographie, used photographs of the nude which were just beginning to be distributed commercially. He even got his friend Durrieu to take photographs of models in previously determined poses in order to be able to use them later when a suitable occasion arose. Delacroix went so far as to write that only these photographs represented the exact truth: 'They are the palpable demonstration of nature's design of which we have never had other than a very imperfect notion.'[20]

Other artists were less ready to welcome this innovation, yet made use of it. It is possible that the famous figure of a nude woman who queens it in Courbet's picture of an artist's studio was painted from a photograph.

But in the majority of cases artists preferred to have recourse to living models. Sometimes the good will of members of their entourage afforded them both convenience and the guarantee of an air of naturalness. Manet was glad to paint his wife, his godson Léon Leenhoff and friends and disciples like Eva Gonzalès and Berthe Morisot. Artists as different as Delacroix, Gavarni and Degas frequently used relatives or comrades in their paintings. We do not refer here to portraits where the problems are different but to compositions in which friends and family appeared anonymously. For example Degas's L'Absinthe was posed by the engraver Marcellin Desboutin and a woman singer who was one of their friends.

But though it might be convenient to use friends and family in domestic or indoor scenes it was less so where vigorous action was involved or where the protagonists took part in dramatic scenes. Nevertheless, Rude used his wife for the figure of The Marseillaise on the Arc de Triomphe: he urged her to shout with mouth wide open, demanding repeatedly: 'Louder, louder!' The artist's collaborators sometimes served as models on occasion. David's pupils posed for his Napoleon at Mont Saint-Bernard. Ingres had one of his pupils represent young Seleucus kneeling by the bed in his Stratonice but was not pleased with the result. So this man of over fifty finally undressed, draped himself and flung himself into the attitude he had conceived while his pupils copied it on paper. He did the same in his preparatory studies for the Virgin of the *Vow of Louis XIII*, climbing up on a ladder with a bundle of rags in his arms to represent the Child while his collaborators were able to note the silhouette he had imagined from below.[21]

In most cases, however, the artists finally had recourse to professional models, a social class essential to the artist and deserving separate study.

The problem was to find a model whose character and appearance were suited to the subject to be represented. So artists noted names and addresses, as Delacroix, for example, used to do. In his 1850 diary we read:

'Mme Carbon, rue Fontaine-Saint-Georges, 44; an elegant model, quite tall, poses draperies.

Mlle Eléanore, rue Notre-Dame-de-Lorette, 40; a very pretty model, a pocket Venus.'[22]

Very young models were to be found, including children, who posed with or without their mothers; there were handsome old men of various types – those with long and flowing beards were much sought after to pose as rivers; there were slender women and Rubenesque women. The cleverest were capable of different types of work: the 'little Aubigny' posed for Puvis de Chavannes' *Hope* as well as for Manet's less idealized women. Caricaturists were always ready to make fun of these young women who specialized in the most unexpected roles: 'Mlle Nina poses angels and virtues at four francs a session. N.B. Payment for capital sins by arrangement to be agreed between the parties.'[23]

Those who followed this profession for a number of years naturally experienced changes in fashion. Dubosc, when a young child in David's time, posed holding the bow and quiver of the god of Love; by 1830 he wore doublet or armour more often than the toga; and twenty years later he was usually asked to put on military uniforms. In a comedy at the Palais Royal called *Le Salon de 1831* a model listed humorously the different types of employment he had undertaken: during the Revolution he posed as a gladiator while his wife was Venus, Psyche or one of the three Graces; then he posed as a grenadier and his wife as a *vivandière*; since the July Revolution he had taken the Louvre and the Tuileries more than once in oil paint while his wife was to be found on every piece of artillery and his son on all the barricades.[24]

As models were seldom of exceptional beauty, some artists used different models for different parts of the body. Not a very satisfactory solution but what better one was there? Delacroix's assistant Louis de Planet has given us his master's opinion on the subject:

'The living model, said Monsieur Delacroix, never exactly renders the idea of the figure one wants to represent; either a model is mean or inadequate in appearance or else possesses a different, perhaps superior, type of beauty so that one is led to change everything. The idea you had escapes you and mere imitation takes its place. An example is the case of *père* Cotte, who is a magnificent model but was mean and round and small in the pose of Pliny; after giving the movement for the first studies and he softened the energy of it for the sketch.'[25]

In the last resort Delacroix reckoned that the model provided the artist with a point of reference, a sort of confirmation of forms which he ought already to have memorized.

However handsome their appearance, models changed and grew old. The men, who were often wrestlers with particularly well-developed muscles, had a longer modelling life than the women, who usually only lasted about ten years. The famous Dubosc, on the other hand, modelled from the age of seven to sixty-two.

Their shorter working life explains why women models were more expensive than the men. In 1852 a woman would ask four or five francs for what was usually a four-hour session while a man was only paid three francs. Around 1885 the rates went up, and women models were paid ten francs a session, more if they were exceptionally pretty, though Italians could be found for five francs; whereas men never made more than five francs a session, six if they worked for sculptors.

The artists had many difficulties with their models. Bad models were unpunctual and demanded more coal in the stove because they were always complaining of the cold. They posed slackly, needing constant reminders. Dubosc, who had so many claims to the gratitude of artists, was exceptional: he had a constitution of iron and showed quite remarkable fortitude when modelling. He gave sessions three times a day, was apparently never tired and sometimes became so stiff when holding difficult poses that he had

75

to be helped to his feet.[26] Dubosc was indefatigable, showed great understanding of the work of those who employed him and was only demanding when it came to getting paid. But those who criticized his meanness were astonished when he retired in 1859 and they learned that this unassuming man had accumulated a fortune that yielded him an income of 3,000 francs a year (which at that time would require a capital sum of one hundred thousand francs). What is more, Dubosc only kept for himself a monthly allowance of 200 francs and gave the rest to the Ecole des Beaux-Arts to help young artists competing for the Prix de Rome – a fine example of generosity on the part of one who was not himself an educated man.

Special problems arose with the employment of women models. It was difficult to persuade good-looking girls to stay with artists who had counted on them as models for several months. If in the meantime they found an easier and more lucrative way of exploiting their physical attractiveness they would be off. From 1845 onwards, whenever the Théatre du Cirque Olympique mounted spectacular shows in which the girls wore tights and costumes which revealed the figure, the models deserted the studios. During the Second Empire Louis Leroy noted that these girls usually appeared in feerie scenes which gave them the illusion of being actresses, and their figures were always appreciated by the enthusiasts in the orchestra stalls. He adds: 'joining the ranks of kept women presents itself to them as an alternative to modelling and the painter can never be sure of finishing his picture with the same hired Venus with which he began'.[27]

Fortunately, at about this time a large contingent of Italian models arrived in Paris, mainly peasant women from the region of Naples, just in time to compensate for the shortage of French models. Towards the end of the century it was estimated that 500 Italians, both men and women, lived by modelling in Paris. Nearly all of them lived in the district close to place Jussier, especially in the rue des Boulangers. However, the market where models were hired was then held in the Place Pigalle around the fountain, and the Italian women in their picturesque national dress were by far the most numerous. In 1885 one of their compatriots by the name of Socci had the idea of opening an agency for models in the boulevard de Clichy to help them find work. Painters and sculptors could make their choice from the available models, photographs and plaster casts supplying them with all the information they needed.[28]

Living necessarily in close contact created ties between artists and models. It was unusual for an artist to do as Bouguereau did: his favourite model was engaged by the month for a regular salary of 300 francs, ate with the family and knitted or helped in the kitchen between modelling sessions. But a good model could learn a lot from contact with the artists, appreciated their jokes, spread good stories from studio to studio, knew how to be an agreeable companion and would clean the palettes or help carry canvases to the salon. Some were proud of their profession, like Dubosc, who used to go to exhibitions to see the pictures he had posed for, or like Bauve who posed for the young boy in Rude's *La Marseillaise* and would repeat to anyone who cared to listen: 'My portrait is on the Arc-de-Triomphe!'[29]

A man who aged too rapidly to carry on modelling often found it difficult to find other work. And for one who became *concierge* at the Ecole des Beaux-Arts there were many who became drivers of horse buses; why it should be this job they took no one quite knows. Others disappeared into poverty or relied on occasional help from artists who took pity on them.

The case of the female models was more delicate. Being an artists' model was apt to give rise to ill-natured gossip. It was one thing to pose for a group of students and another to pose alone with a painter: 'For these students a model is a creature without sex; they regard her almost like an object like a plaster cast who differs from the statues only in her colouring and in the imperfections of her figure.'[30] This report no doubt oversimplifies the problem; the models of the Ecole des Beaux-Arts did not always escape doubtful jokes or propositions. But a young artist alone with an attractive model was prey to other temptations. Delacroix preferred to use Italian to describe his amorous exploits, and his *Journal* leaves us in no doubt that his experiments with certain models were not always aesthetic in nature. In January 1824 Emilie Robert, whose magnificent torso is that of the woman tied to the horse in the *Massacre at Chios*, posed for him. This combination of activities did nothing to blunt his ardour for painting; but as he himself conceded, 'You need to be young for that sort of thing'. He continued to treat her as an ordinary model, and we read two days later: 'Gave Emilie Robert for three sessions for my picture: 12 francs'.[31]

What many of these women were in fact looking for was a permanent liaison or marriage. Monet and Renoir among others married their models. And the hero of the Goncourts' *Manette*

Salomon was one who chose this solution. If the novelists are to be believed, a woman of this type could not but cause the artist to fail by turning him from his ideal – a simplistic thesis and one unconfirmed by what is known of the facts.

CHAPTER FIVE

TECHNIQUE AND EXECUTION

To imagine a subject, work out the composition and sketch its different elements from models, all this is not by itself enough. The actual execution of a painting or statue is a complex and often lengthy task, and the technique cannot be improvised. It is at this stage that the work of the artist most closely resembles that of the craftsman; here too the differences between painter and sculptor are greatest.

The technique of painting and sculpture seems to have changed little over the centuries; recipes were handed down from master to pupil. But apparently, after the end of the Ancien Régime, the teaching of art developed an aesthetic bent and high-flown theories often reduced the role of practice. Louis David was accused of having taught an entire generation of painters to scorn the formulas inherited from the past, thus widening the breach. Degas was expressing a widely held opinion when he said to a friend: 'We live in strange times, it must be admitted. This oil painting of ours – this very difficult art we practise without knowing how. You never saw such inconsistency.'[1] The fact that specialist dealers were increasingly preparing the materials the artists used justified a shorter apprenticeship, but disappointment lay in store for those who had too little respect for the fundamentals of their craft; cracked varnish and darkened colours were often the fate of pictures painted with too little regard for unchanging technical requirements.

Then as now, most suppliers of artists' materials were to be found near the Ecole des Beaux-Arts. Haro is well known to us from Delacroix's papers; Delacroix himself most often dealt with him and he was also Ingres' official supplier. He opened his shop in 1826 in the rue du Colombier, that is to say on the corner of the rue Jacob and the present rue Bonaparte. Haro's own headed paper tells us exactly what artists could expect from him:

'Haro at the Génie des Arts, rue du Columbier No. 30 in the Faubourg Saint-Germain, colourman and picture restorer, stocks everything needed for oil-painting, miniature, drawing, water-colour, tinting drawings and pastel; all qualities of paper, every kind of chalk, gold frames in all widths; mounts and frames prints and drawings and dispatches orders to the provinces and abroad.'[2]

To become a dealer in artists' colours and in paper, then a picture framer and afterwards restorer: such was the path readily followed by successful colourmen. By 1850 Etienne Haro who had succeeded his father had a studio in the rue Marais-Saint-Germain which specialized in repairing damaged paintings, relining canvases and restoring. Eventually he became a dealer in works of art, an expert and the adviser of artists. It was he who found Delacroix the house in the rue Furstemberg in 1857.

The support of the painting was sometimes a panel of wood or board, more usually canvas stretched over a frame. Dealers supplied these in all recognized sizes; they were known by the traditional numbers which corresponded to each canvas size available. The canvas was sized, then primed with three coats of white lead; sometimes a grey or brownish-red ground was used. Few painters preferred to prepare their own canvases – as Daubigny did at the height of his success in 1875 in spite of the time it took. Those who ground and mixed their own colours as painters had done in the past, or who supervised their preparation by assistants, were just as few. Most did as Delacroix when he sent the following note to Madame Haro on October 29, 1837:

'Monsieur Delacroix presents his compliments to Madame Haro and asks her to be so kind as to prepare for him straightaway six bladders of white lead, six of Naples yellow, two of yellow ochre, two of cobalt, and two of peach black, all of them more liquid than the colours prepared for everyone else. He will call tomorrow (Tuesday) morning without fail to collect them at seven o'clock.'[3]

The colours delivered in bladders were badly protected and soon dried; others like lake colours or Prussian blue were unstable and faded rapidly. The use of metal tubes, first of galvanized copper and later of tin, to protect the colours was an innovation which was warmly welcomed, because it meant that they were easier to use and kept better. And soon this English invention, which had won a prize in London in 1824, was in general use all over the Continent. Now that the colours were better protected they were more stable and not so messy to use. They were also easier to carry about, so that the artist could take his painting equipment outside his studio – an indirect contribution to the development of the open-air school of painting.

However, research and experiment were not precluded because of this invention. Not only did each painter compose his palette as he thought best but he might vary it at different times and according to the subject of the painting. Delacroix, for example, has left very full notes on the different palettes he used. Since his pupils collaborated in his work he had to define very exactly the shades he wanted them to use.

Furthermore, many painters believed they could give their pictures a better appearance or ensure their preservation by adopting special procedures of their own. There was hardly one who did not use some personal trick, whether it was his own ingenious invention or an old secret handed down by a teacher or a friend. The less competent painters were the more readily addicted to this type of research, in the somewhat naive hope that a new binding medium or a pigment hitherto unknown would give their pictures a more attractive appearance or else that quality which had eluded them. Artists' memoirs and the treatises which they wrote are full of these definitive recipes which are, however, usually highly debatable. Even the best did not escape this kind of thing: in 1853 we find Delacroix trying to substitute olive oil for the linseed oil or poppy-seed oil which were usually employed in painting; at one time he thought of growing madder for himself. Nor was this all.

At the end of the century Bouguereau and Detaille prophesied a return to egg tempera, while some of their colleagues who had been impressed by the work of Pasteur and Chevreul believed they could reach an exact understanding of the mysteries of colour through the study of chemistry. Yet it cannot be said that their research had much effect on the technique of painting. Many old pictures, painted according to rule-of-thumb methods, have turned out to have lasted better than more recent works which tried to take into account the discoveries of science.

The painter sketched on the prepared canvas the broad lines of his composition, using the preparatory drawings on which he might have spent much time or possibly very little. Horace Vernet, who was a rapid painter, was content to sketch the whole of his *Smalah of Abd el-Kader* on a single sheet of paper with figures an inch or so high, when the finished work was to be more than twenty yards long. But usually the preliminary sketch was prepared with more care; it might be squared for enlargement on canvas, and the squaring and transfer were often the work of a skilled assistant. The outlines were put in first in chalk or charcoal, then one or other of two different procedures was adopted.

Some painters, among them David and his disciples, painted directly on the white canvas, trying to achieve perfection of form even in the details of figures and objects. The other school of thought was the more widespread; and the methods consisted of first painting a monochrome sketch usually in grisaille, so that the overall effect could be judged. The sketch then had to be left to dry for at least a fortnight before work could be resumed. When the composition was a very large one it was usually the masters' pupils who carried out this part of the work. This was the method followed by Delacroix in his decorative paintings. Ingres preferred to paint the sketch himself and then his assistants painted whole sections of the final picture.

Balze has told how he and his comrades in Ingres' studio painted the architecture, mosaics and furniture for the master's *Stratonice*.[4] Naturally the master himself always finished the work, painting in the figures and putting thin glazes over parts of the picture which were already far advanced but where he needed to leave his mark.

The choice of colours was the painters' own, but both tradition and fashion played a part in dictating or suggesting shades to be used or procedures to be followed. The misuse of bitumen around the middle of the century is entirely characteristic of the period. The use of bitumen diluted with wax made it easy for the artist to obtain that transparent yellowish tone resembling the much-prized patina found in old paintings. The resulting shadow which drowned the details and enhanced the attraction of the picture was providential for the less skilful or less scrupulous artists. Unfortunately it cracked with age, as can be seen all too often in some woodland scenes by painters of the Barbizon School.

In their reaction against such methods the Impressionists introduced an entirely new conception of colour which was to revolutionize the history of painting. They chose bright colours like chrome, cadmium and the lakes in preference to the earth colours. They preferred the pure colours of the spectrum and avoided mixing them; even the final coat of varnish which their adversaries used to achieve a certain transparency was outlawed. We know how men like Seurat and Signac gave a more systematic cast to the Impressionists' principles. According to them the little touches of colour laid side by side should blend on the retina of the viewer instead of being mixed together by the painter. This principle of 'optical mixture' which they had found in the works of Chevreul gave painting a more scientific basis. Even if their experiments were only partly successful, they show the extent to which nineteenth-century painters attempted to renew the techniques of their art.

His palette on his left thumb, the long maulstick held out in front of him to stop the paint getting on his clothes, at the same time supporting his right hand in which he holds his brush – here we have our painter at work.

He paints standing up, the more easily to step back from his canvas and judge the effect of each brush stroke from a distance, in the same way as the spectator will judge the finished picture. As Gleyre was always saying to his pupils: 'You may sit in judgment, but you paint standing up.' Of course the painter could sit at his easel when painting small genre pictures, but even then he still had to move in order to look at his work from a distance. And when he was working on an enormous canvas or decorating a wall or a ceiling he would often find himself perched in most uncomfortable positions: on a ladder, a movable platform, or scaffolding. In such cases the dust and the vats of paint he had to use made it necessary for him to protect his clothes by wearing a smock; it might be a white one such as Puvis de Chavannes liked to wear or a blue peasant's smock of the type Corot preferred and which he wore with a cotton night cap.

But many painters were anxious to show that they did not belong to the common people and used to paint in top hat and tail coat, even choosing to wear a velvet coat and a large cravat, the better to distinguish themselves from the common herd. And some wished to resemble the artists of the Quattrocento, wearing a beret with a tassle as Henner used to do, or else a tall round cylindrical hat like Hébert's.

The very act of painting varied from painter to painter; sometimes it was difficult for the outsider to understand the technique, since it was to some extent at least kept secret. Duranty, that fine connoisseur of the arts of the *Pays des Arts*, brings us a little closer to the artist at work in this description of one of his characters, the painter Marcillon:

'The painter's palette was fresh and bright with little patches of colour along the edge.... He dipped his brush into it and with a movement resembling a flick of the fingers placed a light touch of colour on the canvas; or else he filled in the background, or any other large area to be painted all the same colour, with broad, even strokes, afterwards dipping his brush into a darker or a brighter tone and dragging it over the surface of the canvas in order to give a warmer or more vibrant effect. . . . Sometimes he would return to a scumble, i.e. to an area painted lightly and quickly without completely covering the surface and would paint over a few broad horizontal strokes using a fairly thick brush. Sometimes Marcillon would dip a medium-sized brush into a light colour without thinning it in oil and then with a twisting movement would leave an impasto the thickness of a small worm on the canvas. At other times, on the contrary, finding his colours too dry, he dipped a thin brush into a palette cup of oil, picked up a very little paint from the palette and drew the brush very lightly over the canvas, only partly covering the underpainting, so that it still showed through in places. . . . Sometimes his brush worked up and down, sometimes it followed the contour of the object he was painting. At times he was laying on the paint in quick, light touches; at others he used strong movements of the wrist, speeding up or else slowing down and lingering over a brush stroke. Sometimes he applied a good deal of pressure while at other times he was content to merely dab at the canvas.'[5]

Painting methods changed considerably during the course of the century. The classic style of painting was highly finished, carefully following the contours of the forms and all traces of brush strokes were eliminated. Certain portrait painters who sought for easy effects delighted in the virtuoso effect of a *fapresto* technique achieved

84

by skilled brushwork of the kind found in the works of Franz Hals. The Impressionists, by leaving the brushmarks untouched to catch the light, also broke the painter's traditional rhythm of work. Few artists in the second half of the century remained faithful to the ideal of the highly-finished picture and to that air of frigid perfection which pupils at the Ecole des Beaux-Arts had striven so hard to achieve.

In additional to the usual brushes of varying shapes and sizes, painters in the nineteenth century also used the palette knife, originally intended to mix the colours as they came out of the tubes, to apply paint to the canvas. It is often claimed that Courbet was the first to use this method, but both Decamps and Diaz had used it before him to cover large areas with bright colour; with this technique, which some artists abused, a razor is used to cut away any excess of impasto.

'I've been working like a labourer all day: twisting metal bars for the armature of my statue, digging, making *columbins*, that is round boulders of clay, carrying water, cleaning up. . . .'[6]

Thus Chapu, sculptor of *La Pensée* reveals to his parents the nature of the sculptor's daily tasks. Once the artist had 'arrived' he might have assistants to help him, but he could never entirely escape the physical labour which lay at the basis of his art. The sculptor had to come to grips with his material to a far greater extent than the painter, and speculative ideas could not of themselves give birth to a work of art in clay or plaster or marble. It was hard, sometimes heavy work, and required physical strength which was all the more necessary as the sculptor lived in a damp, dusty atmosphere which led to rheumatism.

The sculptor stood before the modelling stand – a revolving stand whose height could be adjusted by a screw – and kneaded the clay, added to it, knocked it out of shape, modelled it with hand or thumb, or used his boaster or roughing chisel to give it the form he had in mind, which would be based on sketches made from the model. Rude used to teach his pupils to use a plumb line and compass to get the muscles in the right place.

Clay is easily modelled, but large masses only retain their shape if supported on a metal armature. This consists of metal bars carefully twisted to form a sort of skeleton. The position of the limbs can be altered without too much difficulty. If the statue is very large the armature must be stronger and has to be welded, when the services of a smith would be required.

Some sculptors preferred wax to clay; they could do finer work, but wax was suitable only for small objects. Barye was one of those who brought this technique back into fashion again. He preferred to leave the iron bars on the outside like a casing in order to make his maquettes easier to handle and give the animals he sculpted that suppleness which was part of their charm.

Once the clay figure was finished it had to be covered with a damp cloth to keep the clay moist and prevent it from cracking. Sculptors often sprayed figures they had abandoned half-way through with a syringe borrowed from an apothecary.

Whether made of clay or wax, the statue at this stage was only a study; the next stage was usually to make a plaster cast which was still comparatively fragile but which could be exhibited to the public. The final work was in marble or bronze and indestructible bar accidents. But the step from plaster to marble or bronze was such a large one and so expensive that it was normally undertaken only on commission. Unless he was able to use a fragment of marble left over from a larger work, the artist usually stopped at the plaster stage until he knew what the fate of his statue was to be.

If fate was kind the sculptor then proceeded to cutting the stone, but this was a long and difficult task. Yet as he struggled with the recalcitrant matter with hammer, chisel and file, having constantly to climb down off his step ladder to judge the overall effect and then clamber up again, the true artist worked joyfully; he would be wearing a white smock, a paper cap on his head and large goggles to protect his eyes against splinters of marble.

The translation from plaster to marble was facilitated by the use of a system involving plumb line and compass to measure the exact depth to hew the stone at each point on the figure. Later, still more ingenious machines simplified the process and made it possible to produce at will figures larger or smaller than the original; for example the pantograph invented by Collas in 1847. With the help of this machine (and also using electrolysis which came into general use at the same time) small statuettes could be obtained cheaply; small pieces were sold to furnish wealthy homes and provided artists with fresh outlets in the absence of commissions for monumental statuary.

A well-organized sculptor had his block of marble prepared by assistants known as *practiciens*; the latter would hew it roughly into shape leaving only a layer a few millimetres thick, or in some cases perhaps certain sections incomplete. Then the master would add the finishing touches, working away meticulously with chisel and file at the surface of his work. In larger works pupils and assistants were sometimes allowed to complete the modelling of an accessory or some secondary drapery. The sculptor who attacked a block which had already been roughly shaped was spared the hardest part of his work and experienced intense joy at the sight of the idea he had conceived emerging from the formless mass and taking shape at each stroke.

When the clay figure was to be cast in bronze, the work was almost entirely out of the artist's hands. He could supervise the casting and reject any pieces which did not satisfy him, but for the rest he had to rely on the skill of the founder. Such work was carried out for example at the foundry of the Susse family in the Passage des Panoramas, and later in the rue Vivienne.[7] Sometimes works were cast in one piece, using the lost wax method (*cire perdue*), but it was more usual at this period to cast different parts of the statue separately and weld them together afterwards; the joins were polished and care taken to achieve the desired patina.

But bronze had the advantage over marble in that it was easier to produce a number of copies so that a sculptor might be represented by several copies of a work in public and private collections – which helped him to become better known.

Both painting and sculpture might be practised by amateurs. But an artist who was engaged on an important work, who was preparing an exhibition and who had to fulfil commissions, knew how much courage and perserverance was required. The *Coronation of Napoleon* was commissioned from David in December 1894 and only finished in 1808. Ingres required four years to complete his *Stratonice;* his *Vow of Louis XIII* took three and a half years to prepare and nine months to carry out. Meissonier had his painting *1807* on his easel for fourteen years before offering it to the public.

Certainly there were artists who were less scrupulous or who worked more quickly: Horace Vernet only needed ten months for his *Smalah of Abdel Kader* which was twenty-five yards long and one of the largest pictures ever painted, and he still found the energy in the evenings to prepare 500 drawings to illustrate a history of

Napoleon. Carried away by an inspiration which had long been maturing, an artist might paint a whole canvas in a record time: Gustave Moreau sketched his *Hercules and the Hydra* in a single day but fainted from exhaustion in the evening![8]

Besides, who shall say when a work is finished? The public considered that the first Impressionist paintings were only half-finished and that the painters were making fun of them by exhibiting mere sketches or studies, first attempts instead of the carefully finished painting which came from the hand of a good craftsman. And the artist himself, when did he decide he should cease work? The completed picture never corresponded to the imagined one; should he rest content with it or try to do better? He might soften one colour, contrast or reinforce another, submerge in shadow a secondary detail which had come too far forward, change the lifeless expression of one of his figures, or repaint the background.

When Manet was working on his portrait of Eva Gonzalès he scraped her head out several times in order to start again. Berthe Morisot, who was present, wrote to her sister:

'Meantime he has begun her portrait again for the twenty-fifth time; she sits for him every day and every evening her head is washed out in soft soap. Now there's a way to encourage people to sit for you!'

A little later she wrote again: 'The portrait is no further forward; he tells me it is now the fortieth sitting and her head has just been scraped off again. He himself is the first to laugh.'[9]

Degas was constantly searching for new techniques and new effects, sometimes painting on oiled paper, sometimes mixing gouache and pastel. He once said to a journalist: 'I've spent my whole life just trying.'[10] Those who were never satisfied, like Degas and Cézanne, had a hard time of it, constantly going back to the beginning and starting all over again. But when it came the final moment was a wrench for all of them, or nearly all, when it was time to put on the last brush stroke and add the signature.

However tired and discouraged he might be, the artist, like the writer, needed a certain degree of self-discipline in his daily work. Those who imagined him leading a carefree life, creating amid joy unconfined, would have been astonished at the amount of work he could accomplish. Meissonier, whose health was excellent, could paint up to thirteen hours a day; Ziem, who specialized in Venetian scenes, spent eight or ten hours a day at his easel. Gleyre would get up at seven, begin the day by making a few sketches, have breakfast at about nine or nine-thirty in a café on the quai d'Orsay, then paint without any interruption; for the painter was the slave of daylight and could do practically nothing by lamplight or candle light.

Delacroix rose at seven and, once he had got under way, worked without stopping to eat until three in the afternoon. Then, though he did not like too rigid a timetable, he usually ate at about four. Afterwards, at the time when he was painting the Chapelle of the Saints-Anges at Saint-Sulpice, he would allow himself a couple of hours' sleep and then go for a walk at about ten o'clock in the evening through the streets of Paris, sometimes covering as much as five miles. 'What do you think of this routine which suits me so well?' he wrote to a friend in 1858.[11]

There were other painters who were no more afraid of walking than Delacroix. For years Puvis de Chavannes, who lodged in the Place Pigalle, used to walk over six miles a day to his studio at Neuilly and back. Painting was hard work and it was necessary to keep fit. Rude practised fencing even in his old age; Doré used the trapeze and horizontal bar in his studio; Meissonier went riding and swimming, and boating on the Seine.

But no less necessary was high morale. In the uncertain days of his youth Delacroix only managed to set to work if there was the prospect of some kind of evening entertainment, music, dancing or whatever. Like Delacroix, many another painter chose to break off when the work was going badly and sing or strum the guitar in the attempt to banish his cares or find fresh inspiration.

When the work went well, when it was more than putting a prepared plan into effect, the artist was said to have the fever (*avoir la fièvre* was how Delacroix put it). Then the painter entered the world of noble visions, of great bursts of inspiration.[12]

At such moments many artists dreaded unexpected interruptions. Delacroix, Fantin-Latour and Cézanne all declared themselves 'not at home' to the visitors they shrank from receiving, in order to be alone with the work which was taking shape. Hence the sometimes violent reaction to intruders that Vollard has described in the case of Cézanne: ' "Excuse me, Monsieur Vollard," he said to me once,

89

standing before a picture he had spoiled when I had interrupted him one day, "but when I'm working I just can't stand all these bloody interruptions!" '13

Even if the presence of assistants or models was unavoidable some artists demanded absolute quiet: 'Monsieur Géricault had to have complete silence,' said Dubosc, 'nobody dared speak or move near him; the least thing disturbed him.'14

But some of the artists who have painted their own studios have depicted them as being very far removed from oases of peace and quiet or artistic retreats. Vernet, Courbet and Bazille, for example, all show themselves surrounded by a surprising collection of friends and visitors. It is true that, to judge from some contemporary witnesses, access to artists cannot always have been so difficult. Gigoux, who was a painter himself, has told us about 'the many idlers who wander round visiting painters' studios, in the winter to get warm, in the summer to drag you off somewhere'.15 The 'friend of painters' was sufficiently common to be included in the series *Les français peints par eux-mêmes*: the *ami des peintres* was rather like the fly in La Fontaine's fable (who buzzed about the horses' ears as they struggled to pull the coach up the hill and claimed a share of the success when it finally reached the top); he talked knowledgeably about artists and their work, ran errands, put more wood on the stove and found happiness 'in seeing his own head appear every year in the background of some painting'.16

A great many people in fact do appear in pictures showing painters at work: Bazille is a case apart: the five in his studio at Batignolles, painted in 1870, are a group of companions. Far more astonishing is the picture painted by Horace Vernet in 1822 which became popular through numerous engravings made after it. Vernet is in the centre practising fencing passes with his pupil Ledieu without either of them having put down his palette; these are still balanced on the left thumb. On the side Robert Fleury is painting at an easel closely watched by Monsieur de Forbin, Director of Museums. One cannot but wonder how it is he remains undisturbed by the hubbub around him. To the right Eugène Lami is reclining on a table and playing the horn accompanied by a young drummer sitting on an open cabin trunk. Also to be seen are a group of soldiers, two boxers resting, a man reading a newspaper and various live animals: a large white horse and a dog barking at a goat.

We know that Vernet's activities kept his neighbours in the rue de la Tour-des-Dames awake at night; but for all that this is not intended to be a realistic picture. Rather the artist has tried to depict the flattering notion of the painter who works and plays at the same time. It is highly picturesque but of doubtful authenticity. As Vernet's friend Charlet very justly remarked: 'People imagine him all the time fencing with one hand and painting with the other: horn-playing here, boxing there. Rubbish! He knows well enough how to shut himself away when he writes his letters and only addresses the envelopes when in company.'[17]

Courbet's *Studio*, painted in 1855, also requires to be interpreted in the sense suggested by its subtitle: *A real allegory representing seven years in my artistic development*. As the composition is an imaginary synthesis we are the better able to understand the simultaneous presence of Baudelaire in reverie, a pair of lovers, a naked woman and a small boy behind the painter who is engaged on a landscape. Allegory apart, the picture aims to give the public a specific, though somewhat debatable image of the artist and his work. Courbet in fact had no more fear of noise than Vernet. His friend Castagnary has shown him painting in company, smoking and singing, indifferent to those around him.[18]

Sculpture presumably requires less introspection than painting. Be that as it may, certain sculptors have also left behind a reputation for preferring noise and bustle to quiet.

Pradier once said to Maxime Du Camp: 'When I'm alone, I'm good for nothing.' He did in fact receive a constant stream of casual callers and also regular visitors, writers like Du Camp or musicians like Auber or Adolphe Adam. His visitors were attracted by the young sculptor's enthusiasm and also by the young and beautiful models who came to pose for him attracted by his fame 'a harem of real beauties – he had first pick and the gallery could admire them at leisure'.[19]

Though Falguière only had a tiny studio he never worked better than when surrounded by pupils busy modelling and a constant coming and going of visitors.

Falguière needed to feel activity, movement, noise about him. His studio was not very large, although he had added adjoining rooms and was crowded with models posing or coming to introduce themselves, with pupils working away in one corner, with visiting comrades, with assistants or architects. And there, where anyone else would have been driven mad, Falguière worked with feverishly youthful ardour and joyous enthusiasm, as if drunk with the living flesh and the joys of creation.[20]

As we have seen, the conditions an artist required to carry out his work could be very diverse. Some fiercely sought solitude while others needed company to stimulate the imagination. But the most important thing for true artists was to be sparing of those precious hours when the inspiration was maturing and to realize that the execution of the work required patient labour. For artists such as these nourished in their hearts the serene joy of creation even at the most difficult moments and cared little for the false ideas the public formed about their work. More than one could have recounted stories like this one that Corot loved to tell: 'When I started painting my father, who thought that painting was for layabouts, said to me, "I would have given you a hundred thousand francs to buy a business but all you're getting now is two thousand a year. That will teach you. Go on, *enjoy yourself*." ' And Corot added, 'I have always remembered these words of my father's! I have always enjoyed myself.[21]

CHAPTER SIX

TRAVELLERS AND LANDSCAPE ARTISTS

Landscape painting, originally considered a minor genre, eventually came into its own. Although the 'open-air school' provoked witticisms from traditionally-minded public opinion, by the end of the century the masterpieces of the painters of the Barbizon School and then of the Impressionists had gradually won acceptance.

As a result of these changes nineteenth-century artists were led to seek their inspiration on the open road to a far greater extent than their predecessors. Ever since the restoration of the Bourbon Monarchy a burgeoning spirit of Romanticism had given everyone a taste for nature, for seeking out ruined monuments, medieval castles, and picturesque sites generally, and had encouraged artists to leave the towns. It was at this same period that the Compagnons du Tour de France (an organization of skilled workmen, a survival of the medieval guilds) set out to work their way round the world, proffering their skills as craftsmen. And it is hardly to be expected that young students of art with no commitments to hold them back should not have been tempted to yield to the spirit of adventure and go off and join them.

But in order to leave it was necessary to have saved a small sum of money first. Those who in their impatience set off too early were soon brought back to reality. The critic Thoré thus recalled youthful memories for Théodore Rousseau:

'Do you still remember our walks in the Meudon woods or along the banks of the Seine on the rare occasions when the two of us had managed to collect a fifty-sous* piece between us after rummaging in all the drawers. What wild rejoicing as we set out! We put on heavy shoes as if we were going to walk all round the

* 1 sous = 5 centimes or $\frac{1}{20}$ of a franc. Worth about $\frac{1}{2}$d at the rate of exchange prevailing at the time.

world, because we always had it in mind that we were never coming back; but necessity tugged at our shoe laces and drew us back to our attic room, condemned never to spend more than twenty-four hours out of doors.'[1]

Daubigny was wiser, saving what he earned by doing little jobs when restoration was in hand at the palace of Versailles. The hoard he and his companion Henri Mignan built up in a hole in a wall finally amounted to 1,400 francs, which for these youngsters was an enormous sum and enabled them to travel all over France in easy stages and even to get as far as Italy.

Travel was not expensive, particularly for those who set out on foot and could endure discomfort. Even at the age of fourteen one could, as Gigoux did, travel a long way with only a hundred francs in one's pocket. Gigoux left Besançon, where he had been born, to visit Switzerland and Savoy, but he has told how when he was lost one evening he burst into tears and called for his mother.[2] In those days nobody was deterred by even longer journeys on foot. When Daubigny was living in Bourg d'Oisans in 1839 he quite coolly considered walking back from the Dauphiné to Paris. All he asked from the friends who helped him to leave was a little money: '150 leagues,' he wrote, 'will take twenty days at most. At forty sous a day that makes forty francs. . . .'[3] In 1828 Paul Huet walked all the way from Fécamp back to Paris; fifty years later Emile Bernard left the capital on foot for Pont-Aven.

Even when their means allowed artists to take the stage coach, journeys were still long: it took four days to reach the Auvergne or the Nantes region from Paris, five to reach Bordeaux. But artists undertook these journeys cheerfully; their gaiety and the easy jokes which enlivened their conversation were usually appreciated by their fellow travellers. Balzac has described for us the punning match between Schinner and the *rapin* Mistigris in the Isle-Adam coach.[4]

The arrival of the railway shortened journeys and made travel easier. But the fact is that only by travelling on foot was the artist able to see every aspect of the countryside, select the most attractive places, linger in some village by an old bridge, a windmill or a waterfall, and discover a subject for a painting. It was easier for him to share the lives of the peasants and shepherds, partaking of their meals when no frugal inn was to be found along the road, sleeping if need be in cottages and peasants' huts or in barns. With his sack on his back and a heavy stick in his hand, our artist set out in search of adventure. He was dressed in a smock or a coat according to the season and wore gaiters; and on his head anything from a top hat, felt hat, or beret, to the black tight-fitting knitted cap sported by Rousseau. He seldom passed unobserved, certainly not a group of artists travelling together. They were sometimes laden with cumbersome equipment: sunshade, collapsible three-legged stool (known as a *pinchard*) and folding easel. Then it was a good idea to do as Daubigny and his friend Lavoignat did when they travelled across the Morvan region in 1853: buy a donkey complete with saddle and panniers for the modest sum of twenty-five francs.[5]

But usually the landscape artist, whether he was collecting material for a future composition or was one of those who produced albums of landscapes, was content to make studies or at most a quick sketch in watercolour, and consequently needed less equipment.

The travelling artist encountered suspicion as well as sympathy, friendship, and amusing adventures on the road. People who saw him working out of doors had no comprehension of what he was doing, and when a group of artists settled down in front of a monument or old house they were soon suspected of carrying out some mysterious survey or else dubbed mad. Champfleury has described one artist installed in front of a timber-framed house alarming the maid: 'He's mad, isn't he, Madame?' she asked. A few passing burgesses stopped some way off to look at the artist and pointed; they were as frightened of his beard as by the proud look on his face; they would have liked to come closer to look at the drawing, but did not dare. The children returning from school formed a circle round the artist, but when he got up to take a closer look at a detail of the carving, they scattered in fright.[6]

Faced with reactions like these one is not astonished to read of the incident that occurred at Troyes, humorously described by the *Journal des Artistes* for November 20, 1836:

'Six artists with long beards and pointed hats who had stopped to look at some medieval monuments set the whole town in turmoil. The authorities, perhaps alarmed by their serious air and their poetically pale, or palely poetic, complexions, thought it their duty to inform themselves concerning the plans of these artists, but eventually found them quite innocent.'[7]

95

Not all travelling artists were landscapists or specialists in picturesque views. Some of them, the 'true wanderers' described by Baudelaire, set out just 'because', from love of a vagabond life. The Goncourt brothers' Rouvillain was such a nomad. As soon as he could lay hands on twenty francs he would arrange to be met at the studio and accompanied as far as the Barrière Fontainebleau; and from there he would set off as fast as he could for the Pyrenees. He would knock at the door of the first priest he came to on the first night, do a head of the Virgin for him or a bit of restoration and leave with a letter of introduction for a priest a little further on; and so he would travel in this way from introduction to introduction, from priest to priest, until he reached the Spanish frontier, when he would return to Paris in the same way.[8]

Rouvillain had many counterparts in real life: when Deveria abandoned Paris he stopped at Rennes, where he found himself commissions for several pictures before leaving again for the South of France. And Charles Saunier, a pupil of Ingres, spent several months in a number of different towns: Dole in 1843, Rethel in 1845, Lyons and Vienne in 1847, Saint-Etienne in 1849, and so on.

And 'Father' Corot himself, who was less dependent on commissions than the others but always ready to travel, spent much of his life visiting friends' houses, happy in a vagabond existence well suited to his carefree bachelorhood which at the same time afforded a great variety of subjects for his paintings.

After tramping the highways and byways many painters came to adopt a favourite corner. They may just have been weary of travelling but it seems that an artist is better able to express the deeper significance of a landscape when he knows it well. Daubigny, with all his rich experience, wrote to his friend Henriet:

'I've done nothing that is any good at Cauterets . . . it's still not like a natural scene where one has lived all one's days and in which one takes real pleasure. Then, one's paintings reflect the inner life and feelings.'[9]

In a series of articles the *Journal des Artistes* in 1839 indicated sites in France worthy of the attention of the painter and very few of the French provinces did not appear on the list. Some of these places harboured colonies of artists and owed their fame to chance encounters quite as much as to their own intrinsic attraction. And

6   Ecole des Beaux-Arts

7   Meissonier's villa in the Place Malesherbes

8   Millet's house in 1870

the role which they came to play in the lives of artists was too large for us to pass over them in silence.

The best known and most talked of region was the Forest of Fontainebleau, which was situated at a reasonable distance from the capital and offered landscape artists a remarkable variety of subjects.

There had been painters at Fontainebleau ever since the beginning of the century: one Bruandet and a Greek called Bulgari. Decamps used to have a *pied-à-terre* there but it did not occur to him to paint the surrounding countryside. Aligny had property at Marlotte, on the southern edge of the Forest, with a view over the Loing valley. It was no doubt he who brought Corot here and Corot was better able than his friend to profit from nearby sites, like the Gorge-aux-Loups and Long Rocher. For Aligny himself was a landscape painter in the tradition of the Ecole des Beaux-Arts and he stylized nature in his paintings to such an extent that, if we are to believe Murger, he began by pulling up the bracken and trimming the turf of landscapes which inspired him.[10]

And then to two not very good inns in Marlotte and the neighbouring village of Bourron came the etcher Chauvel (in 1849, aged eighteen), Cicéri, Celestin Nanteuil and Ménard, later to be followed by Renoir and Sisley. By the end of the century a small colony of artists had settled there. The animal painter Coignard became mayor of Marlotte and even musicians like Massenet and Ernest Reyer came to join Jules Didier and Jules Laurens.[11]

But the most important village as far as the history of landscape is concerned was Barbizon, situated to the north-west of the Forest and soon to become famous the world over. Théodore Rousseau brought his comrades there. Earlier, in 1833, he had stayed at the Hôtel du Cheval-Blanc in the neighbouring hamlet of Chailly-en-Bière; and thirty years later Renoir, Monet, Bazille and Sisley stayed at this very hotel. But once Rousseau had discovered the charm of the region he preferred to settle at Barbizon, where a new inn had just opened.

Barbizon was particularly well placed at the very entrance to the Forest and a bridle-path led to Bas-Bréau deep in the interior. And only a few steps away there were two of the most famous sites, the rocky gorges of Apremont and the lonely sandy dunes of Franchard. In its majestic woodlands, its pools visited by wild animals, its jagged rocks, the artists discovered the natural beauties of still wild forests. And the plain which lay beyond Barbizon to the west, inhabited by rough peasants and broken by clumps of trees and the silhouettes of nearby towns, could provide the setting for scenes from rural life: it was here that Millet set the composition which was soon to become famous as *The Angelus*.

Those who were drawn to this spot, whether for a few days, a few weeks or with the intention of staying, were legion: Paul Huet, Français, Diaz, Barye, Millet, Gérôme and foreigners like the Swiss Karl Bodmer, who left his name to an oak in the forest.

Visiting artists gathered at the Auberge Ganne which has become legendary. Founded in 1822 or 1824 this country grocer's shop was converted by its owners into a very simple sort of inn. For the artists it offered the inestimable advantage of being a place where they were sure to find their fellows and where the owners showed as much understanding of their financial difficulties as of their wild escapades.

Taine came to Barbizon for the same reasons as other writers (like the Goncourt brothers for example seeking material for *Manette Salomon*) and like many who were merely curious to see the artist in his natural habitat; and he has left us this description of the Auberge Ganne in his *Thomas Graindorge*:[12]

'Both the rooms and the food are primitive here: a bed, a couple of rickety chairs and perhaps an arm chair which looks as if it had been in the wars; the walls are whitewashed and daubed with very attractive sketches, indeed yes. . . . Yet the stairs tremble beneath the tread of the guests as they descend; there is a great hubbub in the kitchen, a fastening of bags and a tying of gaiters. They eat anyhow, as the fancy takes them, standing on the stairs, at the dresser, at the table. The little servant girls come down in their white aprons, eyes half closed, still yawning; they accept the buffoonery that greets them without turning a hair. A few well set-up young men toss their sticks on to the path; others who are quieter stare at the dungheap and the hens scratching for food: they stroke the cat and tease the dog. . . . Then each sets off in his own direction, and once in the forest they either work or sleep – and I am inclined to think that the latter is their main occupation.'

The decoration of the rooms mentioned by Taine was the result of voluntary if somewhat disorganized co-operation between artists:

Corot, Français and Diaz worked on it as well as ten others who are less well known, such as Simon, who used to paint charming Parisian women in the forest. The cost of board and lodging varied: from the 2·40 francs paid by Rousseau to 4 francs charged occasional visitors. Generous credit was allowed. The inn's books have come down to us and show that Rousseau owed the quite considerable sum of 1,052·75 francs in 1850 and that he did not pay off the debt until the following year.

The accounts of '*MM. les artistes peintres*' give details of additional expenditure by the artists: we learn that a bottle of vintage wine cost 1 franc and a glass of spirits 3 francs, and that Ganne, who was a good-hearted fellow, would even lend money for trips to Paris.[13] All who lived there were agreed – even allowing for some exaggeration in the warmth of their memories – that the atmosphere which reigned was one of freedom and good humour, highly congenial and, in spite of Taine's insinuations, conducive to work.

Many came back again after a first visit, sometimes for the whole summer. Yet communications with Paris were not all that good. The stage coaches on the main Paris–Lyons route did not like taking passengers who left them so soon after leaving Paris. It was necessary to book one's place several days in advance with the Messageries Lafitte et Caillard, and though there were smaller companies which had vehicles available for short distances, the journey to Fontainebleau took a whole day. It is true that the railway soon reached Melun and then it was only nine kilometres on foot, a distance which alarmed only the women. Later there was a gig which plied between Melun and Barbizon. By 1899, when it was replaced by the tramway, Barbizon had long ceased to be the resort of other than third-rate artists and sightseers and trippers.

Shortly before the 1870 war Ganne's son-in-law had already moved the whole establishment to larger premises which he called the *Villa des artistes*. A second hotel opened to receive an ever-increasing clientele, mainly English and American. The proprietor was Emmanuel Siron, who had the idea of devoting one room to exhibiting the painters' works. And it was here that Napoleon III came in person one fine Sunday to buy paintings from the Barbizon artists.

Apart from the artists at the inn, a number had settled in the village itself. Rousseau eventually came to occupy two small rooms at the bottom of someone's garden and converted a barn into a

99

studio. Millet came with his family in 1849 to escape the cholera. He rented a thatched cottage for 160 francs a year where he lived with his nine children. For a long while he was very poor – as late as 1856 the baker refused him bread – and worked in the garden in clogs. Then Alfred Sensier bought the house and Millet was able to pay his rent in drawings or paintings, but Sensier was later unfairly reproached with having made a fortune out of the arrangement. Charles Jacque, the painter of sheep, occupied another house close to Millet's for a few years and did well out of keeping poultry and growing asparagus.

Basically these men were very close to the peasants, cowherds, cobblers and woodcutters around them, who became so used to the presence of the artists that in 1858 they even suggested postponing celebration of the local saint's day until the summer so that their friends the artists could more easily take part.

Yet with their free-and-easy ways and unkempt appearance they could hardly be mistaken for anything but artists. As the song says of the *'peint 'a Ganne'* (painters at Ganne's):

> *Quand on voit quel'barbe y z'ont*
> *On dit qu'i sont de Barbizon**

Not all the artists who settled at Barbizon were landscape painters. Ziem, for example, who moved into Charles Jacque's old house in 1871, is primarily known for his views of Venice. Some were just looking for a healthy open-air life. Gérôme, who was one of the pioneers and contributed to the decoration of Ganne's inn, liked to paint in the forest. But imagine the surprise of one of his friends who discovered him installed beneath the trees and saw he was busy painting an indoor scene representing Louis XI and Cardinal La Balue.[14]

Models sometimes posed for mythological scenes at a particularly deserted pool, the Mare aux Evées. But the main thing was that the forest afforded painters a vast store of subjects. Each artist had his own way of working. Daubigny often used to set up his easel under the trees while Rousseau or Millet preferred to dash off quick sketches. These first sketches had the merit of being a faithful rendering of nature viewed direct; as Théophile Gautier wrote of Rousseau, he painted 'trees which were not historic trees, rocks

---

* When you see what beards they have, you'll say they're from Barbizon.

where no nymph Echo sheltered, skies no Venus crossed in her chariot'.[15]

In order to become imbued with the atmosphere of the forest, the artists left in the morning to spend the whole day there, carrying their midday snack in their bags. For them midday, when the sun scorched the landscape, 'the hour of chrome yellow', to quote Henry Marger. They were not always idyllic, these days in the forest; smoking a pipe was not always enough to keep off the ants and mosquitoes – not to mention those other pests, intruders who were too inquisitive about painting, like the man whose remarks Daubigny has recorded:

'All the time I was working he was asking "Why are you using yellow? Ah! Now there's a lovely blue! You should use violet for the background! With talent like that one need never be alone, etc." '[16]

Yet of all men the landscape painter is the one who derives greatest pleasure from the changing aspects of nature and there can be few lives more peaceful, or happier, than his.

'Ah you see, it's delightful, the landscape painter's day. He gets up early at three in the morning before sunrise, sits down at the foot of a tree, looks about him and waits . . . it's charming, so he paints it!'

Thus 'Father' Corot on the subject of the most agreeable moments in his life as a painter.[17]

There were other regions, apart from the Forest of Fontainebleau, which encouraged new developments in the history of painting; for whatever reason they were chosen conditions were not necessarily as favourable in every respect.

There were many delightful places along the coast of Normandy and more than one landscape painter found what he was seeking between Dieppe and Port-en-Bessin. But Honfleur became more important because Boudin brought other painters there. In 1859 Courbet met Boudin when he was with Schanne (the Schaunard in the *Vie de Bohème*) and Boudin, who had been born in Honfleur and loved the changing skies and great sand dunes of the Seine estuary, took them both to Honfleur; he also brought Jongkind there. Five years later Monet and Bazille in their turn arrived at this little port which was also visited by Troyon, Diaz, Harpignies, Sisley and many others. There is a letter from Bazille to his parents which describes the attractions of the place:

'The steam boat took us down the Seine – its banks are very beautiful – to Honfleur. Ever since our arrival there we have been looking for subjects for landscapes. They are easy to find, for this country is like Paradise. You will not see richer meadows or more beautiful trees anywhere; horses and cattle graze freely everywhere. The sea, or rather the estuary of the Seine, gives a delightful horizon to these masses of green. We have found lodgings in Honfleur itself, with a baker who has let us two small rooms; we take our meals at the farm called Saint-Siméon on the cliffs just above Honfleur; it is there that we work and spend our days.'[18]

This farm, the Ferme Saint-Siméon, was to become famous because it fed and sheltered and sometimes lodged the artists who came to work before this wide landscape. In 1965 Alfred Delvau introduced it in these terms to readers of *Figaro*: 'It is a real farm, I assure you, and occupies the most marvellous position in the world.' It was run by a woman called 'Mère Toutain' and all who came, like Boudin and Courbet, to 'make a collection of skies' met in the orchard.[19]

The little Breton town of Pont-Aven seemed even less likely than Honfleur to play a role in the history of painting. The village, with its slate roofs and its windmills, is no different from many others in the Breton Peninsula.

Gauguin's only intention when he arrived there in 1886 was to lead the free existence of his dreams, far from Paris, friends and family. Brittany was considered cheap and two hotels in Pont-Aven were known to take in artists. Foreign painters, mainly English, American and Scandinavian, but all called 'Americans', had been staying at Julia Guillou's Hôtel des Voyageurs for some fifteen years. The other establishment, the Hotel Gloanec, was a homelier place and served the pupils of the Académie Julian and Cormon's studio as a holiday centre. All these painters went round in cheerful gangs and were noted for their pranks, the least of which was painting in bright colours the feathers of geese straying in the streets. There was one Granchi-Taylor who was famous for his outlandish costume, consisting of frock coat, clogs and a coolie hat. When Paul Signac visited Pont-Aven in 1891 he was shocked by the influence the young artists had had on the country, writing to his friend Luce:

'I went to Pont-Aven yesterday. It is a ridiculous place full of little corners with waterfalls for the English lady watercolourists. It's a funny nest for Symbolism. . . . Drunken hooligans of painters swagger round in velvet jackets. The tobacconist has a palette for a sign outside his shop and he sells artists' materials. The servants at the inn have "painterly" ribbons in their caps. . . .'[20]

Yet it was here that Gauguin stayed in 1886, coming back again in 1888. He paid fifty-five to sixty francs a month at the Gloanec, which suited his purse, the more so since the Dutch painter Meyer de Haan, the son of an industrialist, helped him out on more than one occasion. But he held aloof from the other painters who made fun of Impressionism in general and of Gauguin's style of painting in particular. During his second visit a small group formed which listened to his ideas, including among others Emile Bernard, Maufra, Charles Laval and the Swiss Amiet. The group also included Serusier, who brought back from Pont-Aven the famous landscape painted in pure reds and greens, which soon came to be called 'the talisman' and showed it to the future 'Nabis'.

However, Gauguin moved some twenty kilometres further away in the summer of 1889, together with Meyer de Haan and Serusier. and stayed at the lonely little inn at the village of Poldu. The proprietress, Marie Henry, known as Marie Poupée, allowed generous credit and went still further to oblige the artists as the daughter she bore to Meyer de Haan was living witness. Free from all constraints, Gauguin and his friends worked hard: they set out for the fields at seven in the morning, had lunch at the inn, returned to their subject until five o'clock, dined at seven and went to bed at nine after a game of draughts or lotto. The group which formed around Gauguin – Laval, Maufra, Seguin and Filiger had joined him in Poldu – evolved a new style of painting using bright and violent colours characteristic of what became known to history as the 'Pont-Aven School'.

Regions closer to Paris also inspired landscape painters during the second half of the century. As early as 1820 some of their predecessors were fond of sites now completely spoilt, such as the slopes of Saint-Cloud and Meudon. Paul Huet used to visit the Ile Seguin and the magnificent bridge across the river, the Pont de Sèvres, from early youth on, as did Troyon, Rousseau and Dupré. We smile now at Huet's enthusiasm when he describes this landscape (now the Renault motor-works): 'Saint Cloud, that enchanting place one talks about when in Italy! I knew its every bush and wept for every tree they cut down as for a lost friend.'[21]

The generation that followed often turned from forests and woodland scenes towards more transient aspects of landscape: sky and water. They found places in the Seine and Oise valleys which accorded with their sensibility: l'Isle-Adam, Pontoise, Eragny, Vétheuil and Giverny, and nearer still to Paris, Bougival and Louveciennes, which for us recall so many paintings by Dupré, Monet, Pissarro or Sisley.

Daubigny seems to have been the pioneer. In 1857 he returned to Auvers-sur-Oise near Valmondois, where he had spent his childhood, and the idea came to him that it would be more convenient for his work to convert a boat into a floating studio in which he could go seeking subjects up and down river at will. The boat was called *Botin*, meaning 'little box', and proved quite comfortable; more often than not it remained moored to the banks of the Oise but sometimes Daubigny sailed down the Seine as far as Pont-de-l'Arche near Rouen, accompanied by his son, who also painted. Life on board was rich in incident, like the day when Daubigny took a step back to judge the effect of one of his pictures and fell into the water.[22]

Botin did not preclude a more settled home. Daubigny also had a house built at Auvers, 'a studio eight metres by six with a few rooms round it'. He decorated part of it himself and part with the help of Corot and of Daumier, who was his neighbour at Valmondois.

Pissarro had lived for some time at Pontoise before the 1870 war: he returned there in 1872 and went to see Daubigny at Auvers, bringing Guillaumin and other comrades from the Académie Suisse. In 1873 he brought Cézanne, whose stay there was of capital importance since it was at this time that he changed and lightened his palette. When he was going through a difficult time Cézanne found support from Dr Gachet who was an art-lover and the confidant and protector of the Impressionists.

Van Gogh took refuge there after the crisis at Arles: 'I'm still afraid of the noise and bustle of Paris and I'm going straight to the country to an old village.'[23] Theo Van Gogh had consulted Pissarro, who had advised Auvers, where at least Dr Gachet could look after Vincent. As we know, Van Gogh took his own life and died at the Pension Ravoux on July 29, 1890.

Monet, too, like Daubigny but more careful of the changing effects of light, had a boat fitted up so that he could paint the river. His base was Argenteuil on the Seine, only eight miles from Paris. He had rented a house there in 1873 where Renoir, Sisley and Manet also came to paint. Manet's painting *Monet in his studio* – a provocative title as he showed his friend in his boat with a straw hat on his head and his wife sitting sewing beside him – fixed the image of the open-air painter in opposition to the traditionalists.

The changing concept of landscape could not but influence the technique and daily work of painters. According to academic principles landscape could not stand alone: it could only be the setting for a scene taken from mythology or history. The romantic landscape was no different in essentials: nature was depicted by some turbulent scene or storm and the tempest dramatized an anecdotal subject. It was the Barbizon painters and then the Impressionists who finally managed to make pure landscape acceptable, depicting what was often a very ordinary scene but with absolute fidelity according to the season of the year and the effect of a particular light.

One can understand how the traditional landscape painter could only make studies from nature. The picture was conceived and composed in the studio like any other kind of subject and reminiscences of paintings seen in museums were often more important than sketches from life. But even Corot seldom worked in any other way. He used a study made in the Valley of Royat in the Auvergne for his *Homer and the Shepherds* but changed the background so that it resembled more closely a scene from antiquity. Rousseau and Millet studied in the open air but did the main part of their work in the studio; they selected and rearranged motifs, eliminated unnecessary or unfortunate detail and accentuated the character of a site.

That Impressionism brought about a revolution in this respect is generally believed, but the fact is that different artists adopted different procedures. Certainly there were some who did not shrink from the brutality of direct vision, believing they could present any fragment of landscape just as it appeared to their eyes under a certain set of circumstances. Baudelaire, who followed the development of landscape closely, was worried by this tendency among certain painters after the Salon of 1859: 'They open a window and all the space contained within the square of the window frame has for them the value of a completed poem.'

Monet was one of those who believed most strongly in the need to paint for the sake of truth directly from the subject and to paint only what he saw. When he was painting his *Women in the Garden* in 1886 he set up his enormous canvas in the garden at Ville-d'Avray and even had a trench dug so that he could lower the painting into it and reach the upper part of the picture more easily. Days without sun condemned him to inactivity, and when Courbet suggested to him that he could use this time to prepared the background he refused for the sake of preserving the unity of the picture. He remained faithful to this method and even exaggerated it when he was painting various river landscapes at Giverny (where he was later to paint his *Waterlilies*). A writer has described how he used to get up before dawn (which was not much later than three o'clock in mid-summer) and, helped by a peasant who carried his canvases, made his way to a boat anchored in mid-stream: 'he has fourteen paintings all begun at the same time, a whole set of studies of one and the same subject, whose appearance may be altered by the time of day, the sun and the clouds'.[24]

Renoir worked in just the same way on the paintings he did at one period in his life when he was living in the rue Cortot in Montmartre. *The Swing* was painted beneath the trees in the garden of this house there. And he also painted his *Dancing at the Moulin de la Galette* in 1876 beneath trees whose foliage dappled the faces and garments of his figures with light and shade. The canvas sometimes threatened to fly away like a kite as he carried it each day from the rue Cortot to the garden where the famous dance was held.

Before Renoir, Daubigny had wished to carry out some of his pictures entirely on the spot. In order to paint his view of Villerville-sur-Mer, exhibited at the Salon of 1864, he set up his canvas in a meadow attached to stakes firmly driven into the ground, without fearing the pranks of the local children or indeed what the sharp horns of the cattle might do. And as he had chosen to paint a windy, cloud-laden sky he had to wait until atmospheric conditions were right before he could start.[25] But before the first experimental stage of Impressionism was over many painters returned to using techniques where the artist's memory or his imagination corrected the raw material furnished by nature. Paul Signac observed in his journal in 1898:

> 'This mania for painting from nature is quite recent. We should collect material, not just copy. . . . What a difference there is between the one who goes out for a walk, stops at random in a shady corner and "imitates" what he finds in from of him, and the one who tries to recall on a sheet of paper or a canvas, by means of beautiful lines and colours, the feelings he experienced at a given moment before a beautiful landscape.'[26]

Seurat, Signac's friend, went every morning for months to the Island of Grande-Jatte, but worked on his great canvas in the afternoons in his studio. And Degas reproached Jeanniot for having painted a landscape on the spot 'A painting is a product of the artist's imagination, it should never be a copy. . . . The air in the paintings of old masters is not the air we breathe.'[27]

Gauguin said to Schuffenecker in 1888: 'Do not copy nature too closely, art is an abstraction; and you must abstract it from nature by dreaming before her and by thinking more about the act of creation than about the result.'[28] But these remarks foreshadow a way of painting which was to be that chosen by twentieth-century artists and which was to take them still further from the external subject.

CHAPTER SEVEN

THE SALON AND EXHIBITIONS

Work when completed must be shown to the public. The artist had to exhibit – his fame and success depended on it. But for the nineteenth-century artist in France there was only one place to exhibit, only one place which could set the seal upon his success: the Salon.

Today it is no longer possible for us to imagine the importance of the Salon in artistic life. It was usually an annual event and crystallized public interest in the arts as well as that of the critics. Enormous crowds flocked to the exhibition halls in the Louvre and later on the Champs-Elysées. Jules Janin wrote in 1844:

> 'This exhibition of painting is the event of the year: people are talking about it two months beforehand – two months of feverish excitement, you never heard such a to-do. What are we going to see this year? The pictures still hiding in the studios, what are they like?'[1]

To be accepted for the Salon marked a turning point in an artist's life. The various prizes and medals awarded by the jury were essential steps in their career for those who wanted to succeed. The contacts made at the Salon with art lovers and potential patrons made sales and commissions much easier to secure, particularly as the general public regarded those excluded from the Salon as bad painters or bad sculptors. Some purchasers would only buy a work of art on condition it was accepted for the Salon. Jongkind even had to take back a picture sold a few days before the opening of the exhibition but rejected by the jury.

Rejection could lead to dramatic consequences. In April 1866 Jules Holtzappel, who had failed to gain admittance to the Salon that year, though his paintings had been accepted in 1864 and 1865, decided to kill himself: 'The members of the jury have rejected me; therefore I have no talent. . . .'[2]

Even the most independent artists found it hard to be excluded, though they might question the principles on which the selection was made. All his life Manet set his hopes on the Salon and showed little enthusiasm for the exhibitions organized by his Impressionist friends. Cézanne could never console himself for not being accepted. However, the protests against the official selection increased and grew stronger. Many good artists were among those excluded and since it proved impossible to effectively widen the basis of a jury which was dominated by the Institut and the narrow academicism of its members, a wide gulf eventually opened between the art which received the blessing of the Salon and real living art.

When the National Assembly abolished the old Académies in 1791 it completely changed the nature of the Salon. Under the Ancien Régime it had been organized by the artists themselves as a body. The authorities of the revolutionary period involved the state in its affairs and thought that by throwing the Salon open to all artists and by instituting a system of awards they were introducing a greater measure of liberty. But the creation of a jury acted as a barrier and soon modified the original intention. The jury was originally responsible for the organization of the exhibition but soon it began to exclude the weakest entries and then to attempt to regulate the moral or political position of some of the others.[3] The result, when the Académies were re-established, though not along the old lines, was that the jury came to consist of members of the Académie appointed by the Director of the Museums Service, so that as the years passed the jury came more and more to embody a twofold constraint: that of the state and that of a small coterie with narrow tastes. Discontent grew among artists outside the circle of Academicians and those who aspired to join them. The fight was all the fiercer because it coincided with the wind of revolt which the new Romantic movement had raised against tradition.

In September 1830, their hopes raised by the prospect of a more liberal monarchial régime, the artists got up two petitions: some of them preferred to petition the King direct while others preferred to approach him through the Chamber of Deputies, but both parties were in agreement in asking that the Salon jury should be chosen by the artists themselves. As so often during the reign of the 'King of the French' the government dashed their hopes and even strengthened the authority of the Institut: the entire Académie des Beaux-Arts was henceforth to be responsible for the admission of works of art to the Salon. 'This jury', wrote Gustave Planche, 'only escapes hatred by inviting ridicule; the fate of painters and sculptors is in the hands of musicians and architects'.[4] And although musicians no longer participated after 1833, discontent increased. In 1844 there was talk of a strike of exhibitors.

It is hardly surprising then that one of the first acts of the provisional government after the 1848 revolution was to abolish the jury. And it was replaced for the Salon of 1848 by a hanging committee chosen by the artists. This committee, which was the choice of 801 electors, found itself obliged to accept the record number of 5,180 works of art. The experiment was not repeated. A return to the old system was assisted by changes in the political situation, though the regulations underwent constant alteration between 1849 and 1870. Sometimes it was the Institut that asserted itself and won the day, as happened for example in 1857. Sometimes it was the government which sought to replace the duly constituted bodies and have its say in matters of artistic choice. The spirit of the times in either case favoured severity; in 1857 it was the Director of the Museum Services who insisted on the need to separate the wheat from the chaff. But until 1865 never had anything been seen like the occasion when the government representative (it was old Field-Marshal Vaillant, who might have been thought to know more about swordsmanship than painting) uttered these incredible words: 'But the principal benefit to be derived from this gathering will elude us if I do not follow the praises which I have been so happy to bestow with a piece of advice. . . .'[5]

It is of course true that this was the year when the jury in some fit of aberration had accepted a picture which was the laughing stock of true connoisseurs of art: Manet's *Olympia*.

The Imperial government also tried to court popularity and conciliate the artists by allocating seats on the jury to their representatives. They were given half the seats in 1852 and nine out of twelve in 1864. However, since the right to vote was restricted to those who had already won medals at the Salon, the new juries were certain to follow the line of their predecessors, as indeed was shown by the result: in 1861, for example, only 4,097 works were accepted out of an entry of more than 7,000 and only 2,217 out of 5,000 in 1863.

Nor did the first years of the Third Republic bring artists the freedom they had once again hoped for. The different procedures adopted for selecting the jury were all criticized in turn and it proved extremely difficult to find a formula which would reconcile all points of view. In the 1875 elections, when only former winners of the Prix de Rome and those who had already won medals at the Salon were eligible to vote, forty-five artists were elected and the fifteen jury members chosen by lot from these. But for whatever reason, sheer force of habit, fear of giving offence or simply poor choice, all the elections gave members of the Institut a majority on the jury, just as in the days when they were officially appointed. The few independents who managed to slip in felt all the more ill at ease because the majority continued to judge according to the same old criteria in perfect good faith. In 1875, when Daubigny wanted to give all artists the right to vote, Cabanel, who was chairman of the jury that year, replied: 'My dear Daubigny, you are only interested in bad painters; the jury does not make mistakes today!'[6] But the following year the jury rejected Manet's portrait of Desboutin.

The revolution came when no one expected it any longer and without a shadow of doubt too late. When Jules Ferry presided at the distribution of prizes for the 1879 Salon his words sounded a new note:

'Gentlemen, for forty years we have tried to govern and control the arts and have flattered ourselves that we have done so. That great learned society represented here today by the eminent men on either side of me will, I am sure, allow me to speak freely about their illustrious predecessors: the Institut conceived the plan of bringing the artistic life of France under its control and of laying down the law. It took upon itself to be the zealous custodian of the doors of the Salon.'

Two years later the minister's representative commented on the changes which were taking place:

'You have to undertake for yourselves, completely and entirely, the organization of the annual exhibition both from the material and the artistic side, instead of and in place of the administration. The state will no longer intervene in your affairs.'[7]

On December 27, 1880, a decree by Jules Ferry handed over the organization of the Salon to a 'society of artists' consisting of ninety members elected by all those who had exhibited at the Salon at

least once. Bailly, head of this *Société des artistes français*, was an architect who was a member of the Institut; the sculptor Guillaume and
the painter Bouguereau, both members of the Institut, were chosen
as vice-presidents, and two of the four secretaries were also members.

These far-reaching changes, then, which left it to artists to decide
the chances of other artists, had less effect than one might have
hoped. By this time the Salon had lost some of the prestige which it
had retained in spite of constant criticism during the earlier part of
the century. It was not long before the great annual Salon split into
several parallel ones. A rival *Société nationale des beaux-arts* was formed
in 1884 as a result of a split within the *Société des artistes français* itself:
a split which owed more to personalities than to principles. Henceforth there were to be two large annual Salons as well as a growing
number of group exhibitions and one-man shows. The painters and
sculptors had destroyed the myth of a single, official event which had
judged the works of art deemed worthy of the name for nearly a
hundred years and against whose verdict there was no appeal.

The way the Salon was organized explains the feverish activity of
artists as the date drew near. The tension was all the greater since
the opening date changed from year to year and was seldom known
far in advance. At certain periods the exhibition only took place
every two years and sometimes it was still more infrequent: there
were only five Salons in fifteen years under the restored Bourbon
monarchy.

Under the Empire the Salon was held in the autumn, but during
the years that followed the dates varied considerably: in 1817 it
opened on April 24th, in 1824 on November 4th and in 1829 on
August 25th. After 1830 the July government re-established the
custom of an annual Salon and decreed that it should open between
March 1st and June 15th. The Salon of 1849 was an exception in
being postponed until December 15th. After 1870 the date chosen
was usually May 1st or 2nd.

Whatever the opening date the candidates had to conform to the
regulations, which remained the same: to bring or send their works
to the office of the museum during a fixed period of time which
terminated ten days before the exhibition was due to open; each
individual work to be accompanied by a note to appear in the
catalogue; copies and works which had been submitted to a previous
Salon to be excluded. And naturally they had to accept the verdict

of the jury which decided which items deserved to be exhibited. The time limit for submitting work, though supposed to be inflexible, was often evaded, at least before 1831. Every year painters who knew they had the jury on their side delayed sending in their pictures until after the Salon had opened – they would do anything to attract attention if they could get away with it! Not everybody objected, considering it revived interest in the exhibition. But young painters who had been rejected on the grounds that they were two days late in submitting their work deplored such concessions. Ingres, who had asked for the opening to be postponed in 1824, put his *Vow of Louis XIII* on view only on November 12th when the Salon had been open since August 25th. And the same artist's *Oedipus* appeared on the Salon walls only in 1828 in the middle of April, a few days before the exhibition, which had opened five months earlier, was due to close.[8]

Lively scenes occurred when the works for the Salon arrived, particularly during the last few days. In their studios the artists were busy putting the finishing touches to their pictures or statues before they left them; some added the final brush stroke or gave a final working over with the chisel at the very last minute. It is said that Pradier on more than one occasion retouched a statue in the street when it had already left the studio.

Then came the question of transport. No problem at all with the smaller pictures; bigger ones called for a porter's dosser or something of the sort; while the largest and heaviest arrived in wheelbarrows or handcarts pushed by the artist himself with the assistance of two or three of his friends. Valuable marble statues and heavy bronzes were brought in on trolleys; wagons rolled up with cases containing works sent in by provincial candidates which had been entrusted to the transport companies. The consequence was a jam of vehicles large and small and frightened horses in front of the entrance to the Louvre. Jokes and insults were exchanged amid the general uproar. The small wine-shops near the Place du Carrousel did a roaring trade. And the Doyenné district, until it was pulled down in 1852 when extensions were being made to the Louvre, was quite exceptionally lively and animated.

After 1857, when the Salon moved to the Champs-Elysées, there was more room but the same confusion and uproar; and an unbroken line passed before the employees who received the entries.

Once he had handed in his entry the artist endured a period of agonizing suspense while he wondered whether he would be accepted or refused. During the second half of the century a small number of artists were accepted without further question; the rules varied slightly from year to year, but members of the Institut, former prize-winners and artists who had won more than one medal at previous Salons were usually regarded as 'exempt' or, as it came to be called later, *hors concours*.

But the others did not know the result, and unless they had an obliging friend among the jurors, one prepared to break the strict seal of secrecy, they had to wait until the Salon opened to find out whether their names were in the catalogue. Then all that was left for those who were rejected was to collect their pictures – which had been marked on the back with an infamous 'R' and could not be sold until they had been relined – and to curse the jury. After 1849 the organizers at least took the trouble to inform the unhappy victims once a decision had been taken against them.

It was hard for the rejected artist to accept his fate, even though he knew that people like Delacroix, Rousseau, Corot, Millet and Courbet had had pictures refused or had only managed to gain admittance to the Salon after repeated failures. That so many great men had shared his plight was poor consolation to the artist who had everything to hope for from success at the Salon.

In his book *L'oeuvre* Emile Zola has given a vivid description of the jury at work under the Second Empire. Though the membership of this respected tribunal varied, the procedures adopted certainly changed little in the course of the century. Whether works were brought forward more or less at random to be examined, or grouped according to the genre to which they belonged, as was done from 1841 onwards[9], or whether alphabetical order was preferred, no system could have prevented bizarre confrontations, harsh judgments, weariness and mutual concessions.

The attendants arranged the large paintings against the wall so that the jury could file past them; these paintings could only be judged at the cost of a great deal of walking on the part of the jurors.

'Every afternoon at one o'clock they set out again on their rounds until all the letters of the alphabet were exhausted. At their head marched their chairman armed with a little bell. They gave judgment standing up and skimped the job as much as possible, rejecting the worst canvases without calling for a vote. Sometimes, however, the group stopped to argue, and then, after quarrelling for some ten minutes or so, they would put the painting aside until the evening revision. Throughout this proceeding two men held a rope ten metres long four paces away from the paintings to prevent members of the jury surging forward in the heat of the debate. Even so the fat stomachs of some jurors pushed the rope out of the straight. A squad of seventy attendants in white overalls under the command of a foreman followed the jury. When the secretaries announced a decision they separated the received from the rejected and carried the latter away like the bodies of the dead from the field of battle.'[10]

Small works on the other hand, i.e. those less than 1 m 50 cms, were presented one by one to the jury as a whole; and the jurors were able to sit down. If no immediate decision was taken, they could be brought forward again for a second look at the end of the day. Sometimes all the paintings would be reviewed on the last day, quite haphazardly amid a chaos of rejected pictures, if it was considered that the final selection was too small. Incidents sometimes occurred when work by a member of the Institut or by an artist who was *hors concours* got by mistake among the work of run-of-the-mill artists before anyone had noticed the signature, and failed to obtain the spontaneous approbation which was its due.

The enmity of some jurors displayed towards artists they disliked went to the lengths of conspiracy. Before they had even seen the artist's works they would warn those they thought they could count on in order to present a united front to the waverers. They would see to it that the victim's pictures were put up to the jury at the right moment. A friend of Théodore Rousseau has described the manoeuvres which succeeded in keeping his landscapes out of the Salon for years:

'At the very moment when the attendants brought his pictures forward at a carefully packed session Bidault, Raoul-Rochette and their friends could be heard to sit up and call out: "Ah, there he is, watch it, that's him" as if to encourage each other in their joint collusion.'[11]

Sometimes one of the jurors would support an unknown artist with a disturbing style; it might be his own personal taste, but quite often he acted out of bravado or sheer contrariness.

The pundits counted on the votes of their pupils to be elected to the jury. It was mutual self-interest: teachers saw to it that their disciples were accepted and they in their turn became entitled to vote. Artists from certain studios were hardly ever refused.

Young Bazille was surprised to be canvassed, but was not taken in; and he described his astonishment to his parents:

'As an elector I have been approached by several big shots in the painting world. Daubigny called round to see me as if by chance, and Stevens, whom I often see at Manet's, has invited me to one of his evenings: it is strange how people can be so ambitious for so little! It goes without saying that I shall eat Stevens' cakes but remain incorruptible.'[12]

Another practice, one which was openly recognized, was for each member of the jury to be allowed to choose a single picture which was known as his 'charity'. In this way a mediocre work by an artist in need would be passed without further scrutiny at the request of a single juror. It was thanks to this custom that Cézanne who had been rejected by the Salon every year since he first entered in 1864, managed to appear once – in 1882 – when his picture was accepted as the 'charity' of his friend Guillaumet.

Further problems arose when it came to hanging the pictures in the rooms used for the Salon. Even in 1849, an exceptional year, when there was no jury, a hanging committee seemed essential. It was impossible to ignore such factors as the size of the work or the fame of the artist. And, like it or not, there were good positions and bad ones.

Arrangement in the alphabetical order of the artists' names, which was customary until 1861, merely increased the problems created by hanging together pictures which clashed, especially as a few places of honour were still kept for particularly famous artists.

As soon as the Salon opened every artist was eager to see whether he had been banished to some dark corner or distant room, or whether, as happened in those days, his colleagues had hung his picture high up on the wall out of spite, where it was placed above several others and difficult for visitors to notice. Poor Corot, who had been hung in the worst positions for fifteen years, used to say: 'Alas I am in the dungeons again this year.'

It is only fair to recognize that the hanging committee did not have an easy task, as the exhibition rooms were often unsuitable. During the first half of the century, as in the preceding one, the paintings were shown in the Salon Carré of the Louvre, which gave its name to the exhibition; the ceiling was very high and pictures could be hung in four or five rows above each other. In theory the largest were hung at the top, but paintings and engravings of the 1800 and 1824 Salons, for example, show incredible pyramids of pictures crowned by tiny ones difficult to see from below.[13]

But in spite of the way the pictures were hung with their frames touching, the Salon Carré soon proved too small and the exhibition began to spread into adjoining galleries, beginning with the Galerie d'Apollon. Soon the Grande Galerie itself was invaded because of the ever-increasing number of exhibits: 542 in 1800, 1,294 in 1812, 2,219 in 1835.

A protest in 1831 by the editors of *L'Artiste* mentions other disadvantages of these exhibitions.[14] The pictures in the museum's permanent collection were no longer taken down but concealed behind a false wall or screen. Apart from the danger of damage to the museum's masterpieces, visitors and artists were denied access to them for the duration of the exhibition and also during the time taken to prepare it, some four months in all. The cost of mounting the exhibition was estimated by *L'Artiste* at 80,000 francs, and even though this figure is probably exaggerated one can agree with the journal that the money would have been better spent on making purchases from artists.

Sculpture had long been exhibited in the basement of the museum, where it was practically impossible to stand far enough away from the works to study them properly.[15] Such were the inconveniences of rooms so ill adapted to their purpose. Many suggestions were made, the most popular being to hold the annual exhibition in the new building which had been proposed to link the Louvre with the Tuileries; for the artists regretted leaving a palace where they could feel they had joined the great masters of the past, even if only for a few weeks.

But in the meantime it was necessary to find somewhere else. Holding the exhibition in the Tuileries itself, which was tried in 1849, turned out to be unsatisfactory because the rooms were not well lit. The artists preferred the Palais Royal, which was used in 1850 and 1852, where their works were exhibited both in the palace itself and in a temporary building erected in the courtyard. But after the Universal Exhibition of 1855 the Salon finally moved to the Champs-Elysées. The Palais de l'Industrie had none of the disadvantages of the Louvre; it was empty, isolated and spacious. But it had its critics, who claimed that this rather uninteresting building, which was used for many different kinds of events from trade fairs to displays of horsemanship, resembled a shed or a railway station. No longer was the Salon housed amid the majesty of a royal residence. Nevertheless, even if the greenery and floral arrangements – not to mention the little lake with a waterfall introduced in 1859 – and the armchairs and sofas for rest and relaxation, did not furnish the building sumptuously, they did confer upon it a certain air of worldly frivolity combined with bourgeois comfort, which suited the official art of the second half of the nineteenth century. The building was demolished in 1897.

The artists anxiously awaited the opening day: would their works be accepted and, if accepted, where would they be hung and what would their colleagues and the critics and the public have to say? Between 1830 and 1840 the Salon did not open till towards the end of the morning on the first day, at eleven or twelve o'clock; but a crowd collected in the vicinity of the museum at least an hour beforehand, consisting mainly of the exhibitors and their friends. Maxime du Camp describes the scene:

'At about a quarter to twelve the crowd began to mass before the closed doors; there was a great deal of pushing and shoving . . . at times a ringing youthful voice, the voice of a young artist, would make itself heard: "Hang the Institut!" There would be laughter and some elderly man belonging to the old school could be heard to say "Good grief, what are we coming to?" As the clock struck the first stroke of twelve the double doors opened and the fat Swiss in red, wearing knee breeches and three-cornered hat, his halberd in his hand, appeared on the threshhold. The shout went up, "Long live Père Hénault". Everyone surged forward up the stairs; at the top every artist looked frantically through the catalogue to see if his name was there, then entered the Salon Carré.'[16]

By the end of the century things were different. The day before the official opening was a sort of 'dress rehearsal' for the artists and their families, the critics and a few specially favoured souls. These *vernissages* (varnishing days), as they were called, were appropriately named as the painters usually applied a coat of varnish to their paintings after they had been hung; and the illustrated magazines show them up tall step-ladders doing just this, surrounded by a sparse but select public.[17]

It was the done thing on those days to have lunch at a restaurant in the Champs-Elysées beneath the trees. The most exclusive of these was Ledoyen's, where famous artists went with their models; the traditional menu at Ledoyen's was always the same, salmon served with a green dressing and *rosbif à l'anglaise*.

But the Salon public did not only consist of artists and society people. One is in fact surprised to see that all classes of society attended, including the working classes. In order to understand the popularity of this annual event it should be remembered that there were far fewer public entertainments than there are today. The public went to the Salon as it went to the military tattoo or the fat stock show.

The fact that it was free was a further inducement. Until 1849 it was completely free – at most one day a week was reserved in some years for ticket holders who wished to avoid mingling with the common people. In 1850 the custom was instituted of entry on one day of the week at a cost of 1 franc; in 1852, there was one day at 5 francs and one at 1 franc. After 1857 the position was reversed and only Sundays were free. On other days you had a choice: to go between eight and ten (or nine and eleven) in the morning, pay five francs and rub shoulders with famous visitors like the Empress; or else pay 1 franc to go during the rest of the day until four or six o'clock as the case might be. Even though entry charges were justified by the need to increase the money available for purchases from artists, they were strongly criticized and the public continued to be admitted free on Sundays and sometimes on Thursdays as well.

The crowds were enormous. Zola has described the scene on some Sundays under the Second Empire:

'There were even groups of countryfolk, and soldiers and nurse-maids, pushing their way through the exhibition on free days to account for the truly staggering figure of 50,000 visitors on some fine Sundays. There was a whole army of them, the rearguard of the lower classes, ignorantly following their betters and filing wide-eyed through this great picture shop.'[18]

This figure may appear excessive but tallies with that quoted by Daumier in 1857, though it is true he was being ironical about the quality of the public: 'None but true connoisseurs – all 60,000 of them!' In 1831 *L'Artiste* estimated a million visitors for that year. There were 518,892 visitors in 1876, and 185,000 of them paid to go in.

It was because they were afraid of the unpredictability of the reactions of such crowds on Shrove Tuesday that the organizers of the 1840 Salon postponed the opening for a few days. They remembered that during the Carnival in 1831 the excited populace had sacked the archbishop's palace. But usually the only fear was of pickpockets, who had a field day. The police on duty at the 1841 Salon caught no fewer than eight of them in the act in a single day.

From the very first years of the century the fastidious shrank from the crowds; and it was asserted that the dust they raised in the Salon Carré sometimes made it difficult to see the pictures. Fifty years later the exhibition was more spacious, but public enthusiasm had not diminished: the poor wood-engravings in newspapers and magazines, and the occasional poster to be seen on walls in the town, could not compete with the enormous brightly-coloured compositions displayed on the walls of the Salon. Taine has given a good account of this 'wider public' in 1867:

'They come as they would to a pantomime or a circus. They want melodrama or military scenes, undressed women and *trompe-d'oeil*; and they get it: battles and *auto-da-fé*, scenes of slaughter in Roman arenas, Andromeda on the rocks, stories about Napoleon and about the Republic, illusionistic jugs and dishes.'[19]

The success of the catalogue can be accounted for in the same way, even though the first illustrated catalogue did not appear until 1879. But the *livret*, as it was called, described the exact subject of each picture, sometimes, in the case of a history painting, even devoting some ten to fifteen lines to it. The success enjoyed by the catalogue extended beyond the followers of art to reach a wider public; as long ago as 1801 the Salon catalogue had sold 12,571 copies.[20]

Criticism of the Salon was also sold at the doors, and pamphlets in both prose and verse: *L'Arlequin au Muséum* for example, which was published annually at the beginning of the century. Ingres raged in vain against what he called literature for lackeys. At least the lackeys of those days were interested in pictures and artists. Reporters and cartoonists took pleasure in representing the different types of Salon visitor: the silent, thoughtful ones; the talkative ones giving long explanations of their aesthetic theories; serious folk making notes in the margin of the catalogue. They show us the artists themselves, close to their work and ready to explain it to passing friends, eyeing their rivals and sometimes condemning them with cruel, clever remarks which their little comrades would hasten to spread around. Nearby stood the models, who considered that part of the credit generally given to the painters was rightfully theirs. And then the small fry of the art world: the copyists, the amateur artists, the young society ladies, all happy to be near the great men everybody was talking about and whose works they imitated.

The Salon also served as a suitable meeting ground between artist and patron. The bourgeois who had had his portrait painted or whose bust was there on a plinth brought his friends to admire it and the artist might find more clients. The average collector spent long hours at the Salon seeking to base his collection on certain values; it was not difficult for him, as the best works of the year were there, guaranteed by the government, and true masterpieces which had won medals were available for his inspection.[21]

Not only did the state organize the annual Salon – its official name was The Exhibition of Living Artists – and intervene in the choice of works to be accepted; it attempted also to select the best of those chosen for the exhibition. Purchases of paintings by the government, and even more the whole system of prizes, medals and distinctions, crowned a concept of artistic judgment which was generally approved by most of the public, as it spared them the uncertainty involved in choosing for themselves.

There was also one whole class of artists who profited from the system: those who saw the prescribed hierarchy of honours as the well-trodden path which led from the Ecole des Beaux-Arts to the Institut, and beyond that, though less surely, to artistic immortality.

The system of awards was complex and changed too often over the course of years to be summed up in a simple formula. Roughly speaking, third-, second- and first-class medals were awarded, followed by the Grand Medal and the Grand Medal of Honour for those who came highest in the jury's estimation. But many did not get as far as that. There were also 'honourable mentions' and what were known as *rappels de médaille* (for artists whose works were considered worthy of a medal but who had already won a medal of the same class at a previous Salon). After the middle of the century any artist who had won a second-class medal at least twice was afterwards exempt or *hors concours* and his works were automatically accepted. By the 1880s an average of eighty-five medals was distributed annually.

These awards caused intrigues, jealousy and protests. Why did Corot, who had won a second-class medal in 1833, have to wait fifteen years to win a first-class medal? He was proposed for the Medal of Honour in 1865 but saw Cabanel preferred to himself after twenty-six ballots. When proposed again, nine years later in 1874, he only got three votes and his friends opened a subscription in order to offer him a gold medal in compensation. Meissonier, on the other hand, won a third-class medal in 1840 and a second-class one the following year; two years later he won a first-class medal; he was awarded the Grand Medal in 1855 and the Medal of Honour in 1867. Alfred Roll, awarded a third-class medal in 1875, received the first-class one only two years later. Examples like these could by multiplied indefinitely. Looking back they seem like a mockery of those prizes to which contemporaries attached so much importance.

The medals were presented at an impressive ceremony which added to the glamour. It was usually held when the Salon closed, or sometimes several weeks afterwards. Some important personage presided; sometimes it was the head of state himself. Napoleon presided on several occasions. In 1808 he made the ceremony the occasion for presenting Gros with the cross of the Legion of Honour in a somewhat theatrical fashion, taking the one he was wearing from his breast and giving it to the artist. In 1824 and 1828 Charles X presented the awards. Louis-Philippe, who was present in 1831, had to endure listening to the murmurs of discontent which arose when the list of prize-winners was read out and the experience encouraged him to stay away during the years that followed. In 1848, in order to re-establish the solemnity of the proceedings, the Salon awards were presented at the home of the Minister of the Interior. In 1849 the Prince-President came in person, and afterwards the ceremony was held in the presence of the Minister of the Interior or, later still, of Field-Marshal Vaillant who represented the Imperial household. After 1864 the names of the winners of the Prix de Rome for the year were announced at the same time as the Salon awards. And finally, under the Third Republic, it was the Minister of the Interior who presented the awards until such time as the artists themselves took over the entire responsibility for the Salon.

The medal-winners were the triumphant victors of the year, but at the other end of the scale the *refusés*, those who had been rejected for the Salon, considered themselves pariahs. In face of the injustices and the arguments caused by the jury system, could they not institute some kind of 'court of appeal'? Hence the idea of a *Salon des refusés*, where the public could appreciate the worth of those who had been excluded.

Little is known concerning the first attempt of this nature, which took place in 1827. On December 8th, that is to say one month after the opening of the Salon, an announcement was made concerning 'a complementary exhibition of paintings, comprising some of those not accepted for inclusion at the Louvre, on view at the gallery at 4 rue du Gros Chenet'. This was a private exhibition, but the *Journal des Artistes* claimed on December 16th that 'some of these rejected pictures are very much better than many of those which were chosen'. But the attempt made in 1841 to show the rejected pictures in the art galleries of the boulevard Bonne-Nouvelle does not seem to have met with much success.[22]

However it was not until 1863 that the artists benefited from a larger and more important venture. For some years the decision of the jury had given rise to the gnashing of teeth and protests. The storm finally broke when it was announced that more than half the pictures submitted had not been accepted. The discontent was so great that the Emperor decided to make a gesture. This time, opening a fortnight after the Salon, there was an official *Salon des refusés*. There were no fewer than 7,000 visitors on the opening day – though it is true that a section of the public came in hope of making fun at the expense of works so clearly deserving of ridicule. They came to view paintings bearing the signatures of artists such as Fantin-Latour, Harpignies, Manet and Whistler among others. Only half the canvases which had been refused were in fact exhibited; many artists preferred to accept the verdict of the jury and try and do better next time. In 1864 the experiment was less successful, having lost something of its novelty, and there was to be no third

Salon des refusés in spite of the demands of the artists concerned.

Because of their nature these exhibitions of rejected artists bore the stigma of official disapproval and necessarily followed in the wake of the official Salon. Were there then no other ways for an artist to show his work to the public?

It would be going too far to say that there were no private exhibitions in the nineteenth century. But though their number increased over the years it still bore no comparison, even during the last three decades of the century, with what we experience nowadays. Moreover, if we are to go by the reactions of public and critics, or indeed by the opinions of the artists themselves, it would appear that the latter could not expect to make their reputations in this way. The *Journal des Artistes*, ever ready to criticize decisions of the jury, yet had no hesitation in stating in 1845 that 'Private exhibitions are certainly becoming fashionable. . . . There is no harm in this as long as one does not seek to evade the tribute which every right-thinking man owes the annual Salon.'[23]

Most of these exhibitions were arranged by charitable organizations or artists' mutual-aid societies and consisted of collections of pictures formed without any specific aesthetic aim. This was the case, for example, with the exhibitions held in aid of the Greeks in 1826, to help the victims of the July Revolution in 1830 and the poor of Paris in 1832. The largest of the regular exhibitions were those of the *Société des amis des arts*. This society, which dated from before the Revolution, was reorganized in 1816 and had many imitators in the provinces. It used to buy works from artists with funds raised from the subscriptions of members and from the lotteries which it organized. Although the society was also allowed to use the buildings of the Louvre, the artistic level of their exhibitions seems to have been low.[24] The association founded by Baron Taylor to help artists in want also organized exhibitions; the profits went into the association's relief fund and the high level of these exhibitions is attested by numerous reports. The first of them was held in 1846 at 22 boulevard Bonne-Nouvelle and was partly retrospective; it saw the triumph of Ingres, who had boycotted the Salon for some years but who had agreed to be represented by several canvases. But one can imagine what the atmosphere was like at these affairs from reading Baudelaire's description of the exhibition. They were 'calm, tranquil, serious like someone's private study', not resembling the tumult of the Salon in the least.[25]

Dealers, like Susse in the Place de la Bourse, where Dantan's caricature statuettes could be bought around 1835, also exhibited work for sale. The most famous of these dealers' shows were those at the gallery opened by Louis Martinet in the boulevard des Italiens. It was here that Manet showed his *Spanish Guitarist* in 1861 and in 1864 fourteen pictures by this artist were on exhibition, causing an uproar in the press.

But one-man shows were rare, though the public was often ready to go and see a single picture. David's painting of the Emperor's coronation was shown all by itself at the Louvre from February 1808 onwards, long before the opening of the Salon, which did not take place that year until October 14th. It was not the first time that crowds had come to see David's work: in 1800 his *Sabine Women* was on show in the painter's studio and could be seen on payment of an entry fee. People must have flocked to see it as different authorities have estimated that the exhibition earned for David a sum ranging between 20,000 and 65,000 francs.[26] Happy days when an enthusiastic public appreciated the chance to see a new work by a master everyone was talking about!

There are many other examples of artists opening their studios to connoisseurs: Isabey showed his *Review by the First Consul in the Court of the Tuileries* in 1800, and Regnault showed three canvases in 1801. Amaury Duval in 1837 and the sculptors Auvray and Pradier in 1845 did the same. The most famous example was when Horace Vernet showed no less than forty-five paintings in 1822. In his own fashion Vernet was a *refusé* that year, as several of his compositions, like the *Battle of Jemmapes* and the *Defence of Clichy*, had been barred from the Salon for political reasons.

The cases of Courbet and Manet are different, because it was their artistic ideas that brought them into conflict with the Salon jury. In 1855 Courbet, whose canvases had not been accepted for the Universal Exhibition which was taking the place of the Salon that year, decided on a grand gesture. He managed to get a temporary building erected in the very shadow of the Universal Exhibition itself. 'It will cost me ten or twelve thousand francs,' he wrote to a friend. 'I have already rented the land for six months for two thousand; the construction will cost me six or eight thousand. . . .' The entry charge was one franc at the beginning; later it was halved as visitors began to fall off. But many did come – as they were to attend the *Salon des refusés* eight years later in search of amusement. And it seems that the 'realist' painter must have covered his costs, because he repeated the experiment in 1867 and had a pavilion built at the Pont d'Alma which he modestly called 'a cathedral in the most beautiful place in Europe'. The pavilion was a veritable museum, containing all his most striking works, but it had cost him 30,000 francs to build and even though he sold a few pictures Courbet was still out of pocket.[27]

This was the year that Manet copied him by exhibiting fifty of his own paintings elsewhere. His introductory brochure began as follows: 'Monsieur Manet has been exhibiting his work or attempting to exhibit it ever since 1861. This year he has decided to show all his paintings directly to the public.' He enjoyed no great success.

It is surprising, when one considers all these initiatives and also the difficulty some innovators found in winning acceptance at the Salon, that they did not think of banding together in order to present their work to the public under better conditions. Lack of money goes a long way to explain their lack of daring. After their failure in 1867 – a critical year for them – Monet, Courbet, Renoir and other young painters considered the question of a joint exhibition; but they had to abandon the idea as they could only muster 2,500 francs between them, although Bazille at least had means of his own. After 1870 they were more successful and in 1874 the first exhibition of what came to be known as the Impressionist School was held in the premises of the photographer Nadar. It was successful enough, in spite of the sarcastic comments of the majority of the public, for eight Impressionist exhibitions were held between 1874 and 1886.

The new trend which had been put in motion was fostered by the changes which occurred in the Salon after 1881. Group exhibitions were held reflecting artistic trends (Synthetism, the Rose-Croix), grouping practitioners of a particular technique (watercolourists, pastellists) or painters of special subjects (orientalists, animal painters), and gradually transformed the artistic climate. Public interest was shifting from the Salon to the private exhibitions and for the artists the time was coming when it would be easier for them to make their work known, if not for its value to be acknowledged.

Even if he won no prizes and nobody bought his works the artist could still hope that the critics would recognize his merits. A favourable review in a well-known journal was nearly as good as a medal: the subject would consider that criticism reflected impartial opinion, independent of the artistic cliques and official influence. And if he were attacked he would blame the ignorance of journalists or that sheeplike mentality which led them to try to please their readers instead of enlightening them.

The importance of the Salon could still be seen in the amount of space most journals devoted to it, while ignoring private exhibitions. The number and scope of such articles was related naturally to the state of development of the press itself, which was strictly controlled under the Restoration. It was freed by the July government, then muzzled again, and it was only after 1848, and particularly under the Third Republic, that the press really expanded. But even during periods when the press was controlled, editors of journals gave their readers long articles on the Salon, knowing their eagerness for them. Picture by picture, statue by statue, the critics carried out their task in lengthy commentaries. And as they sometimes found themselves faced with three thousand pictures, four miles of paintings, they needed time and space and had to take great pains. Weekly publications like *L'Artiste* after 1831 or bi-monthly journals like the *Gazette des Beaux-Arts* devoted four or five main articles to the Salon. But the daily press was still more verbose and the Salon critic was allowed to spread his study of all aspects of the exhibition over several weeks. Théophile Gautier, who wrote the art column in *Le Moniteur Universel* under the Second Empire, used to give twelve or fifteen articles in succession to this important subject. The author of work of any importance was almost certain of at least a mention.

The so-called *salons comiques*, published by humorous journals like *Le Charivari* and *L'Eclipse*, also demonstrated in a different fashion the public interest in this annual exhibition. These series of caricatures by Bertall, Gill and Nadar – this was the famous 'Nadar Jury' – parodied aspects of the works on exhibition; hardly serious criticism, they limited themselves to superficial attacks, but nevertheless contributed towards making the artists known.

The articles by art journalists showed little more understanding of works that did not keep to the beaten track. We can only mention here the growing gulf between artists and public opinion which occurred with the emergence of the Romantic movement and became still wider when the so-called 'realist' painting made its appearance. Delécluze, a man in the Davidian tradition, never ceased his attacks on Delacroix. The famous Albert Wolff, who wrote the art column in *Figaro* during the Second Empire, was still fiercer in his attacks on Courbet, Manet and their generation, while more lucid critics like Thoré-Bürger, Baudelaire and Castagnary could not always find the platform their views deserved. When Zola courageously undertook the defence of Manet in *L'Evènement*, the editor thanked him for his services after three articles and he was unable to finish his series on the Salon.[28]

The artists needed all their courage not to give up in despair when faced by a lack of understanding which reflected the feelings of the general public. After 1885 the number of small reviews under progressive editors multiplied and with them the number of articles favourable to progress in the arts. Men like J. K. Huysmans, Félix Fénéon and Aurier who approved of the Impressionists and their successors helped to make them known. But however agreeable such encouragement might have been for the artists it did not always console them for being misunderstood by the public at large. They were often more pleased by a qualified mention in one of the big newspapers than by unrestricted praise in a journal read by few. Virmaître said as much in 1890: 'An artist prefers two unkind lines in *Le Figaro* because of their publicity value to twenty-five in *Le Petit Journal*.'[29]

To be talked of where it mattered, in circles frequented by wealthy art lovers and in that section of the press read by society people, this was the artist's dream. Happy those who having achieved this satisfaction knew how to resist the temptation to facility and were not turned from their ideal by praise which was fulsome but not always sincere.

9　Landscape artist

10   Wood engravers at work

CHAPTER EIGHT

COMMISSIONS AND MARKETS

In theory artistic creation is a response to an inner need, but who could spend a lifetime painting and sculpting with no other motive than to satisfy himself? Every artist, however few his wants, needs a public, however small, if only to give him encouragement. Life's necessities act as a brake on creative freedom. Even the artist with private means has to negotiate the sale of his works, still more the artist who depends on his art for his living. Degas, himself from a middle-class background, reminded his friend Renoir: 'Why do we paint pictures if not to sell them?'[1]

In the sphere of art the interplay of supply and demand had to correspond to special circumstances. The artist's inclination was to work in accordance with his own vision of the world and his own taste, but he had greater success with the public if he conformed to public taste, which was not necessarily the same as his own. It was during the nineteenth century more than at any other time that the original artist found most difficulty in becoming established. Therefore even for the greatest artists, whether they liked it or not, there was an almost inevitable conflict between what the artists wanted to do and what they were asked to do. Happy the artist whose works, just as he had conceived them, were to the taste of a wide public who were ready to buy everything that left his studio. Most artists managed to strike some sort of balance between work of their choice and work chosen for them by others. More to the pitied were those who accepted commissions and found themselves reduced to repeating the same theme over and over again in a style which they could not abandon without disappointing their clients. Still worse the lot of those who had not even reached this level and were forced to undertake routine tasks, turning out large numbers of items on a production-line system, making copies or doing minor decorative work. Many great artists went through this stage at some point in their lives and, though this type of work was not necessarily to be despised and was often useful, it had the drawback of clipping the wings of the artist's inspiration.

Biographies of artists are marked by details of the material difficulties almost all of them had to surmount. But the degree of success achieved by them varied quite astonishingly: some lived in poverty while others made their fortune. But the fame they enjoy today bears little or no relation to the success they won during their lifetime. However, it will be interesting to understand the problems that faced them, the markets that were open to them and where they found their commissions; and also the kind of lives their material necessities and the prices they obtained for their works allowed them to live, be it like great lords or poor beggarmen.

The artist's first source of support was the state. For him the state was the wealthiest of potential patrons and also perhaps the most honourable; and in a country like France, which prided itself on being the 'mother of the arts' it was natural for some part of the national resources to be allocated to the encouragement of the arts. The young artist who had received his chance of training from the state at the Ecole des Beaux-Arts and who might have been lucky enough to benefit from the Prix de Rome would naturally seek further support from the same source.

The ideal might be permanent support from the community, but only a very few individuals were so favoured. David was appointed first painter to the Emperor, which should have assured him an easy life had not the political situation turned against him. The 12,000 francs per annum which went with the title did not preclude payment for pictures commissioned from him. In making this appointment Napoleon had revived a post which originated under the monarchy; and under the restored monarchy Gérard was awarded the title of 'first painter to the King' and the perquisites that went with it but renounced both at the time of the Revolution of 1830.

The honoraria of members of the Institut, though not comparable, were of the same kind and rose from 1,000 francs a year at the beginning of the century to 1,200 francs later on. Some artists still received substantial sums from the state. Sigalon, who copied the *Last Judgment* in the Sistine Chapel for Thiers, also received an annuity of 3,000 francs.[2]

Some artists who had fallen on hard times also received help. In his memoirs Chaptal, who was Minister of the Interior under the

Empire from 1802 to 1804, boasts of having spent 120,000 francs annually on charitable help for artists.[3] But this was not unusual. Louis-Philippe gave 59,900 francs to writers and artists in 1832 alone, and the Republican government after 1870 granted the aged Daumier a pension of 2,400 francs.

However, the most effective form of official protection of the arts – and indeed the very basis of it – remained purchases from artists and commissions. None of the many régimes which succeeded each other in France, from the Empire to the Third Republic, ever questioned their responsibilities in this respect, though they sometimes followed different criteria.

Ever zealous for his own prestige, Napoleon devoted enormous sums to the construction of monuments to his own glory and to the embellishment of the Imperial palaces, seeing himself as the successor to the kings of France. Architects and sculptors were the main beneficiaries: his bounty was widely shared – one has only to remember that the seventy-six episodes on the Vendôme Column provided work for thirty-six artists. Painters too shared in a vast programme to celebrate the Emperor's great deeds. The day after his coronation the Emperor gave his favourite painter David the task of depicting various moments in the ceremony. A decree of March 3, 1806, announced that eighteen pictures had been commissioned for the Salon of 1808, eleven of them taking their subjects from the recent Austrian campaign. In 1809, only two days after the battle of Wagram, Napoleon sent from Vienna a list of twelve paintings to be shared among various painters. In each case Vivant-Denon, his Director of Museums, was to draw up a detailed programme and discuss its execution with the artists. None of which prevented him intervening personally to make sure his own role had been given sufficient importance. David had to alter many details in his scene of the coronation and Gros had to rearrange the composition of his *Pesthouse at Jaffa* in order to give Bonaparte's presence among the lepers its full humanitarian and symbolic significance.

Thus the artists learned to their cost the bondage attendant on official commissions.

It was still worse when the government which had commissioned them changed and its glorification was made inopportune by the ups and downs of politics. Gros was a victim of both the restored monarchy and Napoleon's Hundred Days when he was given the task of decorating the cupola of the Pantheon. He had to change the composition no fewer than three times and Louis XVIII and the Duchess of Angoulême finally replaced Napoleon and Marie-Louise who had been required by the original design.

There were fewer prestige commissions under Louis XVIII and Charles X, but the total number remained high. Nine different painters worked on decorating the interior of the church of the Madeleine; others painted the ceilings of the Louvre and the halls of the Conseil d'Etat and the Stock Exchange. From the Salon catalogues of the period, which indicate when a work on exhibition was the result of a commission, we can see that a large number of them had been painted at the request of the royal household, the Minister of the Interior, the Prefect of the Seine or the Duke of Orleans.

Artists seem to have had more freedom in the choice of subject, though Napoleonic or Revolutionary scenes were barred. It was in aesthetic matters that official influence made itself felt, under pressure from the Institut which was trying to stem the tide of the emerging Romantic school. A work as controversial as Delacroix's *Dante and Virgil Crossing the Styx* exhibited at the 1822 Salon was however eventually purchased for the state. But in 1827 the director of the Beaux-Arts warned the self-same Delacroix that after the reprehensible tendencies shown in his *Massacre at Chios* he ran the risk 'of being irrevocably excluded from the list of painters employed by the state', *if he did not change his style*.[4]

Although he ultimately became the object of severe criticism it should be recognized that Louis-Philippe took a great interest in the arts. It was during his reign that Delacroix was given commissions for his great mural decorations: the Salon du Roi in 1833, the Library of the Palais Bourbon in 1838, and the Library of the Chambre des Pairs in 1840. Ingres was given the ceiling of the Throne Room in the Luxembourg on his return from Rome in 1841. But the main project of Louis-Philippe's reign was the transformation of Versailles into a 'museum of the glories of France' which gave work to a whole army of artists. The King drew up a programme for decorating the walls of the galleries with great scenes from French history. Alaux, one of Louis-Philippe's favourite artists, spent nine years on eighty-six panels in the Hall of the Etats-Généraux illustrating the history of parliamentary assemblies.

'Out of more than 3,000 works of art commissioned during his reign there is hardly one where the King did not inspire the original idea, examine the sketch and decide the final composition.' This testimony from Montalivet – who was Intendant of the Civil List under Louis-Philippe – goes far to explain the disappointments some artists suffered. Though Horace Vernet was showered with royal favours he had to endure constant niggling demands. When Couder painted the Fête de la Fédération he had to recast his picture completely in deference to the opinions of Louis-Philippe, who had been present in person and was a stickler for historical accuracy.[5]

It is hard for us to imagine nowadays the amount of detail included in official commissions. Here is the programme for a statue to be erected at Toulouse to the *Spirit of Navigation*, commissioned from the sculptor Louis-Joseph Daumas:

'The stance to be upright, calm and energetic, the weight on the left leg with the right foot in front. The right hand holds the tiller of the frail marine craft on which the statue is standing. The left arm is held forward, a sextant in the left hand. The head is crowned with stars and looks straight in front, gazing into the distance. At the statue's feet are various attributes of marine navigation, including a compass. Four bas-reliefs to decorate the pedestal, each of them to be in harmony with the sentiments expressed by the statue and to illustrate different stages in the history of navigation.'[6]

So detailed a description of a work which was still no more than a project was calculated to quench the artist's inspiration. One can understand Pradier's annoyance when the Ministry of Commerce, which had commissioned a statue representing *Public Order*, obliged him to replace the pike in the statue's right hand with a lance and the reigns placed to its left by the 'hand of justice'.

But though some of his demands were open to question, Louis-Philippe must be given credit for good will towards contemporary artists. While the Salon was open he used to visit nearly every day after the public had left: he could do so quite conveniently owing to the proximity of the Tuileries to the Louvre. The King used to go round, pencil in hand, examining every picture and making notes.

The observations he made formed the basis of further commissions and purchases, and it has been estimated that some fifty million francs were spent on the arts during his reign.

The Revolution of 1848 and the Second Empire caused upheavals in commissions to artists who once again found themselves the victims of a change of regime. Couture, who had received a commission from the July government, was unable to contain his rage when in 1851, instead of the picture he had already begun of the enlistment of volunteers under the Revolution, he was given a completely different assignment: the decoration of the Chapel of the Virgin in the church of Saint-Eustache. Soitoux, who had won a prize for a figure of the Republic, preferred to abandon his statue rather than transform it as suggested into an allegory of Justice.

By and large Napoleon III followed the prestige policies of his predecessors. Haussmann's remodelling and transformation of Paris afforded few openings for artists,[7] but they found many opportunities for work in the construction of the new Opéra and the completion of the Louvre; on the latter project two hundred artists worked on fifteen hundred sculptural motifs. We now deplore and find excessive the restoration of castles and churches undertaken for the most part under the direction of Viollet-le-Duc; but this opinion would not have been shared by all the artists who found work on them.

Where painting was concerned the Emperor at first followed his own personal taste, which was for small genre pictures and military scenes. But after the Universal Exhibition of 1855 the level of his purchases rose and he bought works by Bouguereau, Cabanel and Hébert, choices which were in line with majority taste. He even bought works by Corot in spite of the reservations of his Director of Museums, Count Nieuwerkerke.[8] Artists discovered they could approach their Deputy to procure themselves commissions and the Fine Arts service was besieged by members of the Chamber of Deputies who wished to help their protégés and at the same time enrich the churches and museums of their constituency with works of art.

Excesses of this kind continued under the Third Republic and too many mediocre artists filled the museums of small towns with uninteresting works. In spite of changes in taste and in the relative importance of the different genres, official purchases continued to favour history painting, no longer practised by artists like Monet, Renoir, or Gauguin. At the Salon of 1893, organized by the Société des Artistes Français, Henri Bouchot observed that the painters of grandiose historical reconstructions had not given up the struggle, offering as an explanation:

'Reasons of state. The state can most easily dispose of these reconstructions, the more so if they have been tailored to meet official taste, with a plethora of vibrant patriotism. Destined as they are for provincial museums; such works can spread themselves at leisure.'[9]

Sculptors have seldom been happier than during this period. From the reign of Louis-Philippe onwards municipalities erected statues paid for by subscription, on public squares. David d'Angers received many commissions of this kind in Béziers, Strasbourg and La Ferté-Milon. But it was after 1870 that 'statuemania' really became rampant: the pretexts, commemoration of battles which took place in the recent Franco-Prussian War, or homage to local glories. Paris only possessed nine statues of kings or great men in 1870, whereas by 1914 a hundred statues had been erected. The artists were the last to deplore this overcrowding.

However much an artist might want a commission, it often caused him considerable trouble. Apart from changes in the programme and unexpected requirements which he might have to accept, the material difficulties were many, and the administration moved slowly, whatever the regime. Artists' correspondence is full of letters to heads of departments claiming advances which had been promised.

The sculptor was the more to be pitied under these circumstances as he had both to pay his assistants and to pay for the marble; but painters who undertook vast decorative schemes had similar difficulties: the cost of of scaffolding and assistants' wages were a charge on their budget from the first. Delacroix found more than once that the condition of the walls or ceilings to be decorated was such as to cause complications and he was obliged to be constantly pressing for supplementary credits or simply for prompter payment of what he was owed.

In painting contemporary scenes problems began with the elusiveness of models. When Landelle was commissioned to paint the visit of the Empress to the state glass-works, the Manufacture de Saint-Gobain, he had to include some thirty-four official personnages and very few of these agreed to pose for him. Neither Emperor nor Empress would come to his study and he had to make do with photographs by Disderi; the Empress, however, sent one of her ladies-in-waiting to sit for him in her place. But for the Bishop of

Soissons, Landelle had to be content with a photograph and with arranging some of his clothing over a lay figure. When the picture was finished the Empress insisted on changes; in particular she wanted the artist to give prominence to the kiss-curls she had taken to wearing recently.[10]

Another privilege the state granted artists was to be sent on mission. All their living expenses were met by the administration while on mission and they accumulated the documentary material required of them on the spot. A whole team of draughtsmen followed Napoleon or else returned to the field of battle to make sketches and studies. Marinet, Bourgeois, Zix and Vivant-Denon all built up a collection of documentary material which they either used themselves or gave to the artists who were to depict the imperial campaigns. In order to commemorate the Battle of Navarin, the government of Charles X sent a marine painter, Garneray, to the scene, accompanied by young Decamps. The mission was hardly a success: Garneray, who had set out in December 1828, returned to Marseilles a year later a sick man and go involved in a duel, while Decamps failed to paint the figures on the sketch sent to the museum at Versailles. But the journey which took him to Smyrna was the inspiration for his pictures of oriental subjects.[11]

Horace Vernet was sent several times to Africa and even to Mexico to study the sites of battles and to collect documentary evidence and eye-witness accounts. At other times painters were directly attached to army units as observers, a role which ceased to be useful when they could be replaced by reporter-photographers. Ary Scheffer was attached to the Headquarters of the Duke of Orleans during the siege of Anvers in 1822. Meissonier followed the campaign in Italy under the Second Empire in the same fashion and received 50,000 francs. He is said to have been struck with horror at the scenes on the battlefield, which need not surprise us as it was the humanitarian reaction to the carnage of Solferino that inspired the creation of the Red Cross organization. Meissonier's picture of the battle carefully avoids showing the slaughter. As late as 1881 Detaille and Berne-Bellecour followed the campaign in Tunisia.

There were other, more peaceful, missions: for example, Charles Blanc arranged for Eugène Fromentin to go and paint in North Africa in 1849; his secret idea was to rival Delacroix, who had become famous on account of the paintings he made of Morocco and Algeria after his journey there in 1832 with Ambassador De Mornay.

It might seem that favours such as these were many and diverse, but only a small minority in fact benefited. The others resented their exclusion, considering, often with reason, that government policy was open to question in this respect. They did not complain so much when purchases or commissions went to Salon medallists, but that there were so many political or personal reasons for government action.

Viel-Castel wrote in 1831: 'The authorities have had no other purpose in the help and protection they have extended to artists than to attach this important class so their interests.'[12] A harsh judgment maybe, but well-founded at least in part, in that the choice of artists was too often made on no defensible aesthetic grounds. Nor was the result necessarily better when the sovereign followed his personal taste, but in any case the responsibility was often delegated to the Directors of Museums or to those in charge of the Fine Arts: hence the importance of Vivant-Denon under the First Empire, of Count Montalivet during the reign of Louis-Philippe, Charles Blanc at the time of the Second Republic, Count Nieuwerkerke during the Second Empire, and at the beginning of the Third Republic, of the Marquis of Chennevières.

And if it was decided that the choice of a committee should replace the choice of the sovereign, then who should there be seen at the head of the objectors but Delacroix opposing the decision:

'Government encouragement is the only support of artists in many branches of art. . . . The undersigned, in reminding the administration of the encouragement they should be giving, do so because it is their belief that help given in this way affords least scope to the preferences of cliques and coteries. Those in authority have only to consult the voice of public opinion, which is enough to indicate the artists truly deserving of notice. . . .'[13]

Another system, that of public competitions, often seemed fairer. The choice was made publicly and the prize was awarded to the work and not to the artist. It was without doubt more democratic, but the system had undeniable disadvantages: the unsuccessful candidates had worked for nothing; there was the chance that a sudden burst of inspiration would allow some young unknown to carry the day against more talented or more deserving artists. Rudé wrote to his friend Moine that he would never again commit the folly of entering for competitions:[14] And Delacroix also attacked the whole idea with particular energy:

'It is not being obliged to depict this or that subject that I object to; it is having to pass through the pitiless sieve of competition, being lined up before the public like a team of gladiators vying with each other for its impertinent approval, their pleasure to sacrifice themselves and each other in the arena. What an ordeal for the modesty of the true artist!'[15]

Delacroix, of course, had unhappy memories of the competition held in 1831 for the decoration of the Chamber of Deputies, the theme set being Boissy d'Anglas at the Convention, when Court's picture was preferred to the one he had submitted. The 1838 competition for the Tomb of Napoleon in the Invalides provides another example of the equivocal situations which could occur: Victor Baltard won first prize but this young artist, then thirty-three, received a gold medal as his only reward and was passed over in favour of the better-known and much-decorated Visconti, who was given the commission.

However, numerous competitions for public monuments, statues of great men and vast decorative schemes were held throughout the century; the drawbacks of the system no doubt explain why many talented artists declined to take part.

It is certain that all too many of the thousands of paintings and sculptures exhibited at the Salon did not find purchasers, even though this great annual fair was so well suited to awaken interest, bring artists and buyers together and encourage sales.

As we have already seen, official commissions accounted for a proportion of the works exhibited. Others were already paid for; for example, portraits which had been purchased by the sitter. But what of the others? The reporter of the *Bulletin des Arts* asked himself this question concerning the 1846 Salon, which comprised 2,241 entries, excluding architecture, engraving and lithography. According to this reporter

'Nine-tenths of these paintings, watercolours, pastels and sculptures will never be sold. Allowing that there are 741 portraits, busts, medallions and other items that are a gamble on the vanity of the bourgeois or on political patronage in the form of the recommendation of a deputy, there still remain 1,500 pictures and statues to place.'[16]

In the preceding year the same journalist had estimated that a little over half the works shown at the Salon were unsaleable – a more optimistic estimate. Even so, the number of unplaceable works was still high. Small sculptures, bronzes of animals or ornaments might eventually find their way into the shops; paintings were exported at reduced prices to England or America or Russia, the painter receiving twelve francs including the frame. This was the 'bargain-basement' of art and many artists preferred to take back their work and either keep it or destroy it. Delacroix in 1847 recalled the little garden belonging to the sculptor Maindron 'peopled with unfortunate statues that the unhappy artist has been unable to dispose of.'[17] Some works were bought by private individuals but these, as we have seen, were few.

Contemporary observers were unfailing in their denunciations of the effects of social change on the artists' clientele. There were fewer Maecenas, fewer great lords who were interested in art. There was, of course, the Duke of Luynes, who asked the architect, Dubon, and then Rude and Ingres to decorate his castle at Dampierre. The Duke of Orleans, who died young, was a champion of contemporary art, even supporting the art of his day in opposition to his father Louis-Philippe. He was a friend of Ary Scheffer and bought canvases by Rousseau and Huet and sculptures from Barye and Feuchère. Another of Louis-Philippe's sons, the Duke of Aumale, threw Chantilly open to artists and, though he set too much store by Meissonier, was prepared to pay well for any painting he wanted. Other examples could be quoted and money was sometimes to be found among the lesser nobility and even on occasion among the demi-monde. Baudry was responsible for the decoration of the town residences of Madame de Nadaillac and Madame de Galliéra, but also for that of La Paiva.

'Will they never understand', wrote Balzac in Les Paysans, 'that great art is impossible without large fortunes, without large and secure private means.'[18]

But now it was the bourgeoisie which was getting richer and this class had their own special requirements: their homes were small, so they needed small-scale works of art; art was a luxury and they did not want to pay too much; and finally their taste followed in the wake of official decisions. The sculptor Etex wrote in 1859:

'A man who goes quite mad when buying carpets and thinks nothing of spending 20,000 or 50,000 in furnishing his apartment for one season or his drawing room or his town house, if you speak to him of paying 2,000 francs for an excellent bust, or a fine portrait of his wife or daughter . . . will utter cries of protest.'[19]

Sculptors found still fewer private buyers than painters. The critic Thoré referred to the paralysing effect on sculpture of the demands of the Salon jury when he wrote in 1847:

'Where can a plaster group or a marble statue be exhibited? And who will buy them? There are not half a dozen sculptors in Paris who can make a living without the publicity of the Salon and state patronage.'[20]

Most private commissions were for portrait busts. Otherwise, the only demand was for small sculpture: medallions – those of David d'Angers were small masterpieces; ornamental statuettes – Pradier produced many of these, all of them with licentious subjects; and finally ornamental figures for clock surrounds.

But was this art?

The growing importance of middle-class attitudes influenced positions adopted in aesthetic matters and goes far to explain the divorce between the more belligerent and combative artists and a public whose level of taste was usually low. To attempt to woo this public an artist had to be completely without illusions.

It is hard to catch a glimpse of these clients. There exist numerous anecdotes pouring ridicule on their behaviour; such anecdotes are, however, significant in as far as they sum up the difficulties of the artists' relationship with their public.

For example, there is the story of a certain village notary. When Jules Laurens painted his son's portrait the notary asked the artist to give his painting a *second coat*, and never mind the expense.[21] There was the society lady who returned her portrait, demanding the colour of her dress be changed, because she had just gone into mourning.[22] And there must be at least twenty stories about people who judged the value of an artist on the basis of the number of decorations he had received or the cost of his pictures. The client of Balzac's Pierre Grassou said to his wife: 'Do you think I would have our portraits painted by an artist who has not been decorated?' A sitter paid 1,000 francs for his portrait and contracted to pay the artist another 2,000 if the picture was accepted for the Salon.[23] And the banker Pillet-Will told Renoir: 'In my position I have to have expensive pictures. That is why I must go to Bouguereau at least until I find another painter whose prices are higher'.[24] And the famous shopkeeper Chauchard, owner of the *Grands Magasins du Louvre*, dreamt of having his most expensive picture carried before his hearse.

It was this public who influenced the changes in the relative importance of the different genres. In the nature of things, the *grandes machines* (large history paintings) were the subject of official purchases; small pictures, canvases which were easy to hang, enjoyed wider popularity: Meissonier's success was to a large extent due to these factors. The bourgeois liked amusing genre pictures or touching sentimental scenes; he asked for landscapes too, but pure landscape 'did not tell a story'; and above all he wanted portraits – a reporter once wrote that portraiture was the artist's bread and butter.[25] But Ingres, who had had to paint more portraits than he wished while he was in Italy, used to answer proudly anyone who asked whether this was where the portrait painter lived: 'No, Monsieur, he who lives here is an artist.'[26]

Photography soon came to compete with the portrait and the bust; but the latter retained their prestige and maintained their price.

The public did not hesitate to demand repeated variations on a theme which had taken its fancy. Troyon was obliged to call on the help of Boudin in 1861, so popular had his meadows with their white cattle become. Landelle painted no fewer than twenty replicas of his *Fellah Woman*, which had had a fantastic success at the 1866 Salon. She was, however, only a Norman peasant woman dressed up in a borrowed Oriental costume.[27]

Anyone who wanted to make a good living had to accept the situation. As Baudelaire said in his introduction to his critique of the 1845 Salon, not without irony: 'The bourgeois, being bourgeois, is much to be respected; we have to please those at whose expense we live.'

In contrast to this public, who could not be disregarded but whose influence and reactions were often much to be deplored, stand the figures of a few true art lovers who supported the best art of their day in defiance of current opinion. These middle-class Maecenas include, for example, Alfred Bruyas, who sat for no fewer than seventeen painters and who helped and supported Courbet in his difficult early days. But Bruyas, who was the son of a Montpellier banker, possessed a substantial private fortune. More remarkable are those with quite modest means whose taste proved better than that of more illustrious lovers of art. Victor Choquet was a customs official who bought one of Delacroix's paintings as soon as he had saved a little money and eventually came to possess a magnificent collection of early impressionist paintings at a time when so-called connoisseurs were turning scornfully away from the works of the innovators.

The dealer took his ten per cent on every work he sold, but he was a natural intermediary since the artist was spared the trouble of looking for clients himself. However, it was not until 1825, with the rise of the Romantic school, that the sale of contemporary works of art by dealers was instituted.[28]

At first the sale of pictures was only a sideline for those selling paper or dealing in artists' colours. Alphonse Giroux on the corner of the boulevard de la Madeleine and the rue des Capucines was one of the first to enter this field, but he was selling games and luxury goods before he began to deal in pictures. The shop kept by Susse on the place de la Bourse was popular with those who wanted fine leather goods; however, it was here that Dantan exhibited and sold his famous caricature-statuettes, including one of Balzac carrying a stick as thick as himself. Soon Susse began buying small pictures for which he paid 100 or 200 francs at most, in the knowledge that he could easily sell them to adorn bourgeois interiors, especially at the New Year when people exchanged presents.

As for the firm of Durand-Ruel, which was to become so important, in the beginning it was only a stationer's shop in the rue Saint-Jacques where artists bought their materials. They sometimes left a sketch or watercolour or lithograph as payment and so an art department gradually grew up. Durand-Ruel moved to the Right Bank and opened a larger shop stocking artists' materials and pictures in the rue des Petits-Champs in 1833. In 1839 he opened in the rue de la Paix. He earned more from hiring out paintings than from selling them. At that time people were quite ready to rent a picture by the evening or by the week; it might be in order to furnish an apartment for a special reception, or more commonly in order to make a copy of the work. In such cases the clients were colleges, drawing schools in Paris and especially in the provinces, or young society ladies. Berville in the Chaussée-d'Antin and Esnault-Pelterie in the rue de Paradis also had pictures for hire, as did several others.[29]

There were some shops which sold engravings before beginning to deal in pictures. Martinet's, in the rue Coq-Saint-Honoré, noted ever since the Empire as dealers in engravings, was later transformed into a picture gallery. Goupil on the boulevard Montmartre since 1827 did good business out of the lithographic reproduction of his pictures, and the market he could offer artists was far from negligable. Ingres sold the reproduction rights of his *Odalisque* for 24,000 francs, having disposed of the picture itself for only 1,200 francs.[30] Goupil in his turn opened a picture department, making contracts with artists like that signed by Landelle on March 15, 1845:

'M. Landelle undertakes not to dispose of the reproduction rights of any of his compositions, pictures or drawings without first submitting these to MM. Goupil and Vibert. M. Landelle will be paid reproduction rights equivalent to twenty-five francs for every franc of the publication price of prints published by MM. Goupil and Vibert after M. Landelle's works. Furthermore M. Landelle agrees to sell two pictures by him at present on exhibition at the Louvre entitled *L'Idylle* and *L'Elégie* to MM. Goupil and Vibert who agree to accept them for a price 2,000 francs, to include exclusive reproduction rights and the frames, which they will pay him at his convenience.'[31]

In the year this contract was signed, the critic Thoré estimated that there were a hundred art dealers in Paris. It seems an enormous figure. Thoré continues: 'There are as many dealers as there are purchasers, or more.' And he reckons that a mere 200 canvases were sold annually by dealers[32]. We should form a strange idea of the business sense of the age if we did not know that such dealers usually only became involved in the sale of works of art by accident. However, it was about this date that galleries specializing in modern pictures began to be opened. Souty showed a famous collection of works by Vernet and Charlet, and Durand-Ruel exhibited a collection of works in the rue de la Paix which he considered important enough for it to be worthwhile reproducing the most outstanding in an album in 1845, which also included a view of his own gallery. The art trade grew under the Second Empire and from this time onwards the dealers began to play a decisive role in the lives of artists. Théophile Gautier wrote in 1858 in *L'Artiste*:

'The rue Lafitte is a sort of permanent Salon, an exhibition of paintings which lasts the whole year through. Five or six shops display pictures in their windows. They are regularly changed and lit up at night.'[33]

Beugniet's elegant shop was in this street, where Delacroix preferred to sell his pictures rather than deal direct with art lovers, unless he went to Thomas or Tedesco. The shops grew in number and expanded their business abroad. By 1865 Goupil, no longer content with two establishments in Paris where works by Gérôme and Delaroche were regularly on view, had opened branches in London, Brussels, The Hague, Berlin and New York. Paul Durand-Ruel had been at the head of the firm since 1862; he believed in the future of the Barbizon painters and would soon be backing the first Impressionist paintings in the face of the common opinion; about to open on the rue Lafitte, he too was making contracts in America.

Just at the time when the market for works of art was taking on international dimensions, new relationships were forming between dealers and artists. Certainly there still existed a number of small dealers who were often useful in meeting modest needs. That they were, unlike their more famous colleagues, only one step away from being dealers in second-hand curios, did not prevent them having taste and flair. But though they might do good business it was all too often at the expense of poverty-stricken artists. D'Aubourg, known as Père Lacrasse, was established on the Place Pigalle around 1870, and Fantin-Latour and Ribot were only too glad to sell him canvases for five to fifteen francs at the beginning of their careers. Martin used to buy works from Jongkind and Corot and also from Pissarro and Monet for twenty francs or forty according to size and sell them afterwards for sixty or eighty francs. Père Malgras in *L'oeuvre* is a composite portrait of several real individuals and Zola shows him picking up canvases by Lantier for ten or fifteen francs and offering him a lobster on condition he painted a still-life. A few years later one of these men was to become famous. This was Julien Tanguy, a colour dealer in the rue Clauzel, a rough diamond and a former volunteer with the forces of the Commune, who showed amazing intuition concerning innovators like Cézanne and Gauguin and Van Gogh. And because Père Tanguy had managed to collect together in his shop works by the best exponents of modern art, his became a sacred name to a whole generation of painters, from Pissarro to Seurat and the Nabis.[34]

The big dealers, and they were not always the discoverers of the greatest artists, established themselves by other methods. In 1860 Arthur Stevens, brother of the painter, offered Millet a contract which guaranteed him a minimum of 1,000 francs a month for three years plus such additional sums as might be paid him for any pictures he painted. This contract should have assured Millet a good living; instead, such complications arose that already by the end of 1861 the painter had experienced some very difficult moments.[35] As for Durand-Ruel, he was the first dealer to acquire a monopoly of a painter's works, achieved when he purchased seventy pictures from Théodore Rousseau in one transaction for 130,000 francs.[36]

There were other, more equivocal procedures. In his preparatory notes for *L'oeuvre* Zola has described how Braume forced up the price of the painter Roybet. Braume would visit Roybet:

'You are a genius. How much have you sold that picture for? 1,200 francs? But that's crazy. It's worth 2,000. What about this one, how much do you want for it? Good God! 2,000! Look, you don't understand; it's worth 4,000. I'll take it for 4,000, do you understand? From today you'll only work for Braume.'

Then the dealer would sing Roybet's praises everywhere, and sell a picture for 5,000, promising to buy it back for 6,000 the following year if the purchaser became tired of it. But the latter was afraid to let go of something which was increasing in value. In this way Braume eventually managed to sell a Roybet to Chauchard for 40,000 francs.[37]

Other dealers stirred up speculation by organizing fake auctions where works were bought back by the dealer at exaggeratedly high prices.

On the other hand painters who were shunned by public opinion benefited by assistance from dealers. After 1870 the stir caused by exhibitions by young artists organized by Durand-Ruel, Georges Petit, and later on Le Bare de Boutteville, and their financial success, compensated for and to some extent replaced the Salon. Durand-Ruel came to act as banker to the Impressionists and gave some of them monthly allowances. He advanced large sums to Degas as and when the artist needed them instead of on the basis of sales of pictures.[38]

The dealer was a newcomer to the world of the arts who had achieved a somewhat ambiguous position by the end of the century. By contributing to the making and unmaking of reputations he falsified the laws of supply and demand. But by organizing exhibitions, supporting painters who were too advanced for public opinion and introducing artists to patrons, the dealer came to fill an irreplaceable role in the artists' lives.

CHAPTER NINE

MONEY MATTERS: EARNINGS AND EXPENDITURE

Needs and expenses vary with the individual. Nevertheless, for any given period one can say that a certain sum of money will be enough for bare subsistence or a comfortable living, as the case may be, or else that it represents wealth. We need some basis for comparison if we are to assess the standard of living enjoyed by artists. Fortunately, the considerable degree of price stability that prevailed throughout the nineteenth century makes calculation easier. The cost of goods and services varied little over a hundred years; wages, on the other hand, showed a marked rise under the Second Empire and a still more marked rise at the end of the century. But rises of 20 per cent or even 50 per cent did not cause any great upheaval in the French economy. They merely made it possible for careful people to save. And in those days the gradual accumulation of a small capital sum ensured a steady income not subject to tax. These favourable economic conditions must be borne in mind if we are to understand how the artists organized their finances.

In 1829 Henri Dutilleux made a living from copying paintings and giving Latin lessons. His lunch could hardly have been more frugal: 3 sous' worth of bread and 1 sous' worth of cheese. In the evening he had a more lavish meal costing 17 sous. His lodgings in the rue Gît-le-Coeur No. 5 cost 17 francs a month (firewood included). Hamon's lunch when a student at Delaroche's studio was different but just as sparse: 2 sous' worth of bread and 2 of sausage. He had dinner near the Ecole des Beaux-Arts for 9 sous: beef, soup and bread bought from a bakers; in all, 70 centimes a day for food.[1] Bazille, who was well off as a student, enjoyed a less spartan diet; in 1863 he spent 15 sous on lunch: 'soup, bread and a chop'.[2] Courbet, who was better off in 1850 than he had been at the beginning of his career, used to spend 1·35 francs or 1·50 francs on lunch at the Brasserie Andler, including beer and coffee, his monthly bill amounting to between 97 and 100 francs.[3]

147

When Zola was encouraging his friend Cézanne to come to Paris in 1859 he drew up the following budget for him:

'A room at 20 francs a month; lunch for 18 sous and dinner for 22 sous comes to 2 francs a day or 60 francs a month, plus another 20 for the room makes 80 francs a month. You then have your studio fees to pay; Suisse, which is one of the cheapest, is 10 francs a month I think; allow another 10 for canvases, brushes and colours, which makes 100. You have 25 francs left for laundry, light, the hundred and one small necessities that arise, your tobacco and little luxuries. But you can create other resources for yourself! Studies made in the studio, copies from the Louvre, all sell well. . . . It is all a matter of finding a dealer and that is only a question of looking for one.'[4]

It was estimated in 1850 that Parisians spent an average of between one franc and one franc and a quarter on food; bearing in mind how enormous some people's meals were at that time, there must have been all too many who had barely enough to eat. Some people's daily earnings at that time were no more than fifty centimes, and if, like the building workers, their work was seasonal and the slack period long, they knew real poverty. At this time average expenditure on food was estimated to lie between 365 and 460 francs a year. Sixteen years earlier in 1834 the *Nouveau Tableau de Paris* had set the figure at 352 francs; the increase is, as we have seen, small.

Working-class annual incomes in 1850, excluding the most underprivileged, ranged from 900 to 3,000 francs a year. It was then possible to live modestly on 1,500 francs per annum. But it is a measure of Rude's simplicity of character that he considered his problems were over when he had managed to acquire for himself an annual income of about this figure and refused Thiers' offer of 30,000 francs to visit Italy. 'I appreciate your generosity,' he wrote, 'but I want for nothing.'

Other artists wanted a fuller existence. In order to assess their standard of living it is as well to compare their earnings with those in other, similar fields.

Let us take the case of two dramatists, as popular in their own day as they are forgotten in ours: Emile Augier and Scribe had unearned yearly incomes of 5,000 and 6,000 francs respectively, plus large royalties and occasional earnings from other sources. Victor

Hugo himself said he had earned 550,000 francs in the twenty-eight years between 1817 and 1845, which averages out at 19,640 francs a year. One can say in his case that he was very comfortably off indeed.[5]

Mlle Beaugrand, who was a *danseuse étoile* at the Paris Opéra, was given an engagement there in 1857 at 300 francs a year – on which she could easily have died of hunger. But her earnings increased rapidly with success: 1,000 francs in 1860, 5,000 francs in 1863, 14,000 francs by the end of 1867; and in 1875 she was earning 30,000 francs.

Let it also be noted that the Great Chamberlain and the chaplain at the court of Napoleon III were paid 40,000 francs a year and that even the first *valet de chambre* received 6,000 francs, i.e. twice as much as the most prosperous working man.[6]

'Of all the branches of industry practised by man there is none where the raw materials used are less costly than painting, both in themselves and later by comparison with the value added to the painting by the labour of the artist. A picture which costs two or three hundred francs to paint, will, if of average quality, be worth three or four thousand *during the life-time of the painter*. And after his death the price will double or treble in the course of time.'[7]

These comments by the painter Bergeret are not without a certain acuteness, but the ultimate value of a work of art is dependent on a great many circumstances. His remarks do however focus our attention on the 'cost price' of a work of art. Low as this may be, it is not to be disregarded altogether.

An easel might cost fifteen francs or 100 francs if it were well made and the height adjustable. The painter needed palettes, maulsticks, palette cups, and about sixty brushes, which cost him 200 or 300 francs alone. Colours were expensive: twenty-five centimes a tube, or more often one whole franc: and rarer colours cost ten or fifteen francs a tube. A large canvas could absorb 300 to 500 francs' worth of colours, so a painter who painted regularly might have bills of between 400 francs and 1,000 francs a year for colours. As the money spent on one tube of paint would buy a day's food, it is not surprising that when Claude Monet found himself in the most dire poverty and unable to feed his wife and child he was obliged to give up painting because he had no colours. Dealers were accused of charging high prices which allowed them to give credit in their better days. According to Zola, Baudry owed his colour dealer as much as 60,000 francs but the latter did not go bankrupt for all that.[8]

Prices of canvases and frames varied according to size. A medium-sized canvas, the size called 120 (1 m. 95 × 1 m. 30), cost thirty-three francs. A prolific painter of small pictures could easily spend 200 to 300 francs on canvases. The cost of five or six frames a year must be added, 500 to 1,000 francs, and also the expense of models, which might vary considerably. In 1898 it was calculated that a small canvas (1 m. 25 × 0 m. 80) which took 100 francs' worth of colours and 300 francs in models' fees would cost the painter 558 francs; naturally a landscape the same size, less handsomely framed, might cost him under 200 francs.[9]

The rent of an artist's studio was estimated to lie between 1,000 and 1,800 francs per annum at the end of the century. Prices seem to have doubled over the half a century since the *Journal des Artistes* mentions a studio to let in 1841: 'elegant furnished studio with annexes, suitable for history painter or portraitist: 500 francs a year or 50 a month'.[10]

The sculptors' expenses were even heavier than the painters'. Certainly they could set themselves up for 400 or 500 francs with modelling-stand, tubs, buckets, chisels, files and various other tools. But a big commission could involve them in expenditure rising to 1,500 or 1,800 francs a year: there was the clay, armature, plaster cast (600 to 800 francs), models (400–1,000 francs), hire of costumes (200 to 300). The artist could postpone the final execution of his work in bronze or marble if he did not have a definite commission, as this stage caused him far greater expense. Fine Italian marble cost 1,500 or 2,000 francs a cubic metre and a seated figure required two cubic metres. A simple marble bust for which the artist was paid 8,000 francs cost 300 francs for the marble alone. Add to this 200 francs for the plaster cast, 700 or 800 to pay the sculptor's assistants, and 100 francs for incidental expenses, and the artist will have laid out 1,400 francs, leaving himself with 6,600 francs as the price of his labour and his inspiration and on which to live.

The stability of the cost of living during the nineteenth century makes the wide range of prices paid for works of art, paintings in particular, all the more astonishing. The value of a picture varied according to its subject and size, and still more according to the fame of the painter. A work specially commissioned from a well-known artist often commanded a higher price than a work of the same type purchased at the Salon. But other factors played their part. It is hard to see why pictures by Troyon, which he had earlier found difficulty in selling for 500 francs, should have sold for 6,000 or 10,000 francs after 1849, except for the fact the painter had just been decorated. And what was the reason for the infatuation with Meissonier which made him one of the most expensive painters of the century, whereas now, a hundred years later, he is one of the least prized?

Prices were high under the First Empire, at least for artists who were supported by those in power. David, who was already in receipt of an official salary of 12,000 francs a year as first painter to the Emperor, asked 400,000 francs for four pictures of the coronation. The price was reduced, but even so he eventually received 65,000 for his painting of the Emperor's coronation. This sort of price seldom occurs again during the nineteenth century, even for history paintings. In 1849 Horace Vernet sold a picture to the Czar of Russia for 99,000 francs but this was exceptional even for Vernet. Delacroix was content to accept 4,000 francs in 1840 for his *Justice of Trajan*;[11] and Paul Delaroche received only 25,000 francs for his greatest triumph, the Hemicycle of the Ecole des Beaux-Arts. It was another thirty years before Meissonier was to earn higher prices than these, when his *Cuirassiers of 1805* was purchased for 250,000 francs in 1878.[12]

David had demanded 22,000 francs for his portrait of the Pope; two copies were however included in the price. But a portrait by Horace Vernet was only worth 500 francs in 1815; in 1824 he received 9,950 francs for his famous painting of the Duke of Angoulême, an exceptionally high price. The 4,000 francs which Ingres asked from the Duke of Orleans for painting his portrait was generally considered ridiculously high. Here again, the only artists to obtain better prices were Cabanel, who asked his sitters 10,000 or 20,000 francs, and Carolus-Duran, whose usual price was 25,000 francs.

The highest price paid for any painting during the century was for Millet's *Angelus*, which was sold for 553,000 francs at the Secrétan Sale in 1889; a few years later it was to be purchased by Chauchard for 800,000; and Millet had let it go for 1,000 francs in 1860.

Fabulous prices such as these are not our concern here. They were the result of speculation at public sales and the money did not benefit the artists. Nevertheless, such prices exerted an influence on the value assigned to works of art.

Vivant-Denon, who was shocked by David's exorbitant demands, wrote in a report in 1806 that he and his like should be brought back to 'that modest simplicity characteristic of true artists in every country, whose glory it has always been to work hard and live well but without ostentation'.[13] The shade of Vivant-Denon can rest in peace. A few artists may have made their fortune but many experienced poverty and many, even the greatest, had difficulty in managing to live well.

The most fortunate were those who had private means and did not need to fear the rebuffs of public opinion or of potential purchasers. They were fortunate on the strictly material plane, that is, for a painter could hardly be happy to go on painting indefinitely without ever making a sale. Cézanne, who is often regarded as a very unlucky painter, had no real financial worries: an allowance of 200 francs (later 100 francs) a month from his father and a larger income after the latter's death, allowed him to be independent in a modest way. Neither was Van Gogh without means, as his brother Theo, who worked for the firm of Goupil, gave him a monthly allowance of 150 francs. Degas, who came of a banking family, could afford to disregard outlets for selling his pictures until the time when those difficulties arose which were to complicate his life. Of the others, Delacroix and Manet had no need of immediate success at the outset of their careers. Yet at the age of thirty, Delacroix still found it difficult to win for himself 'independence and enough to live on'. During the last years of his life he had an income of 10,000 francs a year.

In our discussion of those who had a hard struggle to earn the most meagre living, we shall refer in this chapter only to those men whose works are nowadays among the glories of French art, and we will deal later with those others whose fate was hardly less enviable but which appears to us to have been less unjust because they overrated their talents.

The greatest artists went through difficult periods when their resources were inadequate. Ingres lived poorly for many years, happy that his wife was able to contribute to the household budget by taking in sewing. When Granet called to visit him during his stay in Florence between 1820 and 1828, the great painter greeted him at the entrance to his lodgings with these words: 'Do not enter here, you will find poverty within.'[14] His situation changed for the better when he returned to Paris and Louis-Philippe asked him in 1841 to undertake the decoration of the ceiling in the Throne Room of the Chambre des Pairs for 100,000 francs. And whereas his *Odalisque* sold for 1,200 francs at the Salon of 1821, Count Duchâtel purchased *The Source* for 23,000 francs in 1856.

Moreau-Nélaton has calculated that Manet spent about 20,000 francs a year between 1862 and 1866, while earning practically nothing from his art. He was only able to organize his private exhibition in the avenue de l'Alma in 1867 thanks to a loan of 18,300 francs from his mother. To be able to do such things it was necessary to have private means. Manet was fifty when Durand-Ruel made a large purchase from him of twenty-four canvases. Even so the total sum was not more than 35,000 francs. Towards the end things were better. In 1879 alone he made 11,300 from his paintings.

The case of Eugène Deveria was just the opposite. At the age of twenty-two he put all his genius into *The Birth of Henry IV*, which was the star attraction of the Salon of 1828 and which he sold for 10,000 francs. Fourteen years later he was glad to find a commission for four pictures at 500 francs each when on his way to Fougères,[15] and some few years after that it was claimed that he was turning out portraits at 20 francs each.

Sculptors often found it still more difficult to make a living than painters did. The following letter by the sculptor J.-J. Perraud to a friend of his youth is a harrowing testimony to the hardships underlying the careers of some artists who were socially successful but weighed down by the burden of hidden poverty. Perraud, born in 1819, had won the Prix de Rome in 1847; nor did he later become a forgotten man, for he was elected to the Institut in 1865. Yet this is how he describes his life at the age of forty-nine:

'I have savoured to the full the praises showed upon me. I have inhaled the fumes of incense, as much as I deserved and more besides. But the smoke vanished and I had to take my plaster casts back to the studio, since I did not have the means to exhibit my work in marble. They gave me first-class medals, the medal of honour, the cross of the Legion of Honour, their homage; but that was all. I had to take everything back to my studio where it lay collecting the dust indefinitely and I found myself out of pocket for the removal expenses.

'Architects needing sculpture to adorn their buildings gave me the occasional statue or bas-relief to do, along with everyone else, along with the small fry and the youngsters. And I was glad of the work as it was the only thing that made it possible for me to live – as thriftily as any poor shoemaker. Even now I just scrape by because I have very simple tastes. Three years ago I replaced Monsieur Nanteuil as a member of the Institut. I have a silk-embroidered gown, olive wreath, cocked hat and even, if you please, a sword to wear on important ceremonial occasions. But I don't go because these solemn affairs cost too much when you have to hire a carriage and anyway I don't care for them.'

And this humble man concludes resignedly: 'You see, having talent does not of itself make one rich.'[16]

At the time when they were the target for public hostility most of the members of the Impressionist school experienced some very difficult moments. Boudin, who was their precursor in the matter of luminous open-air effects, could obtain only seventy-five francs *a dozen* in 1861 for his beach scenes which are so much sought after today. One cannot but wonder how he managed to live, knowing that even twenty years later he was asking Durand-Ruel only 100 francs or 250 francs a picture.[17]

Claude Monet was receiving money from his parents at the start of his career, but they cut off his allowance when they learned that he refused to break with his mistress who was expecting a child. His friend Bazille, who was the son of a wealthy family, then bought one of his pictures for 2,500 francs, but paying for it in instalments; Monet used to wait with ill-concealed impatience for these fifty francs a month from his friend. In 1866 his portrait of Camille was accepted for the Salon and bought by Arsène Houssaye for 800 francs. In 1868 he enjoyed the hospitality of a Le Havre ship-owner who commissioned him to paint a portrait of his wife. But in 1869 Monet knew real poverty: 'Renoir brings us bread from his own home or we should die of hunger. For a week now we have been without bread, without fuel to cook by, and without light. It is dreadful.'[18] His position was hardly better after the end of the war with Germany in 1871, though Durand-Ruel bought two pictures for 300 francs each. In 1875 he was asking Manet for twenty francs and in 1876 he asked the Roumanian Doctor de Bellio for 200 francs. The years which followed were still difficult. He rejoiced when one of his paintings was sold for 2,000 francs at the second Impressionist exhibition in 1876; yet in the autumn of 1877 he was asking Choquet the collector to take two of his paintings at almost any price – forty or fifty francs if he could not afford more – his need of money was so urgent. He knew better times after 1881 when Durand-Ruel, to whom he gave all the canvases he was unable to sell to the occasional rare collector, sent him money regularly.

Ten years later his standard of living was sensibly better. It was in 1890 that he bought his house at Giverny and his prices were slowly rising. In 1883 he was asking 500 or 600 francs each for views of Pourville or Etretat. The following year he fixed the price of the pictures he had painted at Bordighera at between 600 and 1,200 francs. At the Universal Exhibition in 1889 one of his canvases was sold by Theo van Gogh to an American for 9,000 francs. In 1899 the prices of the seven paintings in the *Waterlilies* series ranged between 5,000 and 7,000 francs. Monet had found his reward and spent the last twenty-seven years of his life in relative prosperity.

Monet's career may be regarded as typical of the Impressionists, and those of Renoir and Pissarro followed a similar pattern.[19] But by contrast there were other painters who had always managed to make a good living from their art.

Horace Vernet was without doubt one of those who enjoyed the greatest success. He came from a family of hard-up painters and his precocious talent, so it was said, could have made him self-supporting from the age of thirteen. While still adolescent he painted miniatures, did drawings for the *Journal des Modes* for which he received six francs each, and sold his first paintings for twenty francs. We know exactly what he earned from the account book he kept after his marriage in 1811.[20] In 1812 he was already earning 13,537·50 francs, which included 8,000 francs for a painting commissioned by the King of Westphalia. In 1814, which was a troubled year, he earned only 6,322 francs, but he was never again to be as low as that. His *Death of Poniatoswki* sold for 1,200 francs in 1816, but in 1822 his *Battle of Montmirail* brought him 10,000 francs. He made 64,685 francs in 1827 and 63,826 in 1828.

His earnings fell off slightly in the years which followed, but this was because he had been appointed Director of the Académie de France in Rome, which left him less time for painting. However, he received an official salary of 6,000 francs as Director, and in addition another 6,000 francs for household expenses and the upkeep of his stable; nor should the 100 francs a month he received as a member of the Institut be forgotten. In 1839 he made 78,604 francs and his earnings for the ten-year period 1835 to 1844 reached a total of 652,022·70 francs.

On his return to France, the work he did on the galleries of Versailles accounted for a large part of his income. Vernet, in fact, received 834,000 francs of the money spent by Louis-Philippe on acquisitions and commissions. Such large sums are the reason why his earnings for 1849 soared to 139,146 francs, though it is true that this was the year when he sold a single painting to the Czar of Russia for the colossal figure of 99,000.

Few artists enjoyed such continual prosperity throughout their careers as did Horace Vernet. But there were others who managed to make similar amounts, after passing through leaner times. Bouguereau, who was a brilliant Rome prize-winner, was already selling paintings for 5,000 francs when he returned from the Villa Medici in 1855. Twenty years later he would be demanding 30,000 francs for comparable work. By 1885 his prices were so high and he had so many commissions that he was reported to have said: 'I lose five francs every time I piss. . . .'[21]

Meissonier's case is one of the most remarkable. He began his career very poor, churning out pictures for export with Daubigny at five francs apiece. The first painting of his accepted for the Salon found a purchaser at only 100 francs. But his meticulously accurate reconstructions of eighteenth-century life, and his small, microscopically detailed military scenes, eventually became the rage with collectors. By 1862 he was estimated to be earning 150,000 francs a year and soon the prices paid for his works were to reach fabulous heights. Degas said of his *Cuirassiers of 1805* that everything was iron except the breastplates of the *Cuirassiers*, but the picture was sold in 1878 for 250,000 francs. Eleven years later the Duke of Aumale had no hesitation in purchasing it for 400,000.

There are other less well-known artists whose successes and earnings are still more amazing. Charles Landelle is barely remembered today except by a rather humdrum portrait of Alfred de

Musset. But the United States Ambassador bought his paintings at the Salon of 1842, only the second occasion the painter had submitted work. The state and the city of Paris gave him commissions: for the Audit Office, Hôtel de Ville and various Paris churches. He reached the peak of his success in 1866 with his *Fellah Woman*. Collectors competed for this piece of sham exoticism, the Emperor finally buying it for 5,000 francs; it won for the artist a series of commissions of the same kind. Landelle's record book mentions thirty-two canvases which were either copies, small copies, or variants of *Fellah Woman*, and for which he was paid anything from 800 to 10,000 francs. In 1872, which was his best year, Landelle earned 114,800.[22]

Fantin-Latour commented bitterly after Manet's studio sale in 1884: 'What a ridiculous idea to think that good painting sells as well as bad!' Some of the prices paid for works of art during the nineteenth century seem to confirm this pessimistic observation. In 1846 Ary Scheffer sold two paintings on themes from *Faust* for 45,000 francs. The subject was fashionable, and in the same year Delacroix painted his *Marguerite at Church*, for which he received 1,000 francs. Many good judges of painting were scandalized when *Bernard Palissy*, a picture in the 1861 Salon by a very obscure artist called Vetter, was bought for the state for 25,000 francs. But it was considered quite acceptable when the Emperor paid 40,000 francs for Cabanel's *Venus Anadyomène*. We have already seen what Manet's and Monet's prices were at this time.

A hundred years later, when the table of values has been turned so completely upside down one might consider that good painting had taken a just revenge. But even if the artists who were once scorned had hoped for such posthumous glory it is hard to think that this hope was enough to compensate them for the difficulties of their daily existence.

CHAPTER TEN

ENGRAVING AND OTHER SIDELINES

In 1862 there were between 4,000 and 4,500 known artists in Paris alone. But how many really deserved the name and how many actually made a living out of paintings and statues worthy to be considered works of art?

The greatest masters were obliged to undertake routine pot-boiling work, especially in the early stages of their careers. Not even a Delacroix or a Courbet could paint a *Death of Sardanapalus* or a *Burial at Ornans* every day. As for the unlucky and the failures, unless they were ready to turn their backs on their youthful ambitions, for them the necessity to undertake less glorious tasks was still more pressing.

We can rule out the decorative arts, in those days more generally called the industrial arts. Right up to the end of the century these were the concern of artisans closer to the working class than to the artists. There remains a whole range of activities, none of them to be despised. Those whose skills were greater than their creativity could usefully exercise the former as painters' or sculptors' assistants, or as restorers. Other types of substitute employment were far harder to accept, which is why, in order to achieve the standard of living they wanted, some artists preferred to have a second job and only devote their free hours to the pursuit of their ideal.

One hesitates to include engraving among secondary activities, since engraving is not a minor art. Chassériau's etchings and Toulouse-Lautrec's lithographs rank with the masterpieces of the century. Engravers had shared the Prix de Rome ever since 1804 and engraving had been part of the curriculum of the Ecole des Beaux-Arts from 1863 onwards. However, the finest engraved work of the period was almost always executed privately by painters as a means of expression. The public seldom saw what they produced, or if it did, failed to appreciate its true worth.

What the public knew and liked was the work of professional engravers. There was a whole army of them and they supplied the prints which were sold in single sheets or in albums and illustrated books and magazines. By 1900 the profession was dying. The discovery of photography, and more especially of the process of photogravure around 1870, soon made engraving of very small account as a reproductive technique. Until that time engraving had been essential, both to make works of art known and to illustrate an ever-increasing number of books and magazines, and it provided a very large market for work which varied greatly as regards both intrinsic interest and quality.

But the demand was so great that a good engraver was certain to find work and a secure job – one reason why many talented artists turned to engraving. Lepère, who was the son of a sculptor, took up engraving. Still more typical was the case of Henriquel-Dupont. He was a pupil at Guérin's studio and doing very well, but his father encouraged him to become an engraver to be sure of earning a good living. Disenchantment only set in after the 1870 war when the increasing use of photomechanical processes caused commissions to fall off.

The expansion which had occurred in the production and dissemination of prints since the beginning of the century was the result of two important technological innovations: the discovery of lithography and changes in the technique of wood-engraving – we shall be returning to the latter. Lithography, invented in 1797, was new to the nineteenth century and spread rapidly, as it required no special skill other than being able to hold the chalk. Many painters, among them Delacroix and Renoir, enjoyed drawing on lithographic stone. And the ease and cheapness of the process commended it to publishers. There were highly skilled executants like Daumier, Deveria and Gavarni, but also a host of medicore draughtsmen whose work was sold for a few sous on stalls in open-air markets.

Lithography could be used for everything. At the lowest level for purely commercial purposes: headings for bills and letter paper, prospectuses, small posters. Bouguereau made a little money in his young days by drawing labels for boxes of prunes.

Next came prints for use in schools, for decoration in inns, and for adorning the humble dwellings of the poor. Portraits of politicians, star operatic roles, romantic scenes showing lovers drifting past banks dotted with picturesque ruins, reminiscences of the Napoleonic era or of the heroic 'July days' (the 1830 Revolution), all provided an inexhaustible supply of subjects. Publishers commissioned prints such as these, intended for an undiscriminating public, by the dozen. Jean Gigoux was paid twenty-four francs for his first series of lithographic drawings in 1824. But on a higher plane the best lithographs reached the level of works of art. Achille Deveria, who was both very skilful and a rapid worker, managed to earn 200 or 300 francs a day at his peak, which was a colossal amount.[1]

Lithographs reproducing works of art at the Salon or in museums only gave a very approximate impression of the originals and their quality was questionable. The large and medium-sized sheets and albums issued by specialist publishers for artists and collectors were another matter. These were usually line-engravings, and this technique was colder and lengthier, sometimes tediously so. Aquatint, which was particularly suited to conceal weaknesses in the drawing, was also used for reproducing pictures where *chiaroscuro* predominated. Etchings were not appreciated until after 1850. Although this technique was more rapid and more flexible than line-engraving, it ranked beneath it in the hierarchy which was as unquestioned here as that which prevailed in painting.

Clever publishers saw to it that such reproductions had a wide circulation and reached occasional as well as habitual collectors. Goupil, who had been established on the boulevard Montmartre since 1827, had not only contemporary paintings engraved but old masters as well. In this way both Leonardo da Vinci's *Virgin of the Rocks* and Delaroche's *Virgin with the Infant Jesus* came to adorn elegant apartments or took their place in artists' portfolios to be studied and copied. Spcialist journals like *L'Artiste* from 1831 onwards, the *Gazette des Beaux-Arts* after 1851 and *L'Art* in the years following 1875, had engravings or lithographs made of the most successful paintings appearing at the Salon, and sometimes of refused pictures too. These publications kept many engravers supplied with regular commissions. Both line-engraving and etching, particularly the former, were slow, painstaking work and it took several months or even several years to complete a large plate. To place such commissions publishers needed long-term organization and adequate capital.

Whether he used the burin or the etching-needle, the nineteenth-century engraver proceeded in the same fashion as his forerunners and his studio was not very different from that shown in Abraham

11   Charles X distributing prizes at the end of the 1824 Exhibition

12 A rival's work

13 Artists bringing
their work
to the Palais
de l'Exposition

Bosse's famous print of 1642. The engraver sat facing a window, its light filtered by a blind of translucent paper or by a pane of frosted glass inclined at an angle of 45 degrees, and pushed the sharp graver or burin across the polished copper like a miniature plough or else scratched with the etching needle on the resinous ground which covered the metal, using techniques unchanged for centuries. From time to time he consulted the model reflected in reverse in a mirror. The work was as minute and as detailed as that of a jeweller or goldsmith. The Goncourt brothers, who had themselves practised etching, described the lengthy concentration required:

'It was as if his life was held temporarily in suspense with this calm bemused state which took hold of him, this concentration which made his eyes ache and this emptiness he felt inside his head. . . .'[2]

The etcher knew moments of excitement when he watched the acid bite and observed the mysterious chemistry of the process. The only innovation was that the 'bath' was now made of gutta-percha.

Engravers, when the final stage was reached, almost always pulled at least the trial proofs themselves, using the traditional heavy press. They watched with mingled anxiety and emotion the birth of the child of their long and patient toil.

The work was so engrossing that engravers liked to introduce an element of variety by working on several plates at the same time. This was the procedure favoured by Calamatta, who was official engraver to several of the great painters of the era. He kept several works in hand at the same time and was happy following this method, which avoided the boredom inherent in the engravers' work, or at least compensated for it to some extent by constant change. While he was working on the plate of Francesca da Rimini (after Ingres) he began Delaroche's portrait of Monsieur Guizot and soon afterwards the portrait of Monsieur Mole, also after Ingres.[3]

When Henriquel-Dupont had to reproduce Delaroche's famous decoration for the Hemicycle at the Ecole des Beaux-Arts, he engraved three plates with a total length of 2·60 metres. The work took six years but was considered a masterpiece of engraving for all time. Henriquel-Dupont received a medal of honour at the 1853

Salon, though there were those who thought it a derisory award for an artist who was already a member of the Institut.

Long tasks such as these were well paid. When his *Vow of Louis XIII* was a success at the 1824 Salon, Ingres wanted to have his picture engraved and Calamatta had already made a fine drawing after it. But it was not until 1830 that a friend of the painter was able to make an advance of 25,000 francs to Calamatta. Ingres supervised the work very closely, but it was not finished until 1837! Gavard published the *Galeries historiques de Versailles* at the request of Louis-Philippe to make the pictures the King had collected there known to the world, A sum close to one million francs was shared between the draughtsmen and engravers engaged on this gigantic enterprise.

Etching was a more rapid process than line-engraving. Léopold Flameng, who worked for several art publishers, had some 700 plates to his credit. All the same he was paid 1,200 francs for his etching of *The Source* after Ingres. Jasinksi, who was of Polish origin, began his career at a time when photogravure was beginning to compete seriously with the old engraving techniques. Nevertheless, the *Gazette des Beaux-Arts* paid him 800 francs a plate in 1888, and the publisher Hautecoeur gave him 1,000 francs to reproduce Meissonier's *The Trumpet*. In 1891 the same publisher offered Jasinski the even higher figure of 8,000 francs to go to Milan and do a plate sixty centimetres long after Leonardo da Vinci's *Last Supper*, on the condition that the job was completed in eighteen months. Jasinski had plenty of other commissions and had no hesitation in refusing the offer.[4]

Engraving an old picture did not involve the same problems as reproducing a contemporary work, where problems arose from the often difficult relationship between painter and engraver. When there was much talk about his painting, many approaches would be made to the artist and he could afford to be demanding and claim high fees from the publisher. Ingres sold the reproduction rights of his *Odalisque* for twenty times as much as he had received for selling the painting itself.

The engraver would often ask to retain the picture in order to reproduce it the better and painters suffered from seeing their work put out of circulation in this way. In 1836 Delaroche regretted being unable to show the Austrian Ambassador the pictures he wanted to see because they had been with the engraver for several months.[5] When Delacroix agreed to his *Massacre at Chios* being lithographed he preferred to let the draughtsman use the small copy of this enormous work which his pupil Louis de Planet had done, instead of letting him have the original.[6]

The most serious disagreements arose concerning the interpretation of the work. The resources of black and white are limited, though a skilled engraver is able to manipulate this narrow range to represent the tone values of a picture. Gérard requested a great number of modifications in a line engraving by Toschi after one of his canvases, but always with the utmost courtesy:

'I have made numerous comments, but all on points of detail . . . I have to admit that most of these minor errors are my responsibility and I ask it of your friendship as well as of your talent to put them right. . . .'[7]

It was rare for differences to reach the pitch attained by this letter written to Manet by François Flameng (son of Léopold). Manet had been astonished to see in a catalogue a very poor reproduction of his *Bon Bock*:

Sir,
The engraving after *Le Bon Bock* is very bad because it is a good reproduction of the painting. I have, Sir, the honour to be,
Yours truly[8]

Even though the engraver had as his excuse the general lack of comprehension of Manet's work shown by the public, yet one must agree that it would be difficult to find cases of greater rudeness.

The gifted line-engraver or etcher were both of them people of some importance in the art world, but the place of the wood-engraver was closer to that of artisan. Yet his was a sphere which had grown enormously ever since the innovation of blocks cut 'across the grain' had made it possible for this technique to be used for purposes of illustration right up till its eventual replacement by photography. Wood-engraving between 1820 and the end of the century was mainly a commercial technique which made possible the emergence of numerous illustrated magazines: *Le Monde illustré*, *L'Illustration*, *Magasin pittoresque*, and many others.

The consequence was the creation of joint studios like that headed by Smeeton round 1860 in the *Magasin pittoresque* building near the rue de Sèvres. The engravings published in the illustrated magazines were sometimes 45 × 30 cm. in size. But these weekly publications claimed to keep up with the news, i.e. to contain illustrations of events which had taken place no more than one or two weeks before. The drawings, therefore, which might either have been done on the spot or else executed from eye-witness accounts (or later still based on photographs), had to be engraved within the space of a few days. The work was shared out among a team of engravers, divided into four, eight or even twelve sections, and the engraved blocks joined together before printing. Each engraver would handle the same material on each piece: one would do the backgrounds, another the trees, a third the architecture, while the most skilled was responsible for the figures. The head of the studio distributed the work and supervised it, giving it the final touch if need be by himself engraving some important motif.

Auguste Lepère, whose name stands out from among a crowd of virtually anonymous hacks, entered just such a studio in 1862 at the age of thirteen. The deed of apprenticeship he signed shows the strict conditions imposed on the young wood-engraver: five years' apprenticeship without receiving any wages; ten hours' work a day; the only rest days Sundays and occasional public holidays; time lost through illness or absence or for any other reason to be added to the five-year term. It is true that this contract is no harsher than those imposed on other young workers and the work more interesting. Nevertheless, it meant spending ten whole hours bending over the block of boxwood to cut the wood to the depth required with graver or gouge.[9] A young adolescent subjected to this sytem could hardly do otherwise than envy his comrades preparing for entry to the Ecole des Beaux-Arts in comparative freedom to dispose of their time and their talent as they would. But success for them was uncertain whereas the engraver was sure of a living, and had he become an artist he might perhaps have failed to shine.

This is what a character from one of Champfleury's novels has to say on the subject:

'Know then that all these snivelling people, who make such great claims for their art and say they are victims of society while earning a good living at engraving or lithography, are swollen with pride. They give all that they are capable of giving. Born to be workmen, they launched themselves into the world of art, impelled by a mania all too common today. They have remained workmen, that is to say they are mediocre interpreters of the creators. They are not even worthy of this role and yet they complain.'[10]

These words are harsh but just, where certain engravers were concerned. But Lepère was truly worthy to reproduce the works of the masters and even to compete with them, and he never failed to devote part of his meagre leisure time to drawing and painting. In 1878, after sixteen years in his profession, he became draughtsman and engraver for *Le Monde Illustre*. His work for the week over by Thursday evening, he was free to spend the last three days of the week working to please himself and developing his own talent.

Few artists enjoyed greater freedom than the draughtsman. All he required was a sheet of paper or a sketch book, pencil and charcoal, or perhaps pen and brush and a bottle of Indian ink. Nor did the draughtsman need daylight; he could work at a table by the light of a lamp; better still he could make his sketches anywhere, standing or seated, at the theatre or on the omnibus. And all that remained to be done was to complete them afterwards.

Illustration, including caricature, provided a market. Draughtsmen who made drawings for illustrated magazines were sometimes no more than skilled craftsmen without great talent. It became more and more customary for them to be asked to draw directly with pen or brush on to the block engravers were to cut. Though their work was closely connected with that of engravers, it was more independent and less mechanical.

Publishers who were anxious to produce books of high quality were more demanding of the talent of their draughtsmen where book illustration was concerned. As a result good artists like Gigoux, Raffet or Gavarni often found additional work in book illustration. Horace Vernet, in spite of large commissions for history paintings, was ready to spend his evenings illustrating vignettes for a history of Napoleon.

Sometimes a publisher was prepared to place confidence in young artists. In 1838 Trimolet shared a set of illustrations for the publisher Curmer with his friends Steinheil and Daubigny. Curmer gave them twenty francs per vignette, which was considered good pay. Gustave Doré was undoubtedly the most gifted and prolific of draughtsmen.

It was in this field that he excelled, in spite of his pretensions as a painter or even as a sculptor (like so many minor artists, he retained a certain nostalgia for 'great art'), and he far surpassed many other competent illustrators. Doré was gifted even as a child and managed to sign a contract with the astute Philipon of *Le Charivari* when only sixteen years old and still attending classes at the Lycée Charlemagne. This contract guaranteed him the publication of one drawing a week for three years; he was to be paid between fifteen and forty francs per drawing during the first year and up to sixty francs during the third year. But the contract states that this was only a minimum, 'if he should not have time to do more, whether on account of homework while still studying, or on account of holidays which he shall be free to enjoy, or on account of illness. . . .'[11] A vast distance separates this agreement with a young 'artist' from the terms imposed fourteen years later on the apprentice Lepère, a mere engraver on wood.

To his skill and imagination Doré owed a career as brilliant and as lucrative as that of certain painters of the era. Publishers offered him all the great works of world literature in turn and he illustrated the Bible, Cervantes and Rabelais with the same verve. It is claimed he worked so quickly that he could complete twenty drawings in one morning. And since he was sometimes paid 500 francs for a drawing it is hardly a matter for surprise that he should have earned some seven million francs in the twenty years between 1850 and 1870 – which made him one of the wealthiest artists of the century.

It was less common for caricaturists to work on commission. Or at least it was rare for them not to choose their own subjects. But the inspiration which enabled them to seize upon the humourous side of a situation could not be summoned up at will. The caricaturist was fortunate who was retained by a newspaper and sure of placing one or more drawings a week. He was fortunate, that is to say, so long as fatigue and weariness did not paralyse his inspiration, so long as the editor, or the readers, were in agreement with his interpretation of events, and so long as the censor did not threaten to reward his daring with fines or imprisonment, as happened under Louis-Philippe and also under the Second Empire. Daumier was imprisoned in 1832 for his caricatures against the King and in 1860 was sacked from *Le Charivari* after twenty years of collaboration on the pretext that readers were cancelling their subscriptions because of his caricatures of the social scene. And poor Daumier, for all his great talent, was condemned to silence while awaiting better days.

Under the Third Republic and with the passing of the law on the press in 1881 opportunities for draughtsmen and cartoonists, particularly the latter, increased. Unlike the engravers they were not much bothered by the introduction of photogravure and even found it to their advantage since mechanical processes rendered their drawings more faithfully than engraving. And when one considers that there were no fewer than two hundred newspapers and magazines in France in 1890 which published caricatures one begins to form an idea of the enormous market they provided for a host of artists of varying degrees of skill.

And yet demand was so great as to foster an atmosphere of production at any price in some journals which was prejudicial to quality.

But these conditions also favoured an outburst of talent which would otherwise have gone elsewhere. With men like Forain, Willette, Robida and Steinlen, the front rank of draughtsmen was particularly brilliant.

Widhoff has left us a satirical account in *Le Courrier français* of 'a day in the life of a draughtsman today' (about 1900). This 'industrialist of the press' accepts commissions over the telephone and directs a team who use tracings, casts and photographs: 'Eight drawings in one hour, you say, that's more than enough. . . .' (adding for the benefit of his collaborators): 'Nothing to do with art, just a matter of meeting public taste.'[12]

Differences in the quality of both the drawings and the journals they appeared in, and also in the fame of the draughtsman, account for the variations in the payment made. When Fabiano began work for *Frou-frou* at the end of the century he was given five francs a drawing and the editor kept back twenty-five centimes of that to pay for the receipt. Willette in 1880 was earning twenty times as much but he had agreed to work for a pornographic magazine, hiding behind a pseudonym, in order to make a living. When Henriot replaced Cham on *Le Charivari* in 1879 he was paid a fixed salary of 300 francs a month. And Edmond de Goncourt was somewhat shocked to learn in 1893 that Forain sometimes received this same amount for a single drawing from the editor of the *Journal*.[13]

There were a number of occupations open to those who preferred to use the brush rather than the pencil or the graver, but who had been unable to win recognition for their original talent. Making copies was one of the best paid, since in those days a good copy was considered almost as good as the original. Students at the Académie de France in Rome were not only given Italian masters to reproduce for the sake of the training this provided, but also because the best of these copies would be sent to Ecole des Beaux-Arts or to the provincial museums. Wealthy art-lovers commissioned copies to adorn their châteaux or their apartments. Thiers would commission copies for his own collection, quite independently of the official programme, and he lived surrounded by reproductions of great Italian paintings, the work of the little-known Bellay.[14]

Schnetz agreed to do a number of copies for the government while he was director in Rome. Ingres had more pride. At the age of sixty-eight, when he was at the height of his glory, Ingres still considered that he needed to make copies after the masters 'in order to learn', but he haughtily refused Thiers' commission of a drawing after Raphael's *Transfiguration*:

'He asked me for a drawing after someone else! He asked me, head of the Ecole, to go to the Vatican with my sketch book tucked under my arm! I told him "Monsieur le Ministre, when I do drawings now I sign them *Ingres*".'[15]

The importance of the copyists can be seen in the facilities the administration accorded them. Certain paintings in the Louvre were transferred to the studios of well-known painters so that they could be copied. As late as 1872 Pils asked Val-de-Grâce for the loan of a canvas by Gros which he needed to copy. Since he added that he would take advantage of the opportunity to restore it, we do not feel greatly reassured on looking back.

Most copies were commissioned by the Fine Arts service on behalf of provincial museums and churches. An example is the copy of an *Assumption of the Virgin* in the Louvre which young Gleyre agreed to do in 1842. It was destined for a church in Doubs and he was paid 1,000 francs for it. Often Deputies asked for such grants to be made – they were a way of helping artists in need or quite simply artists who enjoyed special favour. The fact that many of those who benefited from such commissions were women only adds to the suspicion of favouritism which attaches to them.

Foreigners liked to take home copies of paintings in French museums. From the age of seventeen Fantin-Latour made a living for a number of years from the copies he did for Americans.[16] Not to mention the seldom-acknowledged but all-too-common trade in copies which were carefully aged and given a false patina and then passed as variants of famous works. The regulations forbade copying paintings in the same dimensions as the original, but more than one 'replica by the master' circulated which was nothing more than a copy of this sort.

Most copyists went where the pictures were, above all to the Louvre. The student of art did not exist who had not at some time set up his easel in one of the galleries of the museum. Renoir and Cézanne studied there just as Delacroix and Géricault had. Some copyists were amateur painters who devoted their leisure time, or their retirement, to this innocent occupation. The young girls among them may have had an ulterior motive and have come more in the hope of finding a husband than with the intention of studying great art. But most were professionals who derived all or part of their income from this source.

The galleries of the Louvre had been thronged with copyists ever since they were opened to the public. They are already to be seen in Hubert Robert's view of the Grande Galerie painted in 1796. By mid-century they were so numerous as to constitute an annoyance to visitors, particularly in those parts of the Grande Galerie and the Salon Carré where masterpieces were more than usually thick on the walls. Contemporary prints which record the scene show a veritable forest of easels and movable step-ladders, canvases of all sizes, some very large indeed, and a whole crowd of painters in various attitudes, sitting, standing or perched up on high. Their numbers included long-haired youths as well as dignified old men wearing top hats. A surprisingly high percentage of these curious creatures, who seem to have taken up permanent residence in the galleries were women dressed in the most varied costumes; when they worked up step-ladders they never forget to wrap a piece of serge around their legs to discourage prying glances. And then there were the miniaturists huddled modestly over small tables, working at their painting on china. The Goncourt brothers describe them as 'staring fixedly and grimacing with the effort of copying Titian's *Entombment* in microscopic detail'.[17]

As for the restorers, their work in some respects approached that of the copyists, though being purely technical it was even less rewarding. The nature of the work varied too according to the differing concepts of restoration formed at different times, each generation justifying its own procedures in opposition to those of the preceding generation. Unfortunately, caution did not always prevail in the workshops of the Louvre; it was, for example, very far from being the distinguishing characteristic of Granet who was keeper of paintings between 1826 and 1848, and very high-handed where the care and treatment of masterpieces was concerned. When Daubigny returned from Rome he was obliged to enter the restorers' workshop in the Louvre and was appalled at the rashness of the team working under Granet's orders:

'All his comrades outshone him when it came to repaintings which he was naive enough to try and harmonize with the background. He was unable to touch any of these great masterpieces without feelings of embarrassment. He was abashed by their magnificence and far from possessing the triumphant self-assurance of his colleagues.'[18]

Things were no better under the administration of Villot, who was a friend of Delacroix. Viel-Castel has described Villot's favourite restorer, Godefroy, on the subject of the portrait of Francisco de Moncada by Van Dyck. One can only hope that Viel-Castel was exaggerating. Here are Godefroy's own words as quoted by him:

'You would have difficulty in recognizing that portrait. It's changed a lot since I removed the varnish. . . . The painters who had begun copies have had to start all over again. (Here Godefroy gives way to suppressed merriment.) Moncada's head used to stand out strongly against a light cloud, now it's light against a dark cloud! . . . There was a tree-trunk in the foreground, now there's only a stone! . . . The hindquarters of the horse have disappeared, the contour has vanished. But Monsieur Villot is going to bring me an old engraving after this work and I shall repaint the hindquarters. (Here Godefroy swells with pride.)'[19]

One can hardly speak of unrewarding work in such a case. Restoration along these lines offered ample scope to the imagination.

The restoration of ancient monuments generated a large programme of work and here too the imagination of the restorers was sometimes allowed too free a rein. But there was much to be done in bringing a little glamour and quite often the mere chance of

170

survival to many monuments of the Middle Ages which had long suffered neglect or damage from vandals. Under the direction of men like Viollet-le-Duc, Lassus and Ruprich-Robert, teams of collaborators devoted their skill and labour to sites all over France. Sculptors like Toussaint, Michel Pascal and Geoffroy-Deschaumes found worthwhile outlets for their work in addition to the all-too-infrequent commissions they received from the government or from private individuals.

The work of the sculptors' assistants, the *praticiens*, was still more humble, since their names never appeared alongside that of the master who was considered the sole creator. To rough-hew the marble or touch up the bronze and sometimes execute a statue from a maquette, such tasks would never make a man rich, but at least they enabled him to make a living. But he would have had to have lost any desire to be considered as a creative artist and rest content with the secret joys of the executant.

Some sculptors undertook such work temporarily while awaiting a chance to try their own wings. Rodin and Dalou assisted Carrier-Belleuse, who was overwhelmed with commissions, and made for him a great many *objets d'art* to which the master had only to add his signature.

No more did painters' assistants expect to win fame from their work. There were in fact different ways of collaborating on a painting. The young pupil had no call to jib at painting in the background of his master's canvas or adding minor details. This was how he learned his trade and it was an honour for him to be asked to collaborate discreetly in this way. When Ingres was a pupil in David's studio he painted the bronze candelabra in the latter's portrait of *Madame Recamier*, but it is unlikely that the fact would be known if David himself, his pupil and the portrait had not all become equally famous. Ingres, in his turn, had no hesitation in entrusting part of the background of his *Stratonice* to a pupil, Victor Baltard. Baltard, too, made a name for himself, but in architecture.

Collaboration of another sort occurred when artists working on big commissions, particularly decorative painting, sought assistants; they required skilled men already trained, but who were not concerned about their artistic independence, and they paid well. In 1843 Delacroix employed Louis de Planet at 150 francs a month to paint the background for his *Death of Marcus Aurelius*, which was exhibited at the Salon the following year. In 1838 he had engaged

171

another assistant, Lassalle-Bordes, who was to work for him for thirteen years. Lassalle-Bordes sketched in the cornerpieces in the Chamber of Deputies, and his contribution to Delacroix's great decorative works was a large one. During his best period he was being paid 500 francs a month. But later he claimed paternity of whole fragments of the master's decorative paintings – with some exaggeration, it would seem. The two men quarrelled in 1851, but Lassalle-Bordes never showed convincing proof of his genius, once free from Delacroix's tutelage.[20]

It was all a matter of degree and everything depended on the relationship between the artist and his assistants. Nevertheless, it does seem that in some cases flagrant injustice was meted out to artists' collaborators. For example, although we do not know very much about who Gérard's assistants were, we do know that when his European fame brought him more commissions for portraits than he could paint himself he had a whole team working for him on pictures to which he only added his signature.[21] Pils did the same with his historical compositions, which are well and truly forgotten today. Some of them were painted by the little-known Charles Lhuillier. Yet this unknown journeyman painter became a teacher in Le Havre after 1871 and the pupils he trained include Dufy, Othon Friez and Braque.

Most of these tasks, inglorious though they were, required some creative talent or at least great technical skill. There were other ways of earning one's bread which did not even leave their practitioners with the consolation of still being artists in spite of everything.

Some were obliged to accept what was purely the work of artisans at the beginning of their careers. For example, painting china when the same motif was repeated over and over again on identical objects was practised by men as different from each other as Diaz, Raffet, Rodin and Renoir. Or painting blinds, practised by both Renoir and Guillaumin.

Sculptors awaiting commissions for great works sometimes had to resign themselves to lesser things. Neither Pradier or Carpeaux thought it beneath them to make ornamental statuettes, not to mention the decorative pieces of furniture, copies of antique vases and chimney pieces which also fell to the lot of Carpeaux. Rodin in his youth even sculpted mascarons (the grotesque masks on the keystones of arches) on the façades of houses. Barye began with an engraver of medals who had him design uniform badges and buttons; he also made relief-maps. He did not, however, sink as low as Chapu, who modelled in lard for a pork butcher when he found himself in want soon after his return from Rome; nor as low as Frémiet who, like the Goncourt's Anatole in *Manette Salomon*, worked for some time at the morgue for an embalmer.

Those concerned with the decoration of churches – and at that time they were very much over-decorated – were ready to order saints male and female by the gross. They were also glad to take series of carved or painted stations of the cross like those Gérôme executed with the aid of a team of comrades. To make the work easier, each only put on one colour, i.e. one did the red, one the blue, etc.[22]

Other similar markets might be offered by unscrupulous business men only too happy to satisfy an undemanding public at a low price. Certain subjects were always profitable, either because of their pretentiousness or because of their sentimental or salacious undertones. And so there proliferated scenes from childhood, cats, shepherds and shepherdesses, Spaniards, Swiss landscapes painted without stirring from the room, and women at their toilet, like those painted by Millet – he once sold six for seventy-five francs – until the day when he felt ashamed of them and gave it up.

Nothing more need be said of the painters of 'production-line' portraits than that one of them is said to have put on his sign: 'Perfect likeness twenty francs; nearly like fifteen francs; family resemblance ten francs; people who have been decorated two francs extra.'[23]

Other artists copied the faces of the departed from photographs; young Henner began in this way. A friend of the poet Banville was part of an enterprise which photographed 'story pictures' and made very faint prints; then one artist would colour the clothes, a miniaturist would paint the heads, and Banville's friend would fill in the backgrounds to meet customers' requirements. When Pradier's brother was *massier* in Ingres' studio he made a little extra money from innumerable copies of Napoleon on horseback, traced from a coloured engraving after Carle Vernet.[24] It was better to paint coats-of-arms on coaches as Gérôme did, or shop signs like Charlet, Gérôme and many another who might have exclaimed together with the young man Daumier shows us in *La Caricature* in 1843: 'To think I spent fifteen years of my life copying the leg of the Apollo in the Vatican in order to paint a lump of sugar on a grocer's sign.'[25]

Memories of times like these might evoke nostalgia in those who had put such things behind them, but unfortunately melancholy tasks of this nature remained the daily lot of men who barely qualify for the title of artist. One can understand why, rather than sink so low, some of them preferred to have a second paying job and devote their leisure to art. But even so, there was often a price to be paid. Bonvin, who was first a compositor and later worked for the police, had to draw by lamplight when he left the office and could only paint in daylight in the summer for a few hours in the early morning. He was thirty-three years old when he finally decided to give up his job. Guillaumin was employed for a long time in the Compagnie d'Orléans; Gauguin was thirty-five when in spite of his family he decided to risk everything for art and left his work at the bank.

But the men who eventually came to realize the dreams of their youth are perhaps less to be pitied than those who were forced back into paid employment by the material difficulties of their lives or by a success which in the event proved transitory.

After 1850 draughtsmen like Nadar and Carjat found a less uncertain way of life in photography and one still related to art in some respects.

Teaching others to draw seemed a lesser evil, since even the greatest masters had been glad to transmit their knowledge to their disciples. But teaching at the Ecole des Beaux-Arts was one thing, imparting the rudiments of drawing to young ladies of good family, or to youngsters taking their first lessons, was quite another. Yet many painters and sculptors had to resign themselves to teaching.

Posts as museum curators were better. But even though the museums themselves were not particularly active in those days, the post as curator often involved giving up the practice of art almost entirely. This was what happened to Achille Deveria, who was appointed assistant keeper in 1848 and later on keeper of the Print Room at the Bibliothèque Nationale. It was also the case with Granet, who owed his appointment as curator of paintings at the Louvre to the friendship of Count Forbin, who was Director of Museum Services at the time. But Deveria and Granet, who held important positions in the capital, were still in touch with artistic circles there. Appointment to a provincial museum, to Rouen like Bellangé and Garneray, or Dijon like Célestin Nanteuil, often meant complete withdrawal from active participation in the art movement. Such posts brought social prestige to those who held them, though not artistic fame; but there were of course non-conformists who preferred obscurity to the renunciation of an ideal which they had yet proved themselves incapable of upholding.

CHAPTER ELEVEN

THE ARTIST AND SOCIETY

Because the artist despised the bourgeoisie and the bourgeoisie were suspicious of the artist, it is hardly surprising that the two parties found difficulty in living on good terms together in a society like that of nineteenth-century France, which was predominantly bourgeois in its values. The majority of artists did not integrate easily into this world; they feared its censure and the constraints it imposed. When they laid aside their self-isolating creative activities they readily sought the company of their own kind, attended gatherings or formed associations where they could be together with other artists, or visited salons or cafés where they were sure of finding their fellows.

Times changed, however. The different classes of society drew closer together and the bourgeoisie consented to admit men of outstanding talent to its ranks. Although some artists continued to live on the margins of society, almost like pariahs, there were others who adjusted better to bourgeois precepts and came to accept the values of this class, finishing their careers wealthy and decorated and occupying honourable positions in the best society.

Bohemia has always been with us, but never before had it acquired the aura of glamour it took on during the Romantic era. Henri Murger's *Scènes de la vie de bohème* recalls the blend of poverty and idealism in which the lives of a group of young poets and artists in the 1830s were plunged. The painter Schanne, the landscapist Chintreuil, the engraver Fauchery, who used to install himself in a café with all his equipment, and Nadar, who was a draughtsman for several small journals before becoming a photographer, all of them experienced long days without food or fuel, sordid attics, casual love affairs – and some of them the hospital bed – which were the lot of Murger's heroes.

Murger's picture of Bohemia had its sentimental side and served to establish a myth. 'Bohemia', he claims, 'is the nursery of the arts',[1] a remark calculated to soothe the conscience of a society already over-inclined to accept that hardship was the proper fare of genius and hunger his best sauce. Even those who had themselves been through it sometimes retained nostalgic memories of a difficult stage in their lives when they had proved their defiance of conformism. Throughout the century Bohemian existence was the lot of the more independent artists and sometimes even their ideal.

Although they lived on the fringe of society, the artists had no desire to pass unnoticed and they were usually distinguished by a special costume. Ever since the beginning of the Romantic movement the painters had been the first to adopt the fashions launched by its young followers. A pointed felt hat with a very wide brim, a narrow-waisted tailcoat with long lapels and an enormous bow-tie, these were the main features of the costume adopted by those who were known as Jeunes-France in 1830. Add long hair and flowing beard and moustache and you have the broad outlines of the recognized stereotype of the artist which lasted long after 1900.

About mid-century some of them, the most refined, made additions to the uniform: fancy waistcoats like doublets – the reader will remember the famous red waistcoat worn by Théophile Gautier, who was himself a painter before he became a poet – boots or shoes with long pointed toes, and great cloaks, like the one Deveria wrapped about himself. It was a little later than this that Pradier took a fancy to black velvet jackets and the fashion was copied by his friends.[2]

It is difficult for us to imagine the extent to which the bourgeois public was shocked by such extravagances. At one time the mere fact of wearing a beard or moustache was a black mark against an artist who was a candidate for membership of the Académie. It was one of the reasons why the great sculptor Rude was kept out: 'We cannot, said members of the Institut, admit a man with a beard to our number.'[3] By the Second Empire changes in fashion had transformed the situation and the great beards of Cabanel and Meissonier were completely compatible with their official position. Cabanel taught at the Ecole des Beaux-Arts in a velvet jacket and a cravat which streamed in the wind, and Meissonier was often to be seen in a red knitted waistcoat and high boots.

Then it was the turn of the less conservative artists to shun the style of dress of the art student. Manet was always immaculate, wore a top-hat and endeavoured to appear correctly, even elegantly, dressed. Both Seurat and Signac made a point of always appearing in black or dark blue suits. Cézanne, on the other hand, in spite of his middle-class origins or perhaps on account of the lack of understanding he found there, used to try to shock. In 1878 the critic Duranty described Cézanne's recent appearance in a little café on the place Pigalle in a letter to Zola: 'blue overalls, a coat of coarse white linen covered with brush marks and torn, a battered old hat. He was a success! But such demonstrations are dangerous.'[4]

Unable to integrate into a society they despised, artists preferred to keep to themselves. Numerous accounts throughout the century testify to the existence of gatherings of artists which typified a distinctive way of life. It was pleasant to get together in the studio of another artist of an evening – or during the late afternoon in winter when the nights closed in early – to smoke a pipe and swap aesthetic theories or hopes of success, and perhaps play cards or make music.

There were also larger weekly reunions, often attended by prose writers, poets and dramatists, and enhanced by the presence of actors and actresses who contributed by their talent or their beauty. The lively gatherings, which were the result of contacts in an atmosphere of freedom between creators and interpreters who shared a common love of art, scandalized some and were the envy of others, while for the bourgeois they represented an essential part of his conception of an artist's life.

However, under the restored monarchy most artists' reunions had none of the unbridled character those of the younger generation were to have – Baron Gérard's receptions in the rue Bonaparte, for example, were comparatively austere, though one might profit from the conversation of great minds like Mérimée, Cuvier and Stendhal – and they had something of a homely family atmosphere. We have already described the good-humoured conviviality of the evenings enjoyed by the artists with studios in the Sorbonne prior to 1821. The atmosphere at Duval-le-Camus' in rue Vivienne was similar except that the host played the role of master of ceremonies and organized little games or introduced an entertainer.

At Cicéri's the company was more sophisticated and the entertainments more varied; they danced, played cards and presented short plays. And it was here, according to Jal, that a game very common in artistic circles was born:

'It was there that the game of improvising pictures, if I may call it that, began; the artist had to produce a complete picture out of the inspiration of the moment while a candle-end burned itself out. In this way the album of caricatures was enriched by fine cartoons conceived and executed by Isabey senior, Horace and Carle Vernet and Cicéri.'[5]

The famous soirées held in Nodier's salon at the Arsenal until his death in 1844 were elegant affairs. Readings and recitals of poetry alternated with the dancing, and the artists who attended included Delacroix, David d'Angers, Deveria, Boulanger, Gigoux and other lesser names.

Parties at the Deverias' were family evenings at the home of a mother and five children, two of whom were to achieve fame, at least for a while: Eugène and Achille. These gatherings are frequently described, no doubt because the 'star' was the young Victor Hugo.

The critic Ernest Chesneau has left us this description of that amazing household:

'Everywhere, high and low, in the bedrooms and on the stairs, in the studio and in the salon, people drawing. Achille Deveria, the eldest by five years, directed the work while at the same time executing countless elegant lithographs which were the sole support of this 'phalanstère' of drawing. They copied impressions of antique medals a foot larger than the original. They read Dante, Shakespeare, Goethe, Byron and the old French chronicles. Then straightaway gave graphic expression to the deep influence of their reading upon them when the genius of our nation and that of the great foreign poets had revealed itself for the first time to youthful and brilliant imaginations.'[6]

One can imagine the reception accorded in such circles to a rising young poet who embodied all the hopes of romantic lyricism.

Hugo himself lived a few steps away in the same road and the young painters in their turn used to spend their evenings at his house. The great master of romantic literature attracted many artists: Delacroix, David d'Angers and Boulanger among them, as well as the young poets whose boldness was shocking contemporary opinion. The very names of the painters and sculptors who grouped themselves around Hugo when he moved a short while afterwards to 6 Place Royal – Camille Rogier, Auguste de Châtillion, Gigoux and Jehan de Seigneur – evoke subjects inspired by the new literature.

Some at least of the same group of artists used to meet together in a more free-and-easy fashion at the Impasse du Doyenné in the now-vanished district which used to surround the Place du Carrousel. Nerval, Houssaye and Théophile Gautier shared the same lodgings and Théodore Rousseau, Nanteuil, Gavarni and their friends used to come and join them. Their outrageous dress and behaviour and the noise they made disturbed this quiet district, and the girls they brought to the house were a cause of scandal.

The soirées organized by the Johannot brothers at the rue de Rocher shared the same reputation. A lithograph called *Champagne*, drawn by Gavarni, gives the best idea of what they were like: it shows Alfred Johannot sprawled on a large divan, where another young man and three young women are also reclining nonchalantly; Gavarni himself is making a speech and holds a glass of champagne in his hand; Tony Johannot is standing next to Alexandre Dumas and is holding a glass to the lips of a young woman who has fallen against him. The print is well calculated to confirm the legend of those famous orgies in artists' studios which were denounced by people 'in the know'.

Similar things were said of the Saturday gatherings at Gavarni's in the rue Fontaine-Saint-Georges and then after his marriage in 1845 at his house in Auteil. The Goncourt brothers, who were regular guests, have put the record straight:

'There have been so many legends concerning these supposedly wild parties which were really dreary little evenings when the only drink offered was rum punch, and the usual entertainment innocent party games; and afterwards Balzac used to say with blatantly ingenious cunning and the guileless artlessness of a man of genius: "Now supposing we don't play anymore, suppose we just enjoy ourselves?" '[7]

The gatherings at the Hôtel Pimodan in the Ile-Saint-Louis between 1843 and 1848 were no doubt more like orgies. The 'hashish club' met at the painter Boissard's in search of 'artificial paradises'. Delacroix attended these soirées, Daumier too, and of course Baudelaire; the music was good and Boissard de Boisdenier played the violin even better when under the influence of the drug.

The café offered the solitary artist an even more convenient refuge than gatherings in other artists' studios. There, where he was sure of finding comrades, he could spend long evenings exchanging bantering or cynical opinions about life, women or politics. Though not all their names have come down to us, some of these cafés became famous because of the artists who met there.

The Café Momus at 15 des Prêtres-Saint-Germain-l'Auxerrois, thanks to an indulgent proprietor who had himself been a poet in his youth, was the scene of various episodes described in the *Scènes de la vie de bohème*. The Divan-Le-Pelletier, No 5 in the street of the same name, rang to the voices of Gautier, Musset and Gustave Planche between 1837 and 1859; there they held discussions and exchanged theories with Clésinger and Landelle and later with Gustave Courbet. The latter was a great café-goer and his exuberant personality was the centre of attraction at a *brasserie* in the rue Hautefeuille. The Andler-Keller, as it was sometimes called, had been founded by a Bavarian and on more than one occasion its whitewashed walls resounded to the singing of the apostle of realistic painting. He was surrounded by regulars like Champfleury and Baudelaire, Gigoux and Bonvin, and by occasional visitors like Corot, Daumier, Decamps, Préault and Chenavard.[8]

Courbet was also to be found at the Brasserie des Martyrs, situated on the slopes of Montmartre behind Notre-Dame-de-Lorette, which was the scene of one of the most brilliant meetings of minds in Paris around 1855. Musicians, poets and artists all flocked there; no one was excluded and all theories were allowed to co-exist. Monet used to come, and the Stevens brothers, and a whole band of sculptors which included Christophe, Chatrousse and Aimé Millet.

The regular clientele at the Café Guerbois was less all-embracing, but it can be said that within its walls the theories of realism and impressionism took shape. In the years preceding the 1870 war the Café Guerbois at 11 Grande rue des Batignolles, only two steps away from Père Lathuile's open-air restaurant made famous by Manet's painting, was the rendezvous for all those scornfully dubbed by the critics 'the Batignolles School'. The group which formed around Manet consisted of Bazille, Guillemet, Renoir and Degas, and occasionally Sisley, Pissarro or Cézanne would be present, not to mention other artists who remained on the fringe of the group, like Constantin Guys and that great cabaret-goer Marcellin

Desboutin. It even included painters whose sole aim was worldly success, like Carolus-Duran. Georges Rivière used to claim that he had almost converted him to Manet's style of painting.[9]

The number of artists' cafés rose sharply after the Franco-Prussian War. The most popular ones were in lower Montmartre, a district where many artists had their studios. Most of the habitués of the Café Guerbois found a refuge in the Nouvelle Athènes on the Place Pigalle: Manet, Renoir and Degas were there, Cézanne sometimes, and younger artists like Forain, La Gandara, Henner and Victorine Meurent, who had posed for Manet's *Olympia* and then taken up painting herself. Not far away the Café la Rochefoucauld, on the corner of the rue Notre-Dame-de-Lorette, was popular with Cormon, Gervex and Rochegrosse, but was not shunned by less academic painters either, since Degas, Renoir and Forain were often to be seen there. Two other popular meeting-places for artists living in Montmartre were the Abbaye-de-Thélème, which was established in 1885 in the painter Roybet's former town residence, and the Café Pigalle on the Place Pigalle, which was also known as the Rat-Mort.

There seem to have been fewer artists' cafés on the left bank on the whole, though the poets crowded the establishments on the boulevard Saint Michel and around the Luxembourg from the Vachette to the Closerie-des-Lilas. The Café Voltaire at least, beloved of the Symbolist writers, was also visited by Carrière, Rodin and the young Nabis. Finally there were a number of cafés which had the reputation of welcoming *rapins*. For example, the Café Lafitte was almost exclusively patronized by students from the Ecole des Beaux-Arts. The proprietor, who had himself been a student in Picot's studio, wore check trousers and a velvet jacket and liked to talk shop with the customers.[10]

There was plenty of ill-natured gossip and scandal-mongering at the expense of those who were absent at these café gatherings. But in spite of their competitiveness, artists were not unaware of the advantages of mutual assistance. For those who had belonged to the Académie de France at Rome, their training and their shared memories tended to draw them together, the implicit aim being unconditional support of their clan. As often occurs in the case of men from the same educational establishment, they were accused of constituting a sort of freemasonry to promote their own success and election to the Institut. In 1817 a group of 'Romans', including the sculptors Cortot and Seurre and the painter Navez founded the 'Brotherhood of the Onion', during a simple dinner on the Via Appia. As late as 1850 some people claimed that a man like Alaux owed his membership of the Institut to this group.

Ten years later their successors took the name of *Cald'arosti* from the cry of the sellers of hot chestnuts, adding as their motto *semper ardentes* (always burning). This confraternity included men like Chapu, Robert-Fleury and Falguière, and was headed by Bonnat; it was still very much alive at the end of the century in defence of positions which were coming more and more under attack.[11]

But mutual aid might be disinterested, or more broadly conceived. It was difficult to organize for joint action both out-and-out individualists and artists who had already attained the peak of official success. But any artist might experience passing difficulties and solidarity between artists could help to solve these and to overcome the uncertainties of old age.

Friendly assistance from artist to artist was less rare than might have been thought from the bitterness of the competition for commissions and honours. There must have been many examples which have never come to light. But Jules Dupré, who was indignant at the obscurity his friend Théodore Rousseau languished in, forced him to leave the attic where he was living and let him a studio in avenue Frochot, is frequently cited. Likewise Diaz, who allowed young Renoir to use his account at his colour-dealer's; and Corot, who provided Daumier with a refuge in his old age in a house at Valmondois.

Five young artists, Meissonier, Trimolet, Steinheil, Daubigny and Geoffroy-Dechaumes, came to an arrangement in 1838: each of them was to enjoy a year of freedom while the other four worked and supported the community. Only two of them in fact profited from the arrangement, but none of them ever regretted it.

It was old age which gave rise to the greatest problems. Some artists only won fame late in life and enjoyed success in their old age, but others felt their strength failing them; or, as happened still more frequently, changes in fashion thrust men who had known moments of glory into oblivion. The most tragic of these was Gros, who felt public opinion deserting him after having enjoyed every honour and who finally committed suicide at Bas Meudon in 1833.

Little could be done to combat this kind of unhappiness, but solidarity between artists could give material aid to those in need.

The idea of a mutual aid society was brought back from London by the history-painter Henry Fradelle,[12] but it was thirteen years before it took shape. The project was taken in hand by a dynamic individual, Baron Taylor, who was a publisher and Director of the Théatre-Français. He organized a number of societies intended to give those who lived by the arts some guarantee against misfortune. He began by founding an organization for theatre people, the *Société de secours mutuels des artistes dramatiques* in 1840, followed by similar societies for painters, sculptors, architects, engravers and draughtsmen in December 1844. The Société Taylor, as it became known, won the favour of those most concerned and members soon numbered 3,000. The annual subscription was low, six francs, payable by monthly instalments of fifty centimes.

In spite of the scepticism which always greets an undertaking of this kind and the resistance of men too proud to accept help, the society was able to carry out its task of caring for the sick, paying pensions to the old and helping in cases of emergency. It did not have to rely on subscriptions alone. Baron Taylor managed to interest wealthy art lovers and organized fêtes, lotteries and paying exhibitions. The first was held in 1846 and was a triumph for Ingres who had agreed to show a large number of paintings.

When the Société Taylor was first formed, a journalist writing for the *Bulletin de l'Alliance des Arts* gave as his opinion that it would combat speculation, prevent artists being exploited and generally play the role of a Ministry of the Arts. This is going rather far but at the same time it raised simultaneously a new problem and attempted to offer a solution: in view of the continual wave of discontent provoked by the arbitrary choices of other authorities, should artists not undertake for themselves the organization of their profession?

The first steps in this direction were concerned with the organization of exhibitions independently of the official Salon. Claude Monet and his friends had to abandon this idea in 1867, since they had been unable to raise enough money. The idea came up again in 1873, and this time Paul Alexis, a friend of Zola's, pointed out the advantages for artists in organizing themselves into a trade union.[13] In the meantime Pissarro formed the *Société anonyme coopérative des artistes peintres, sculpteurs, graveurs*, etc., which was very flexible in its organization and was to organize the exhibitions known as Impressionist ever since the opening of its first in 1874.

Soon, as we have already seen, the state itself was to hand over the organization of the Salon to the artists. The creation of the *Société des artistes français* was in this sense truly revolutionary, and in spite of the difficulties encountered in drawing up its constitution, the idea was launched in 1881. The dissident *Société des beaux-arts* put itself at the head of a rival salon and both groups claimed the title of 'independent artists'. Twenty-five years had seen the transition from an almost complete lack of organization to a proliferation of small groups: watercolourists, painter-engravers, women artists and so on. These groups varied in their level of activity and in their staying power, but all were united in their determination to present joint exhibitions.

In 1888 Van Gogh even envisaged the creation of a society for selling impressionist paintings, which would manage the artists' affairs and protect their interests. 'I am inclined to think,' he wrote to his brother Theo, 'that artists should guarantee each other a living, independently of dealers.'[14]

The main obstacle to organizing artists was their habitual non-conformism and disregard of all social obligations. Many of them, for example, considered that marriage was incompatible with their calling. 'A married man,' said Courbet, 'is a reactionary in art'.[15] Gentle Corot's stand was just as uncompromising: 'I have only one aim in life which I wish to pursue resolutely: to paint landscapes. This firm decision prevents any serious attachment.'[16]

Setting up a home certainly brought with it the obligation to earn one's daily bread and hence renunciation of disinterested, uncompromising art, without immediate hope of gain. And could a woman understand the rhythm of the artist's work, consisting as it did of spells of idleness, time apparently wasted, followed by bursts of creative activity, when everything had to be sacrificed to the work in progress?

There were even those who thought that not only married life but any strong feeling for a woman was liable to turn the artist from the path he should follow. The model Dubosc remembered hearing Delacroix vehemently criticizing a young painter who wanted to get married. 'And if you love her and if she's pretty, that's the worst of all . . . your art is dead! An artist should know no other passion than his work, and sacrifice everything to it.'[17] The Goncourt brothers constructed the whole of their novel *Manette Salomon*, which is such a valuable source of information about painters' lives in the 1850s, around the story of an artist who marries one of his models and is driven by his wife to degrade his art and seek immediate advantage at the expense of his ideal.

When Alphonse Daudet published *Femmes d'artistes* in 1874 he, too, embroidered variations on the theme of the complications married life brought to the artist.

He tells of a young woman who is shocked to discover her husband with a model the day after returning from their honeymoon and prefers to pose for him herself; a sculptor who would have been perfectly happy with his wife and daughters, had not the way their house was run and the Bohemian existence that they led frightened off the girls' suitors; an academician worried lest after all he owes his election and some part of his success to the amorous intrigues of his too pretty wife. But it is above all in the prologue, which consists of a dialogue between an artist and a poet, that Daudet proclaims the theme that marriage for the artist, in spite of a few very rare exceptions, is impossible unless he subordinates his talent to material needs and also that the type of woman needed by this 'nervous, demanding, impressionable child-man called an artist' is almost impossible to find.[18]

Ingres, Daumier, Millet and Renoir demonstrated that marriage is not always incompatible with great artistic activity, but Delacroix and Courbet, and others besides, preferred to renounce this social tie. Gauguin's case is particularly significant since he left his home and family at the age of thirty-six in order to dedicate himself entirely to painting.

The artists' failure to adjust to society also marked the least of their relations with society's representatives, beginning with the landlord and his representative the *concierge*. Differences with the National Guard are echoed in many artists' biographies. For a period of forty years, from the accession of Louis-Philippe in 1830 to the inauguration of the Third Republic in 1870, the obligation was laid on every able-bodied citizen to put on uniform and perform a spell of guard duty. This seemed to the artists an intolerable interference with their liberties. Although they were not alone in seeking to evade the obligation, they were only equalled in their insubordination by the poets, and it was the artists who made the prison for the recalcitrant famous. The prisoners' lot does not, however, seem to have been very harsh in the lock-up on the quai

Austerlitz, nicknamed the Hôtel des Haricots. Artists who had failed to fulfil their turn of duty without good cause were incarcerated for twenty-four hours in this easy-going prison, where the beds were comfortable and the authorities provided playing cards and refreshments. There were those who preferred to spend their enforced leisure in some flight of fancy of their art, and cell No. 14 became famous for the sketches left on the walls by different occupants: a Christ surrounded by children by Deveria, bacchantes by Auguste de Châtillon, and a medallion by Théophile Gautier, not to mention the vengeful inscriptions expressive of the confused revolt in their authors' minds against a society which persecuted them; the most spontaneous of these was certainly: 'Down with the jury of the Institut.'[19]

Official positions or the adoption of political standpoints seldom seem to have been reconciled with art; there were nuances, which ranged from complete indifference to deliberate abstention. Gautier's famous lines express the detachment of the poet:

Sans prendre garde à l'ouragan
Qui fouettait mes vitres fermees
Moi, j'ai fait Emaux et Caméesn!

They are symbolic of an attitude for which the critic Théodore Silvestre severely reproached Ingres: 'We see him in June 1948 calmly finishing his *Venus Anadyomène* while the tocsin of civil war rang out and the blood of its victims flowed in the streets of Paris.'[20]

Even an artist who had benfited from official commissions might hold aloof from political strife. Or least this is the attitude that Louis Reybaud attributes to the painter Oscar in his once-famous novel *Jérôme Paturot à la recherche de la meilleure des Républiques*. Oscar in fact declares on the morning after the July Revolution: 'I have ceased to be painter-in-ordinary to His Majesty, so be it, but I have become instead painter-in-ordinary to the Republic; colours have no opinions.'[21]

Not all artists adopted this attitude. Paul Delaroche had the courage to refuse an important commission offered him by Napoleon III, the decoration of the interior of the Arc de Triomphe, and furthermore to give his reasons in his letter of refusal: 'I thank your Majesty for the great honour which you have done me in offering me this magnificent commission, but I have vowed never to do anything for a government to which I am opposed.'[22]

And there were yet others who did not hesitate to undertake responsibilities at times of political upheaval. In so far as they felt that they themselves had not managed to adjust to society, they could not remain indifferent to political revolution. There is therefore nothing surprising in the fact that many artists proved to be republicans. For example, in 1848 Garraud, the sculptor from Dijon, took over the department of Fine Arts and Jeanron undertook the military occupation of the offices of the Museums Service. David d'Angers agreed to become mayor of the 11th *arrondissement* in Paris (at that time the town hall was in the rue d'Assas), and afterwards was elected Deputy for Maine-et-Loire for several months. But Jehan du Seigneur, who had been nominated temporary curator of the Louvre, and its masterpieces which he had spontaneously helped to protect, soon withdrew to his work as an artist. On March 6, 1848, he wrote to the Minister of the Interior: 'Now that order has been restored I believe it to be my duty to ask you to accept my resignation. I shall return to my studio as a sculptor and ask nothing more of the Republic, only marble.'[23]

The most famous example of political commitment and the one which had the most disastrous consequences was the role of Courbet at the time of the Paris Commune in 1871. As a result of his position in the general assembly of artists, the *Fédération des artistes de Paris*, and the destruction of the Vendôme Column for which he was falsely held responsible, Courbet was obliged to end his days in exile.

Towards the end of the century many artists who were disillusioned with, and eager to oppose, a conservative republic where they felt, artists did not receive the position their merits deserved, became attracted to anarchist movements. Pissarro and his sons, Maximilien Luce, Steinlen, Seurat and Signac and others, all played a part in the dissemination of libertarian ideas through their drawings. The violent compositions which were published in *La Feuille* or *Le père peinard* reflected the adoption of very extreme standpoints in opposition to the ideas of the contemporary bourgeoisie. Some of them were implicated in the famous trial of the thirty anarchists which took place in 1894 – though all the accused were eventually acquitted. For a man like Luce lawsuits and even prison sentences were the inevitable consequence of his open fight against the society of the day.[24]

188

Even though their ideas seldom coincided with those of the government of the day, most artists were content to express inconsequential indifference and an anarchism which was confined to words alone; and their principles of hostility to the life of their time did not in fact prevent them from integrating fairly closely with it. Some actually sought out society, prompted either by their own taste or by family tradition, while others became assimilated all the more easily because the success of their work had brought them renown and honours.

Yet mistrust was not all that rare, even among men who basked in the favour of the public but who saw little to be gained from mixing in circles which were motivated by curiosity rather than by genuine interest. Meissonier said: 'The artist should stay in his studio where he is king. What has he to do with society which takes him over, body and soul, when he is famous and serves him up to guests.'[25] Daubigny was even blunter: 'Long life to a few good friends to be found among both men and women and the devil take the official world and all institutions! And that goes for the Institut too.'[26]

Artists in fact were kept at arm's length by a sizeable proportion of what passed for good society at the beginning of the century and would have had difficulty in acknowledging the changes that history and an altered social climate were bringing about. Yet as early as 1803 Le Breton noted in his *Notice Académique de l'an XI*: 'The status of artists has risen since 1789. They have been *ennobled* by the nature of things, by circumstances and by the use which they have made of their talents....'[27] Artists were regarded as 'outsiders', as 'originals', in a society where social differences were tending to diminish. They were seen as disturbing yet seductive, and aristocratic men and women finally came to draw these socially inferior but alluring persons to themselves.

Some artists thumbed their noses at the ostracism to which they were subjected, or reacted with scorn. Others suffered at not being admitted to the most elegant drawing-rooms. A man like Delacroix, who was a complete man of the world, could make people forget that he was a painter; and the esteem which society people had for him compensated for the rebuffs which his aesthetic position, generally held to be revolutionary, earned for him from traditional art circles. But the eldest of the Clarke sisters, lively young English girls who were also friends of Benjamin Constant and Stendhal, once

189

exclaimed: 'How charming and witty Monsieur Delacroix is! What a pity he's a painter!'[28]

Delacroix in fact had many society acquaintances and his evenings were often taken up by dinners at the homes of his eminent friends. To take only one example, between the beginning of 1855 and February 15th the same year he dined twice with the Princess Czartoryska, and once at La Paiva's, visited Thiers three times and Viardot twice, also visited the banker Fould, the architect Lefuel, the chemist Payen and Madame de Lagrange, the friend of Berryer; and attended a ball given by the Duke of Morny! None of which prevented him from working on his picture of *The Two Foscari* as well as on another which included a study of lions.

The clever ones who had determined to make a career in the world knew the importance of decorations; the medals won at the Salon were awarded for the work, whereas decorations were awarded to the man. They were only refused by artists determined to maintain the strictest independence or who wished to receive nothing from a political regime of which they disapproved. Degas, who was far from being an anarchist, used to say: 'I accept orders from no one!'[29]

On the eve of 1870 Daumier refused the offer of the cross of the Legion of Honour from an Empire which was becoming more liberal. Courbet gave the reasons for his refusal at about the same time in a letter which caused quite a stir:

'As a citizen, my political opinions are opposed to my accepting a mark of distinction which pertains to a monarchical order of things. . . . I am fifty years old and have always lived as a free man; let me end my days in freedom. . . .'[30]

The majority of artists, however, even when they were conscious of receiving a patent of gentility, were ready to accept decorations, even to try and obtain them. We have already remarked that the public regarded such distinctions as a guarantee of talent and was more ready to give commissions to artists who had been decorated; why then should artists reject honours which were so profitable to them? As Manet said in 1878: 'In this wretched life of ours which is all struggle, one can never be too well armed!' – words which recall Stendhal's: 'The greater the artist, the more he needs titles and decorations to defend himself.'[31]

All of which goes far to explain the tenacity of some, not necessarily

the greatest, artists in demanding a piece of ribbon or a cross which
they felt had been slow in coming to them from whatever government
was in power or from men in positions of authority. Gros wrote to
the Minister of the Interior in January 1817:

> 'Having failed to discover my name in the list of Chevaliers de
> Saint-Michel which His Majesty has just appointed, may I be
> permitted to set before you what I believe to be my just claims to
> this honour and to protest against Your Excellency's grievous
> oversight in this respect. . . .'

Scandalmongers used to claim that Pradier never missed a chance
to intrigue for a favour or a commission. However, in 1824, when
he was only thirty-two years old, he preferred to set out a direct
statement of his merits in claiming the promotion he expected,
writing as follows to the Director of Museum Services, Count
Forbin:

> 'The time is drawing near when artists chosen by you, whose
> work makes them worthy of encouragement, are due to receive
> their recompense. What I have done up till now, including my
> work at Versailles, gives me ground for hoping that this year I
> may receive the reward which I desire and which I believe myself
> to deserve.'[32]

However, it was another four years before Pradier became a
member of the Legion of Honour.

Napoleon had had the army in mind when he first created this,
the highest honour the state could bestow. The Emperor had,
however, no hesitation in also awarding it to artists, and on one
occasion when he did so he displayed a certain amount of showman-
ship. When he was presenting awards to painters who had exhibited
at the 1808 Salon he handed out a number of crosses but seemed to
have forgotten Gros. Then he turned towards the painter of *The
Battle of Eylau* and, wishing to afford him a special distinction, took
the cross he wore on his own coat and presented it to him with due
solemnity.

The granting of titles of nobility to artists or of honorary political
appointments was rarer and all the more appreciated. David was
made a knight of the Empire in 1808. The restored Bourbon
monarchy gave baronies to a few artists: Gérard in 1819, Gros in
1824, and Guérin, Regnault, Lemot, Bosio and Boucher-Desnoyers

later. The title which without any shadow of doubt caused the greatest stir was Horace Vernet's in 1841, when he became a peer of France. The art world was flattered to see one of its number enter such a closed circle, but his ennoblement was often attributed to his subservience as a courtier rather than his skill as an artist.[33]

During the Second Empire Ingres was made a Senator but Delacroix was not, although many people had expected them both to be nominated.

Preferment of this order, bestowed by the government, remained the exception, whereas membership of the Institut normally set the seal on a successful career. Nevertheless, it was a privilege restricted to a very small group of men. The Institut was created in 1795 to replace the Académies of the Ancien Régime; the fourth section of the Institut was allotted to the fine arts and, enlarged and expanded, became the new Académie des Beaux-Arts, created by royal decree of March 21, 1816. Its membership consisted of fourteen painters, eight sculptors, four engravers and six musicians.

To be elected a member of this *élite* by one's peers was like joining a select club to which the finest minds of the age belonged. It also meant participating in important decisions in the world of art: selecting the winners of the Prix de Rome, giving advice on appointments to the Ecole des Beaux-Arts and to the Salon jury. The artist saw his talent confirmed in the eyes of the public and felt the assurance that posterity would not forget him.

Unfortunately, the theoretical virtues of the Institut were often contested in practice. Attacks made upon the Institut from all sides represented it as a group of self-satisfied mediocrities and an organization for mutual support which was hostile to independents. However, it can be said that during the first half of the century all the great painters belonged. Gérard was elected in 1812 at the age of forty-two, Guérin and Gros in 1815, when the former was thirty-nine and the latter forty-four, while Ingres became a member in 1825 when he was forty-five years old. During the reign of Charles X artists gained admittance at a still younger age. Horace Vernet, David d'Angers and Pradier, for example, were thirty-six or seven when appointed. But Rude, who was refused admittance in 1838, was never elected. And Delacroix, who was a candidate in 1837, saw Léon Cogniet preferred to him. It was only at his seventh attempt in 1857 that he was elected when he was fifty-nine.

14   Contemporary cartoon: Anciens et Modernes

15. Palais de l'Industrie

Delacroix was the last painter of the century, who seems to us to have been truly great, to enter the Institut. The list of Academicians after Delacroix includes Meissonier, Jean-Paul Laurens, Paul Baudry and Jules Breton. Most of those whom we now regard as the great artists of the period were not even candidates to an institution which they despised. But, considered objectively and setting aside both the self-satisfaction of the one party and the disparagement of the other, it is impossible to deny the fundamental role of the Institut in the artistic life of the nineteenth century, nor the respect felt by French society for the Academician. That artistic developments should have taken place outside the Institut or in opposition to its principles is another story.[34]

Although for many it proved a hazardous undertaking, yet an artist's life could lead to a magnificent career in which every stage provided a privileged minority with a wealth of personal satisfaction and social esteem through Salon prizes, decorations, membership of the Institut and exhibition juries. Both David, until the fall of the Empire, and Ingres, after his return from Italy in 1841, were treated by the government and French society as persons of consequence. Louis-Philippe personally showed Ingres around the galleries at Versailles and then kept him for dinner in his palace at Neuilly, where a concert by his favourite musicians was awaiting him. And Napoleon III invited Carpeaux, Hébert and Viollet-le-Duc to Compiègne to share in the entertainments.

Nowadays Meissonier's success appears to us to be disproportionate. However, in order to appreciate its full extent it may be useful to know the full list of the honours bestowed upon him.

Born in 1813, Meissonier was awarded a third class medal at the Salon of 1840, a second class medal in 1841 and a first class medal in 1843; in 1846 he was made a Knight of the Legion of Honour; in 1848 he won the first medal at the Salon of that year. In 1855 he became an Officer of the Legion of Honour and won the medal of honour at the Universal Exhibition. By 1861 he was a Member of the Institut; and in 1867 a Commander of the Legion of Honour; in 1876 he became President of the Institut; and in 1878 he was Vice-President of the jury of the International Exhibition at which he received a 'rappel de médaille'. In 1880 Meissonier became a Grand Officer of the Legion of Honour, and in 1883 he was President of the painting section of the National Exhibition of the Fine Arts.

In 1889 he presided over the international Jury of the Universal Exhibition and also received a *'rappel de grande médaille d'honneur'*. He died in 1891. We have to add to the list the decorations he received from Belgium, Italy, Austria, Sweden and Turkey, and also the Order of Nassau. Furthermore, he was a member of the Academies of Amsterdam, Antwerp, Brussels, London, Madrid, Munich, Turin and Venice, and also the Academia di San Luca in Rome. . . .

A list like the above – which even so is almost certainly incomplete – shows that the man who had the good fortune to please the taste of his contemporaries and who knew how to profit from their admiration could look forward to receiving all kind of honours. Thanks to changes in the social climate a famous artist was admitted to a sort of 'aristocracy of talent', his lowly origins forgotten, so that finally, a few out-and-out individualists apart, and those who were misunderstood in their own day (it is of course true that they included some of the greatest), artists came to occupy their rightful place among the nation's *élite*.

CHAPTER TWELVE

FIN DE SIÈCLE

We have been able, in our consideration of the lives of artists, to draw upon the century as a whole because of the high degree of stability which prevailed in living conditions and to the gradualness of any change in the social climate. But the last two or three decades of the nineteenth century saw more than fresh variations on old themes. A turning-point which occurred under the Second Empire ushered in a period of intense innovation which can be discerned in poetry and music as well as in the plastic arts; it had its effects even in the circumstances of the artists' lives.

Contemporary opinion was strongly aware of living during a *fin de siècle*. The phrase was constantly repeated, usually in a pejorative sense, since many feared moral and intellectual decadence, while others saw a justification for their refinement of their vices.

A new factor had arisen which influenced public attitudes towards the artist: people were beginning to think that art might be an honourable profession or at least a lucrative one – the two were easily confused in a society which set great store on money values. Bertall in 1878 draws attention to this recent development: 'There was a time when if you mentioned an artist to the lowest category of tradesman, to the humblest draper or hardware merchant, he just shrugged his shoulders. To introduce a painter or sculptor into the household of a dealer in cottons or a money-lender was considered a sort of enormity. Even if he was commissioned to do a portrait the daughter of the house would be hidden away from him – "You know what these artists are". But today [continues Bertall], everything has changed and painting can be good business. Didn't Meissonier sell a canvas for 200,000 francs? And isn't he able to paint four like it in a year?' Quite suddenly the artist was considered a good match for an heiress and sons were encouraged to take up painting.[1]

Ten years later Francis Jourdain makes the same point in describing the world of the artist:

195

'At the present time a painter becomes established more quickly than a notary's clerk: he does watercolours in albums, dresses like the Prince of Wales, paints slick portraits of ladies, leads the dancing. He pays his colour merchant in cash in order to get a discount, invests his savings in the railways and, as soon as he is *hors concours*, marries the daughter of a wealthy, if unscrupulous banker.'[2]

Another observer of the contemporary scene sounds the same note:

'Painters today are nabobs, money flows in from all sides; they receive commissions from the state for 100,000 francs; the smallest portrait of a society lady is priced at 750 louis; American picture dealers cover their paintings with dollars several times over; and their sketches are taken off them for ridiculous prices.'[3]

Not that all painters, still less all sculptors, suddenly became rich. Far from it. But the fortunes which some of them made and their display of wealth struck the public imagination more forcibly than the poverty of others. Paul Arène said ironically in 1882: 'There was once a time, though some people may find it hard to believe, when artists were not rich.'[4]

Edmond de Goncourt, describing painting circles at about the same date, commented that he ought to rewrite his novel *Manette Salomon* (which was written around 1865/6), this time taking as his hero a well-off painter in the avenue de Villiers.[5]

The painter in the public eye, of course, who had society clients, aspired to a studio in a private residence, like that extraordinary pseudo-Renaissance construction that Meissonier had built in the place Malesherbes. We have already described how the Plaine Monceau and the neighbourhood of the avenue du Bois de Boulogne became the districts where elegant artists usually settled.

Those who wanted to be considered as such were obliged to follow their example. Boldini let himself be persuaded that his studio on the place Pigalle was no longer worthy of him and was happy to move into the residence left vacant by Sargent on the boulevard Bertier in 1885. Forain, who had become rich through his satirical drawings rather than by his paintings, caused a sensation when he purchased a plot of land in rue Spontini near the Porte Dauphine to build himself a town residence. *L'Echo de Paris* for

April 29, 1897, did not fail to inform its readers that the land alone had cost 62,000 francs.

Successful painters were usually those who painted portraits of society people and they too became difficult to approach. *Le Courrier français* claimed that one had to be recommended by a general or minister if one wanted to be painted by Léon Bonnat.[6] Bonnat never failed to give prominence to his sitters' decorations, be it a rosette or ribbon of knighthood. Women dressed themselves in furs and wore their most astonishing hats to have their portraits painted by Laszlo or drawn by Helleu. A picture might prove all the more expensive to the sitter, since some painters insisted on special dresses which could cost as much as 10,000 francs.

Painters such as these were received in society, or at least in that section of it, consisting of certain members of the aristocracy and upper bourgeoisie, where snobbery reigned. They were to be seen riding the very first bicycles in the Bois de Boulogne, and in all the smart cafés. And though they remained faithful to the Salon, yet they had a weakness for the sort of private exhibition where admission was by invitation only. The exhibitions organized every year from 1878 onwards by the *Cercle artistique et littéraire* of the rue Volney was one of these, and so was that of the *Union artistique*, better known as *Merlitons*, held first in the rue Boissy d'Anglas and then, after 1899, in the place Vendôme.

These society painters included a great many women. The woman artist, of course, was not a new phenomenon; many women, like Madame Vigée-Lebrun, Mlle Godefroy and Rosa Bonheur had occupied honourable places among the century's painters. But the majority of women painters had been copyists and miniaturists, poor creatures for the most part. And the young society ladies who dabbled in watercolours did not try to exhibit outside their circle of friends. By the end of the century the facilities for exhibiting their work made it possible for women artists to present themselves to the public as a group, the *Union des femmes peintres et sculpteurs*, separately from their male colleagues.[7]

The lucky ones were able to claim to be painters and at the same time surround themselves with a salon. The Princess Mathilde, cousin of Napoleon III, set the fashion by painting in watercolour and exhibiting her work, opening her drawing-room to the elite of the world of letters and the fine arts. Both in her town residence in the rue de Courcelles and in her summer-house at Saint-Gratien, north of Paris, artists like Gavarni, Herbert or Carpeaux could meet important people like Count Nieuwerkerke, himself a sculptor, who had become Director of Museums. The Princess continued to hold her receptions after 1870 in the rue de Berry and encouraged younger artists like Chapu and Marcel Baschet.

Madeleine Lemaire was of less noble origin but her friends proclaimed her 'the empress of the roses'. She was in fact famous as a flower-painter and received Robert de Montesquiou and the Duke of Grammont in the rue de Monceau, also Forain, Sem, Helleu, Detaille, Gérôme and many others. Marcel Proust knew her well and had her salon in mind when describing the 'Verdurin clan' and it was of Madeleine Lemaire that he was thinking when he showed Mme de Villeparsis receiving her friends 'with her brushes and palette and a watercolour of flowers already begun'. Albert Flament also caught the atmosphere of these gatherings when he wrote in his journal: 'Mme Madeleine Lemaire's secret is that her Tuesday evenings give the artists a chance to appear elegant and they are most entertaining for society people in Paris to attend.'[8] We have here an example of the blurring of distinctions between artists and society which gave the former their patent of nobility.

Henceforth the artist appeared as a man devoted to values far removed from those of the vulgar crowd. To give oneself to art, to set art above money, politics or morals, was to give proof of a superiority which placed one among the élite.

Many who now claimed to be artists were not creators but simply patrons of the arts or connoisseurs. When Edmond de Goncourt published *La maison d'un artiste* he described his own home, that of a novelist and journalist, where he had assembled a collection of works of art and ornaments with scrupulous care and taste. The ranks of artists were thus swollen by those who made a point of living a carefully chosen aesthetic setting surrounded by beautiful things. After 1881 such men were usually called 'aesthetes' following the example of their English counterparts.[9]

But this was the time when painters and sculptors were also giving thought to the appearance of their lodgings. Consequently the surroundings of the society man or wealthy bourgeois 'artist' and those of the true creative artist who was also becoming something of an aesthete, began to resemble each other.

Artists' studios in smart districts were much sought after by young snobs. They draped them with materials, decorated them with all kinds of ornaments and furnished them with enormous divans. It was in this sort of décor that the heroines of Paul Bourget's novels yielded to their seducers. The painters and sculptors in their turn were influenced by the taste of the period and habitually received their wealthy sitters in studios which were taking on the appearance of art galleries. There was no longer any great difference between the salon-studio of a society man like Robert de Montesquiou, for example, and the studio-salon of someone like Jacques-Emile Blanche, the society painter. Colette has recalled what the consequences of this custom were in *Mes apprentissages*:

'At that time there were already more studios than painters, but painters could not find studios to rent on account of the society art-lovers, eccentric women and ordinary private individuals who vied with them for the pleasure of furnishing their studios with garden seats, pyxes, Japanese sunshades, divan beds and choir stalls.'[10]

What both groups seem to have been after was not so much a convenient place to work as an atmosphere suited to contemplation and reverie, and it was this kind of atmosphere that the accumulation of heterogeneous ornaments, chinoiserie and draperies helped to create. The 'decadent' side of the *fin de siècle* décor was readily emphasized; religious objects like lecterns or chasubles were put to non-religious uses; the burning of incense was sometimes accompanied by the taking of opium or ether.

Contemporary journalists, ever interested in the oddities of their days, took pleasure in describing interiors of this kind. They were usually attributed to fictitious people and based more often than not on real ones. The studio of the 'erotic-mystic' painter Norlinger, described by Jean Lorrain, was typical: it was a meeting place for long-haired artists and writers who came down from the heights of Montmartre to listen to the muse of the aesthetic and literary painter-prophet. Then the poets 'crouched in the gloom' on 'modern-style' stools, read their latest sonnets in a setting which Lorrain describes in the following terms:

'A jumble of heterogenous objects, some connected with religion, others in every day use, fraternized in significant promiscuity and announced the state of mind of the master of the house to new arrivals as soon as they set foot inside the door. There were bellows, chimney hooks and fire-irons from country kitchens, rustic clocks, breadbins and even troughs for kneading the dough from Provence, all rubbing shoulders with church candlesticks, old chasubles, basins of holy water, lecterns, processional crosses, Corpus Christi banners and even altar-pieces. . . . And alchemists' retorts to give this junk-shop a spurious resemblance to a laboratory.'

Jean Lorrain described a similar atmosphere in Claudius Ethal's studio, and we know that here he was inspired by the society painter La Gandara, who was a collector of wax masks. The room was hung throughout with antique tapestries:

'A crowd of figures from the past seemed to throng the walls and here and there a ghost-like face emerges from the shadows in the form of the firmly modelled contours of one of the wax heads, a haggard face with sightless eyes and a painted smile. A dozen large candles burnt in groups of three in enormous church candlesticks in each corner of the room; the dim light made Ethal's studio look larger and the angles seemed to reduce into the darkness.'[11]

The list of imaginary painters could be a long one, but one more example will suffice: Octave Mirbeau's artist, who was particularly concerned for his appearance to harmonize with the décor of his studio and either wore an embroidered Japanese kimono or else a Louis XIII costume. 'What a pretty patch of colour I make,' he would say as he looked in the mirror at his own reflection, a light figure against a Gothic cabinet or a dark one against white silken wall-hangings.[12]

A rather dubious mysticism encouraged the aesthetes in their blend of religion and art, but it was because a confusion of values led them to regard art itself as a true religion. Joséphin Péladan and his followers, who were better known to the Parisian public for their outlandish clothes than for their theories, wanted to revive the medieval tradition of the Rose-Croix and make the artist into an ideal knight. Péladan resurrected the Chaldean title of *Sâr* for his own use and paraded in a doublet of watered silk with lace at the wrist and neck. He was too vain to keep his disciples but nevertheless managed to attract a number of artists who, like him, were concerned to reintroduce idealism to a world dominated by crude reality. His most useful achievement was the creation of the Salons of the

16   1879 Exhibition: private view

17 Exhibition of sculpture at the Grand Palais

Rose-Croix. Unfortunately, the large public which flocked to the first in 1892 was not always motivated by the best kind of interest. They wanted to see the *Sâr* with his Assyrian beard, inhale the fumes of incense, hear the trumpets which announced the opening or the invisible organs which played in muted tones (inspired by Wagner) rather than look at the works on exhibition.

It is true that the latter had been chosen according to strange criteria – all portraits, for example, were excluded – and apart from the pictures by Péladan himself were very uneven in quality.

The Salons of the Rose-Croix, however, continued for another five years, that of 1897 being the last, and they gave young artists hitherto unknown, like Rouault and Bourdelle, a chance to show their early works.[13]

Péladan's attempt to unite artists for a common struggle was doomed to failure from the start, on account of the personality of the organizer and the eccentrics who collected around him. But his venture was only one of many which were dreamed up by men from completely different backgrounds. Such tendencies were fostered by the spread of socialist ideas at that time. For many artists the benefits they imagined they could derive from community living were not just on the material plane but also on the level of the interchange of ideas and the enrichment to be found in the confrontation between differing aesthetic concepts. Feeling themselves faced by a society which was fundamentally hostile towards their problems, they were attracted by the idea of an organized group-life, which could offer them the advantages of both a convent and a commune.

All such ideas remained in the realm of fantasy, however. There was nothing in France like the English Pre-Raphaelite Brotherhood around 1850. But some attempts at communal living were made in certain houses of studios on the Left Bank or in Montmartre, and a few isolated individuals tried to find fresh inspiration in community experiments. When Van Gogh left for Arles in 1888 he persuaded Gauguin to join him. Van Gogh thought that the pictures he dreamed of were 'beyond the power of a single individual and would probably be created by groups of men working together to execute a common idea'.[14] Emile Bernard and Laval had let it be known that they might join their two friends in Provence and Seurat might perhaps have followed. But everyone knows the unhappy end of that adventure.

It was at the end of the same year that some young painters who admired Gauguin proclaimed themselves the 'prophets' of the new painting. A touch of mystery suited the taste of the times and they preferred to call themselves by the Hebrew word *nabi*. But although they dined together and met at 'the temple', that is to say in the studio of one of their number, Paul Ranson, they did not really live together, sharing resources, as would have been the case with J. K. Huysmans' project at Ligugé if he had succeeded in putting it into effect.

Huysmans had had a house built there in the shadow of a Benedictine monastery and the novelist dreamed of leading a quiet tranquil existence, suited to the lay brother he had by then become, in this town in Poitou. But he also hoped to gather about him a small group of Catholic writers and artists. Unfortunately, his friend the draughtsman Jean de Caldain refused to follow him and the painter Charles-Marie Dulac, in whom he placed great hopes for a renaissance of truly mystic art, died in 1898 before Huysmans had finished settling in Poitou.[15]

All these experiments ended in failure. The reasons differed but the deep-rooted individualism of French artists seems in itself to have been obstacle enough to any really community life.

Although by the end of the century the number of artists who could afford to spend money on fantastic luxuries had increased, Bohemia did not for all that disappear; yet even here there were signs of a rapprochement with the public, which had given up the rather patronizing sentimental pity and scorn of Murger's time, dwelling rather on the entertaining aspects of the artist's life; they were readier to approve their free-and-easy ways.

Montmartre, which had hitherto been a somewhat remote district, became more and more popular on account of its countrified air. The heights of Montmartre became the centre for a happy-go-lucky sort of artistic life where the general public came to join in the young artists' fun. A legend was in the process of being formed which was to carry the name of Montmartre all over the world. It was at this period that the slow construction of the Sacré-Coeur gave a new meaning to the name of the 'hill of the martyrs'. But religion was forgotten for the sake of freedom of thought and behaviour.[16]

The artists made a large contribution to the birth of this new Montmartre. They not only attended the cabarets in the district but were also responsible for decorating them, and they organized evening entertainments and spectacles which soon became famous. They were to be found at the Grande Pinte after 1878, a café on the avenue Trudaine which had stained-glass windows designed by Henri Pille, replaced by the Ane-Rouge after 1890, decorated by Feure and Willette. Willette was one of the main organizers of Montmartre cabarets: he painted frescoes for the Auberge-du-Clou and took part in the creation of the Chat-Noir; he painted the sign for the Cabaret des Assassins which later became the Lapin Agile on account of a punning sign painted by André Gill.

The most famous was the Chat-Noir, founded by Salis, a former student of the Ecole des Beaux-Arts and himself a painter without talent. He got together a group of young painters and poets and their girl friends. Their art had a tendency towards comedy, caricature and parody, while the poets cultivated the polished epigram and the well-turned quatrain. But Willy, Maurice Donnay and Alphonse Allais, together with Willette, Rivière, Steinlen and others helped to create a minor art, but one that was not without charm. What was new was that these artists' cabarets appealed to the public and, thanks to clever businessmen, became attractions to both Parisians and foreigners; they made known the studio jokes and traditions till then confined to a closed circle. They even competed with pleasure spots like the Moulin-Rouge and the Medrano Circus, both of them Montmartre institutions and frequented by artists like Degas and Toulouse-Lautrec who were attracted by spectacles and the music-hall.[17]

The public had other opportunities to get to know the world of the artist; events like the Bal des Quat'z'arts, whose ups and downs were fully reported in the press, caused a great stir outside the circles where they were originally conceived.

There had been balls organized by young artists throughout the century, the most famous being that held by Alexandre Dumas in 1833, which was remembered long after the close of the Romantic era. Among his other flights of fancy, he had had an empty apartment decorated in the space of a few days by ten or so of his friends, including Delacroix, Boulanger and Johannot. After his artist friends had vied with each other in decorative skill they joined the hundred ball guests, all in fancy dress, in a riotous uproar which lasted until nine the following morning.[18]

The description Dumas gave of this celebration in his *Mémoires* exaggerated its excitement still further and it lingered in the memory of the bourgeois as the very type of those frenzied parties they loved to imagine but which owed their glamour to legend rather than to reality.

The creation of the Bal des Quat'z'Arts in 1892, on the other hand, was a perfectly reasonable venture with no nonsense about it, in the beginning at least. The idea was that of a student of architecture Henri Guillaume and a group of his comrades who simply wanted the Ecole des Beaux-Arts to have its own annual ball like other institutions of higher education: the four arts – painting, sculpture, architecture and poetry (later replaced by engraving) – were to have their own ball. An unpretentious affair was held on April 23, 1892, in the Elysée-Montmartre (it is significant that a hall in the lower part of Montmartre was chosen) and its success did not extend beyond the art students and their circle. The only rules concerned dress; the young artists had rejected the black garb of respectable folk and felt obliged to demonstrate their originality by refusing to hire their clothes.

The following year things changed. Much in the same spirit the studios of the Ecole des Beaux-Arts wanted to contribute to the décor and costumes; they organized a fancy-dress parade in order to create a sensation, and in an attempt to impose some kind of unity decided that the costumes must be from antiquity. The atmosphere was spoilt by the intervention of the press. Jules Roques, was the editor of *Le Courrier français*, a journal which published gossip and caricatures, was very free in tone and therefore very 'Montmartre'; he took an interest in the students' plans and helped them. In return, invitations were issued to his subscribers, while the remainder were distributed by the *massiers* (senior students in each studio; see Chapter 1) as had been the case in the previous year.

The readers of *Le Courrier français* and also a number of journalists were very excited at the prospect of penetrating the hidden world of artists' studios and they gave the Bal des Quat'z'Arts the kind of publicity it could have done without. The fancy-dress parade was sensational. The regular artists' models took part. Gérôme's students reconstructed his painting *Bellona*, while those of Rochegrosse represented the arrival of Cleopatra. The part of Cleopatra herself was taken by a magnificent red-head, Sarah Brown. She was all but naked under net draperies and the dress of the other members of her train, as well as that of some of the other women present, was closer to that of models posing in a studio than that of Parisian women in street attire. Scandal broke out, there were accusations of orgy and debauchery, and after the ball Henri Guillaume and four models appeared in court and were fined. The students of the Quartier Latin were furious at the sentences, which might however have been more severe, and organized demonstrations which got out of hand and caused one death.

Serious incidents like these were not enough, however, to prevent a celebration which had become an established custom. The following year the students of the Ecole des Beaux-Arts took firm steps: nudity was banned and the *massiers* alone were responsible for issuing invitations. The Bal des Quat'z'Arts, once again a purely private and corporate event, became a tradition helped by a relaxation of public opinion.

In a similar vein Willette and his friends had the idea of exploiting the popularity of artists' celebrations with the public by inviting them to participate directly. In 1896, and again in 1897, they organized a sort of parody of the old fat stock shows in the form of a procession or tableaux presenting the *Vache enragée* (the angry cow, symbol of the hardships of the artist's lot).

The *Vachalade*, as it was called, of 1896 was not particularly successful, but the following year it attracted a great deal of publicity. Willette had inspired tableaux evoking Paris by Night, the Court of Miracles and various other themes, and young artists like Grün, Radiguet and Guirand de Scevola interpreted in their own fashion Imagination, Folly, the Golden Calf and so on; these scenes were represented by young women of Montmartre, models or dressmakers' apprentices. One of them who personified the place Blanche was proclaimed the Muse of Montmartre and music, specially composed for the Coronation of the Muse by Gustave Charpentier, was played by some 150 musicians. The purpose of the celebration was to raise money for needy artists and it took place under the auspices of a committee of honour headed by Puvis de Chavannes. However, the organizers had difficulty in paying off the debts incurred by the venture.[20]

This kind of event may indeed only have served to confirm in the bourgeois the dangerous notion that artists were just happy-go-lucky jokers.

The rapprochement between artists and society which took place during the last few years of the century did not occur only at the level of the upper bourgeoisie and of society artists but also on a more popular level, where ordinary members of the public observed with sympathetic amusement the celebrations and social activities of the artistic community. On the whole, the serious and sometimes slightly snobbish members of the Institut and the young art student, still proud of his wide-brimmed hat and flowing cravat, were both better adjusted in relation to French society. And only the most backward mothers of families were alarmed by them.

But where essentials were concerned the gulf between the public and the innovating artists was wider than ever. Some artists may have become millionaires and others may have managed to make a living after experiencing a period of hardship, but there were yet others who could not succeed in selling their works or even in making themselves known to the critics. Van Gogh, who had originally settled in Montmartre with his brother Theo, fled Paris altogether, while Gauguin sought solitude first in Brittany and afterwards in the remote islands of the South Seas; Cézanne lived completely unknown at Aix – at least until the period 1892–4.

This was the time when Verlaine had just been telling the world about the *poètes maudits*; close by them lived painters who might also have accepted the label *maudit*.[21] Behind the transient festivities and the superficial appearances which constituted the artist's life in the eyes of the public, the continued daily struggle; it was a hard and bitter one for some artists, but fortunately they were rich in the hopes that sustain true creators.

SELECT BIBLIOGRAPHY

The problems treated in this work have not been studied together as a whole before. Certain aspects of them are to be found in:

ROSENTHAL, L., 'Les conditions sociales de la peinture sous la monarchie de juillet' in the *Gazette des Beaux-Arts*, February–April 1910.

LEROY, A., *La vie familière et anecdotique des artistes français*, Gallimard, 1941.

The material conditions of painters' lives are analysed in:

WHITE, H. C. and C.A., *Canvases and Careers, Institutional Change in French Painting World*, Wiley, New York and London, 1965.

MAIN CONTEMPORARY FIRST-HAND SOURCES

AMAURY-DUVAL,—, *L'atelier d'Ingres*, Charpentier, 1878.

BLANC, C., *Les artistes de mon temps*, F. Didot, 1876.

BURTY, P., 'Croquis d'après nature', extract from the *Revue Rétrospective*, 1892.

CHAMPFLEURY, J., *Souvenirs et portraits de jeunesse*, Dentu, 1872.

CHENNEVIERES, P. DE, 'Souvenirs d'un Directeur des Beaux-Arts' in *L'Artiste*, 1883–5.

CHESNEAU, E., *Peintres et statuaires romantiques*, Charavay, 1880.

CLARETIE, J., *L'art et les artistes français contemporains*, Charpentier, 1876.

DELACROIX, E., *Journal* edited by A. Joubin, Plon, 1960. In three volumes. (English translation, *The Journal of Eugene Delacroix*, Jonathan Cape, 1938.)

—— *Correspondance générale* edited by A. Joubin, Plon, 1936–8.

DELECLUZE, E.-J., *L. David, son école et son temps*, Didier, 1855. In five volumes.

FLANDRIN, H., *Lettres et pensées* edited by H. Delaborde, Plon, 1865.

GIGOUX, J., *Causeries sur les artistes de mon temps*, Calmann-Lévy, 1885.

JOUIN, H., *Lettres inédites d'artistes français du XIXe siècle*, Protat, Mâcon, 1901.

—— *Les maîtres peints par eux-memes*. Gaultier-Magnier, c. 1900.

LAURENS, J., *La légende des ateliers*, Brun, Carpentras, 1901.

MORISOT, B., *Correspondance* edited by D. Rouart, Editart, 1950. (English translation, *The Correspondence of Berthe Morisot*, Lund Humphries, 1957.)

SILVESTRE, T., *Histoire des artistes vivants*, Blanchard, 1855.

VACHON, M. *Pour devenir un artiste*, Delagrave, 1903.

VENTURI, L., *Les archives de l'impressionisme*, Durand-Ruel, 1939. In two volumes.

VERNON, P., *Les coulisses aptistiques*, Dentu, 1876.

VIRMAITRE, C., *Paris-Palette*, 2nd edition, Savine, 1888.

—— *Paris-Médaillé*, L. Genonceaux, 1890.

VOLLARD, A., *En écoutant Cézanne, Degas, Renoir*, Grasset, 1938.

Soixante ans dans les ateliers d'artistes, Dubosc modèle, Calmann-Lévy, 1900.

LITERARY SOURCES

BALZAC, H. DE, *Pierre Grassou*, Souverain, 1840.

CHAMPFLEURY, J., *Contes vieux et nouveaux (Confessions de Silvius)*, M. Lévy, 1852.

DURANTY, E., *Le pays des arts*, Charpentier, 1881.

GONCOURT, E. and J. DE, *Manette Salomon*, Lacroix, 1865. Definitive edition, Flammarion, 1925.

JOURDAIN, F., *L'atelier Chantorel*, Charpentier, 1893.

MOREAU-VAUTHIER, C., *Les rapins*, Flammarion, 1896.

MURGER, H., *Scènes de la vie de bohème*, M. Lévy, 1851. (Many English translations published between 1887 and 1960.)

ZOLA, E., *L'oeuvre*, Charpentier, 1886. Also in the complete works edited by Maurice Leblond, Bernouard, 1928. (English Translation, *The Masterpiece*, Paul Elek, 1959; and other earlier translations.)

MONOGRAPHS ON ARTISTS

We have consulted numerous biographies of artists but have listed below only those written by direct eye-witnesses which have enabled us to enter more closely into the intimacy of the artist at work. Particularly valuable are the books of E. MOREAU-NÉLATON in which he presents the painter '*raconté par lui-meme*' (as told by himself):

Corot, Frazier-Soye, 1924. In two volumes;

Daubigny, Laurens, 1925;

Manet, Laurens, 1926. In two volumes;
Millet, Laurens, 1921. In three volumes.

We have also referred to:

BASILY-CALLIMAKI, M., *J. B. Isabey*, Frazier-Soye, 1909.

BLANC, C., *Ingres*, J. Renouard, 1870.

—— *Les trois Vernet*, Laurens, 1898.

CHASSE, C., *Gauguin et son temps*, Bibl. des Arts, 1955.

CLEMENT, C., *Gleyre*, Didier, 1887.

CLEMENT-JANIN, N., *La curieuse vie de Marcellin Desboutin*, Floury, 1922.

DAVID, J.-L., *Le peintre L. David*, Havard, 1880–2.

DELAS, M., *Willette*, n.d.

DELESTRE, J.-B., *Gros*, 2nd edition, 1867.

EPHRUSSI, C., *Paul Baudry*, L. Baschet, 1887. (English translation, *P. J. A. Baudry*, Chapman and Hall, 1883.)

ESCHOLIER, R., *Delacroix*, Floury, 1929. In three volumes.

FIDIERE, O., *Chapu*, Plon, 1894.

FOURCAUD, L. DE, *Rude*, Librairie d'art ancien et moderne, 1904.

—— *Bastien-Lepage*, L. Baschet, 1885.

GAUTHIER, M. *Achille et Eugène Deveria*, Floury, 1925.

LAFOND, P., *Degas*, Floury, 1918–19.

LAPAUZE, H., *Ingres*, Impr. Petit, 1911.

LARROUMET, G., *Meissonier*, L. Baschet, 1898.

LEMOISNE, *Degas*, Vol. I, Arts et Métiers graphiques, 1949.

MACK, G., *La vie de P. Cézanne*, Gallimard, 1938. (English edition, *Paul Cézanne*, Jonathan Cape, 1935.)

MOREAU-VAUTHIER, C., *Gérôme*, Hachette, 1906.

POULAIN, G., *Bazille et ses amis*, Renaissance du Livre, 1932.

RIAT, G., *G. Courbet*, Floury, 1906.

RIVIERE, G., *Renoir et ses amis*, Floury, 1921.

ROOSEVELT, B., *Gustave Doré*, Libr. ill., 1887. (English edition, *Life and reminiscences of Gustave Doré*, Sampson and Low, 1885.)

SAUNIER, C., *Auguste Lepère*, Le Garrec, 1931.

SENSIER, A., *Millet*, Quantin, 1881. (English translation, *Jean-François Millet*, Macmillan, 1881.)

STRYIENSKI, C., *Landelle*, Emile-Paul, 1911.

VACHON, M., *Puvis de Chavannes*, Soc. d'édition artist., c. 1905.

—— *Detaille*, Lahure, 1898.

—— *Bouguereau*, Lahure, 1900.

VATTIER, G., *Augustin Dumont*, Oudin, 1885.

More general works consulted include:

BENOIT, F., *L'art français sous la Révolution et l'Empire*, Baranger, 1897.

LUC-BENOIST, —, *La sculpture romantique*, Renaissance du Livre, 1928.

REWALD, J., *Histoire de l'impressionisme*, A. Michel 1955. (English edition, *The history of impressionism*, Museum of Modern Art, New York, 1949.)

—— *Le post-impressionisme*, A. Michel, 1963. (English edition, *Post-impressionism: from Van Gogh to Gauguin*, Museum of Modern Art, New York, 1956.)

SOUBIES, A., *Les membres de l'Académie des Beaux-Arts*, Flammarion, 1904–14.

TABARANT, A., *La vie artistique au temps de Baudelaire*, Mercure de France, 1942.

PARTICULAR ASPECTS of the subject are covered by references to the works mentioned in the Notes to the Text.

NOTES

ABBREVIATIONS

BN   Bibliothèque Nationale, Paris
GBA   *Gazette des Beaux-Arts*

CHAPTER ONE

MASTERS AND APPRENTICES

1. *Paris-Rapin*, 1855, p. 43.
2. VACHON, *Pour devenir un artiste*, p. 21.
3. TEXIER, *Tableau de Paris*, I, Paulin et Lechevallier, 1852, p. 36.
4. VACHON, *op. cit.*, p. 14.
5. *Caricature sur les brimades* (lithograph by Moynet, 1843).
6. MOREAU-VAUTHIER, *Gérôme*, p. 25 seq.; GONCOURT, *Manette Salomon*, pp. 34–5; POULAIN, *Bazille et ses amis*, p. 18. For more about art students: *Paris-Rapin*, 1855; CHAUDES-AIGUES, *Les français peints par eux-mêmes*, I, 1840.
7. WILLETTE, *Feu Pierrot*, Floury, 1919, p. 60 seq.; ALEXANDRE, *Raffaëlli*, 1909, pp. 31–2.
8. *Croquis de Girodet corrigeant* (BN Estampes, Na 106, Pet. fol.)
9. AMAURY-DUVAL, *L'atelier d'Ingres*, p. 45; BALZE, *Ingres, son école*, 1880, p. 2.
10. REDON, *A soi-même*, 1922, pp. 22–4.
11. JOUIN, *Lettres inédites d'artistes français du XIXe siècle*, p. 346.
12. CLEMENT, *Gleyre*, p. 171 seq.; FOURCAUD, *Rude* p. 280 seq.
13. PROUST, *Manet*, Laurens, 1913, p. 17 seq.
14. RIVIERE, *Renoir et ses amis*, pp. 55–6.
15. *Mémoires de Guéniot* in *GBA*, April 1966.
16. BALZE, *op. cit.*
17. ADHEMAR, *L'enseignement académique en 1820*, Girodet in *Bulletin de la Société de l'histoire de l'art français*, I, 1933, p. 270 seq.
18. ADHEMAR, *La lithographie de paysage en France à l'époque romantique*, A. Colin, 1937, p. 17.
19. BLANC, *Les artistes de mon temps*, p. 108.
20. REWALD, *Histoire de l'impressionisme*, p. 62.
21. PROUST, *op. cit.*, and the same author's reminiscences in *La Revue Blanche*, February 1, 1897.
22. CLEMENT, *op. cit.*, p. 171.
23. REGAMEY, *Lecoq de Boisbaudran*, 1903; JULLIEN, *Fantin-Latour*, Laveur, 1909, p. 6 seq.; BLANCHE, *Propos de peintre*, 1919, p. 75.
24. Courbet papers (in BN Estampes); and *Le Monde Illustré*, March 15, 1862.
25. On the Académie Suisse: DUBUISSON, *Les echos du bois sacré*, p. 14.
26. For the Académie Julian: DEBANS, *Plaisirs de Paris*, 1889, pp. 185–211.

CHAPTER TWO

FROM THE ECOLE DES BEAUX-ARTS TO THE VILLA MEDICI

1. TAINE in *Paris-Guide*, I, A. Lacroix, 1867, p. 845 seq.; TEXIER, *Tableau de Paris*, II, Paulin et Lechevallier 1853, p. 188 seq.; LEMAISTRE, *L'Ecole des Beaux-Arts*, F. Didot, 1889; MUNTZ, *Guide de l'Ecole des Beaux-Arts*, c. 1895.
2. FOURCAUD, *Rude*, p. 59.
3. TAINE, *loc. cit.*; BEULE, *Eloge de Duban à l'Ecole des Beaux-Arts*, 1872.
4. On the competitions for the Prix de Rome see: LAURENS, *La légende des ateliers*, p. 390 seq.; CLARETIE. E. *Hébert in Revue d'art ancien et moderne*, XX, 1906, p. 400 seq.
5. AMAURY-DUVAL, *L'atelier d'Ingres*, p. 8–11. For winners of the Prix de Rome see: *Arch. Art fr.*, V, p. 273, and *Nouvelles Arch. Art. fr.*, II, p. 451.
6. REGNAULT, *Correspondence*, 1872, pp. 127–8 and 390.
7. On the Villa Medici: HERBERT, *La Villa Medici en 1840* in *GBA*, 1901, pp 265–76; BENEDITE, *J. J. Henner* in *GBA*, 1908, I. p. 37 seq.; LAPAUZE, *Histoire de l'Académie de France à Rome*, II (1802–1910), Plon, 1924; BESNARD, *Sous le ciel de Rome*, Ed. de France, 1925; ALAUX, *L'Académie de France à Rome*, Duchartre, 1933.
8. LAPAUZE, *op. cit.*, p. 72, note 1.
9. Quoted by BLANC in *Les artistes de mon temps*, p. 231.
10. REGNAULT, *op. cit.*, p. 32.
11. PLANCHE, in *L'Artiste*, 1832.
12. Letter from Horace Vernet to Gérard in GERARD, *Correspondence de F. Gérard*, Lainé et Havard, 1867, p. 789.
13. RADET, *Histoire et oeuvre de l'Ecole française d'Athènes*, Fontemoing, 1901.
14. FROMAGEOT, *V. Schnetz directeur de l'Ecole de Rome* in *Arch. Art. fr.*, VIII, 1914, pp. 329–41.
15. BENEDITE, *loc. cit.*, p. 41; FIDIERE *Chapu*, p. 40.
16. BENEDITE, *loc. cit.*, p. 54.
17. LECOMTE, *La vie héroïque . . . de Carpeaux*, Plon, 1928.
18. H. Vernet in LAPAUZE, *op. cit.*, p. 217.

CHAPTER THREE

LODGINGS AND STUDIOS

1. MERSON, *Les logements d'artistes au Louvre* in *GBA*, 1881, p. 264 seq., and II, p. 276 seq.; AULANIER, *Histoire des palais et du Musée du Louvré*, I, 1949, and IX, 1964, pp. 46–8.
2. JOUIN, *Les maîtres peints par eux-mêmes*, pp. 264–5.
3. DELABORDE, *L'Académie des Beaux-Arts*, 1891, pp. 176 and 193.
4. DELECLUZE, *L. David*, p. 15 seq. and p. 297 seq.
5. BONNEROT, *La Sorbonne*, P.U.F., 1927, p. 27 seq.; VATTIER, *Augustin Dumont*, p. 27 seq.
6. MAILLARD, *Rodin statuaire*, Floury, 1899, p. 23; MONTROSIER, *J. P. Laurens* in *GBA*, 1899, I, p. 154.
7. Anonymous caricature, around 1840.
8. PYAT, *Les artistes* in *Nouveau tableau de Paris*, IV, 1834, p. 15.
9. MOREAU-VAUTHIER, *La vie d'artiste*, 1892.
10. CLARETIE, *L'art et les artistes français contemporains*, p. 70 seq.
11. JOUBIN, *Logis et ateliers de Delacroix* in *Bulletin de la Société de l'histoire de l'art*

français, 1938, pp. 60–9. Monet and Bazille lived in rue Furstemburg from January 15, 1865, to February 4, 1866.

12. BANVILIE, *Mes souvenirs*, Charpentier, 1882, pp. 84 and 174; GEOFFROY, *Daumier* in *Revue d'art ancien et moderne*, IX, 1901, p. 229.
13. BERTHOUD, *Le singe de Biard* in *Musée des Familles*, 1839, p. 275.
14. BURTY, *L'atelier de Mme O'Connell* in *GBA*, March 15, 1860.
15. BERTHOUD, *op. cit.*, p. 347.
16. FOURNIER, *Un grand peintre, F. Ziem*. Lambert, Beaune, 1897, pp. 74–5.
17. GAUTIER, *Albertus*, 1831, stanzas LXXV–LXXVI.
18. CLEMENT, *Gleyre*, p. 182 seq.
19. VALERY, *Degas, danse, dessin* (*Oeuvres, II*, Gallimard, 1960, p. 1174).
20. FERVACQUES in *Le Figaro*, December 25, 1875.
21. BLANCHE, *Propos de peintre*, 1919, p. 145.
22. VERNON, *Les coulisses artistiques*, p. 26 seq.
23. GONCOURT, *Manette Salomon*, pp. 166–7.
24. For Meissonier's studio see SOUBIES, *Les membres de l'Académie des Beaux-Arts*, III, p. 25, and also an album of photographs (BN Estampes, Na 295 in-4°).
25. TEXIER, *Tableau de Paris*, II, Paulin et Lechevallier, 1853, p. 44.

CHAPTER FOUR

SUBJECTS, INSPIRATION AND MODELS

1. DU CAMP, *Souvenirs littéraires*, II, 3rd edition, 1906, p. 202.
2. LENORMANT, *A. Scheffer* in *Le Correspondant*, XLVII, 1859, p. 478.
3. Described in SILVESTRE, *Histoire des artistes vivants*, pp. 15–16.
4. MOREAU-NELATON, *Manet*, p. 26.
5. CLEMENT, *Prud'hon*, 1872, p. 314 seq.
6. ESCHOLIER, *Delacroix*, III, p. 50.
7. The text is quoted in MOREAU-VAUTHIER, *Gérôme*, pp. 102–3.
8. PLANET, *Souvenirs de travaux de peinture avec Monsieur Delacroix*, edited by A. Joubin, 1929, p. 63.
9. JOUIN, *Maîtres contemporains*, p. 217.
10. ROCHETTE, *Notice historique sur la vie . . . de Monsieur Pradier*, Institut de France, 1883.
11. LETHEVE, *La République de Soitoux* in *GBA*, October 1963.
12. VACHON, *Pour devenir un artiste*, p. 131.
13. SILVESTRE, *Histoire des artistes vivants*, p. 49.
14. LETHEVE, *Le public du Cabinet des Estampes au XIXe siècle* in *Mélanges J. Cain*, Hermann, 1968.
15. BLANC, *Les artistes de mon temps*, p. 48; BERGERET, *Lettre d'un artiste sur l'état des arts en France*, 1848, quoted by NAEF. *Parmi les gravures de la collection Ingres* in *Bulletin Musée Ingres*, December 1965.
16. HAUTECOEUR, *L. David*, 1954. pp. 201–8.
17. VACHON, *op. cit.*, p. 225.
18. TAINE, *Paris-Guide*, I, A. Lacroix, 1867, p. 851.
19. CLARETIE, *Peintres et sculpteurs contemporains*, p. 124; BURTY, *Croquis d'après nature;* DURANTY, *Le pays des arts*, p. 141.
20. DELAÇROIX, *Correspondance générale*, III, p. 195.
21. FOURCAUD, *Rude*, p. 203; BLANC, *Ingres*, pp. 80 and 118.
22. JOUBIN, *Les modèles de Delacroix* in *GBA*, 1936, I, p. 345 seq.
23. Caricatures by E. Beaumont for *Les croquis parisiens* exhibited at Martinet's 1859.

24. Play by Brazier, Varner and Bayard, quoted by DORBEC, *La peinture au temps du romantisme* in *GBA*, 1918, XIV, p. 281–2.
25. PLANET, *op. cit.*, pp. 35–6.
26. *Dubosc modèle*, p. 121. For further information concerning models consult *Journal des Artistes*, II, 1829, pp. 348–50; ZOLA in his notes for *L'oeuvre*, Leblond edition, p. 423; and VIRMAITRE, *Paris-Palette*, pp. 79–87.
27. LEROY, *Physionomies parisiennes, artistes et rapins*, 1868, pp. 106–7.
28. LE ROUX, *L'enfer Parisien*, Havard, 1888, pp. 68–82; *L'Illustration*, January 4, 1890.
29. *Dubosc modèle*, p. 121.
30. DU SEIGNEUR, *Paris, voici Paris*, p. 224.
31. DELACROIX, *Journal*, January 18, 24 and 26, 1824.

CHAPTER FIVE

TECHNIQUE AND EXECUTION

1. Degas to his friend Jeanniot, quoted by BOURET *Degas*, 1965, p. 112. For painting techniques see: MOREAU-VAUTHIER, *La peinture*, Hachette, 1912; *Comment on peint aujourd'hui*, Floury, 1923; PIOT, *Les palettes de Delacroix*, Libr. de France, 1931; ROUART, *Degas à la recherche de sa technique*, Floury, 1945; GROSSER, *The painter's eye*, Rinehart, New York, 1951.
2. JOUBIN, *Haro entre Ingres et Delacroix* in *L'Amour de l'Art*, March 1936.
3. DELACROIX, *Correspondance générale*, I, p. 207.
4. BALZE in *GBA*, 1911, II, p. 144, no. 1.
5. DURANTY, *Le pays des arts*, pp. 174–6.
6. FIDERE, *Chapu*, p. 97.
7. BORDIER, *Les Susse: une dynastie coulée dans le bronze* in *Jardin des Arts*, June 1966.
8. PALADILHE in his preface to the catalogue of the Gustave Moreau exhibition at the Louvre, 1961, p. 16.
9. MORISOT, *Correspondance*, pp. 33–4.
10. VOLLARD, *En écoutant Degas*, p. 80.
11. Delacroix to Berryer, October 18, 1858, DELACROIX, *Correspondence*, IV, p. 50.
12. DELACROIX, *Gros* in *Revue des deux mondes*, September 1, 1848.
13. VOLLARD, *En écoutant Cézanne*. p. 65.
14. *Dubosc modèle*, p. 51.
15. GIGOUX, *Causeries sur les artistes de mon temps*, p. 172.
16. WEY, *L'ami des peintres* in *Les français peints par eux-mêmes*, I, 1840.
17. SOUBIES, *Les membres de l'Académie des Beaux-Arts*, II, p. 49.
18. HUYGHE, BAZIN and ADHEMAR, *Courbet, l'Atelier*, Ed. des musées nationaux, c. 1940.
19. DU CAMP, *Souvenirs littéraires*, I, 3rd edition, 1906, p. 247; *Dubesc modèle*, p. 137.
20. BENEDITE in *Revue d'art ancien et moderne*, II, 1908, p. 67.
21. CLARETIE, *L'art et les artistes français contemporains*, p. 395.

CHAPTER SIX

TRAVELLERS AND LANDSCAPE ARTISTS

1. THORE, *Salons*, 1868, p. 14.
2. GIGOUX, *Causeries sur les artistes de mon temps*, p. 172.
3. Letter quoted by MOREAU-NELATON, *Daubigny*, p. 30.
4. BALZAC, *Un début dans la vie*, 1844.
5. MOREAU-NELATON, *op. cit.*, p. 69.

6. CHAMPFLEURY, *Les Noireau* in *Contes vieux et nouveaux*, pp. 295–6.
7. Described in ADHEMAR, *La lithographie de paysage en France à l'époque romantique*, A. Colin, 1937, p. 17.
8. GONCOURT, *Manette Salomon*, p. 28.
9. Letter to Henriet dated September 30, 1872, and quoted by MOREAU-NELATON, *op. cit.*, pp. 109–10.
10. MURGER, *Adeline Protat*, M. Lévy, 1854.
11. On Marlotte see: *Revue de l'art*, V, 1899, p. 103 seq.
12. TAINE, *Vie et opinions de T. Graindorge*, Hachette, 1867. For Barbizon see also: GASSIES, *Le vieux Barbizon*, 1907; MICHEL, *La Forêt de Fontainebleau*, Laurens, 1909; BILLY, *Les beaux jours de Barbizon*, 1947; FORGES, *Barbizon (Lieu-dit)*, 1962.
13. LECUYER, *Demeures inspirées et sites romantiques*, I, 1949.
14. FLEURY and SOLONET, *La société du Second Empire*, III, p. 349.
15. GAUTIER, *Histoire du Romantisme*, 1874, p. 232.
16. MOREAU-NELATON, *op. cit.*, p. 38; HENRIET, *Le paysagiste aux champs*, Faure, 1866.
17. These lines describing a 'day in the life of a landscape artist' were actually written by Alfred Stevens under the name of Graham (*L'étranger au Salon*, 1863) but they were attributed to, and inspired by, Corot and the painter never disowned them.
18. POULAIN, *Bazille et ses amis*, pp. 40–1.
19. DELVAU in *Le Figaro* in a series called *Les châteaux des rois de Bohême*, 1865.
20. Letter written to M. Luce and quoted by REWALD, *Post impressionisme*, p. 174. For Pont-Aven see: CHASSE, *Gauguin et le groupe de Pont-Aven*, 1921, and the same author's *Gauguin et son temps*.
21. Quoted by MIQUEL, *P. Huet*, Sceaux, Ed. de la Martinelle, 1962, p. 34.
22. HENRIET, *op. cit.*, p. 58.
23. VAN GOGH, *Correspondance complète*, Gallimard-Grasset, III, 1960, p. 465.
24. GUILLEMOT in *Revue illustré*, December 1897 to June 1898.
25. MOREAU-NELATON, *op, cit.*, p. 118.
26. SIGNAC, *Journal* published in *GBA*, April 1952.
27. LEMOISNE, *Degas*, I, p. 100.
28. Letter from Gauguin to Schuffenecker quoted by REWALD, *Histoire de l'impressionisme*, p. 327.

CHAPTER SEVEN

THE SALON AND EXHIBITIONS

1. JANIN, *L'été à Paris*, 1844, p. 148.
2. For Jongkind see: REWALD, *Histoire de l'Impressionisme*, p. 70. For Holtzappel see: TABARANT, *Vie artistique au temps de Baudelaire*, p. 440.
3. A decree of 28 Ventôse year VIII (August 5, 1800) instituted a commission to safeguard morals and exclude politically dangerous works; the text is quoted by AULANIER, *Histoire des palais et du Musée du Louvre*, II, 1951, p. 44.
4. For the reforms of 1830 see: *Journal des Artistes*, August–September 1830 and January–February 1831, *passim*.
5. Field-Marshal Vaillant's speech foreword to the Catalogue of the Salon of 1866.
6. MOREAU-NELATON, *Daubigny*, p. 115.
7. FERRY in the Catalogue of the Salon of 1880, p. VI; remarks addressed to the Committee of the ninety members of the society of artists responsible for the

organization of the Salon on January 17, 1881, and printed in the Salon Catalogue for 1881, p. ix.

8. 'Fresh works of art have come to enrich the Salon; art-lovers have greeted the appearance of Monsieur Ingres' *Oedipus* with satisfaction' (*Journal des Artistes*, April 20, 1828. (See also AMAURY-DUVAL, *L'atelier d'Ingres*, p. 126.

9. *Journal des Artistes*, January 3, 1841.

10. ZOLA, *L'oeuvre*, Leblond edition, p. 301.

11. SENSIER, *Souvenirs sur T. Rousseau*, L. Techener, 1822. p. 90.

12. POULAIN, *Bazille et ses amis*, p. 111.

13. Engraving of the Salon of year VIII (1800) by Devisme after Monsaldy; painting by Heim showing Charles X distributing the prizes at the Salon of 1824.

14. *L'Artiste*, 1831, I, p. 145.

15. GIGOUX, *Causeries sur les artistes de mon temps*, p. 65; LUC-BENOIST *La sculpture, romantique*, p. 30.

16. DU CAMP, *Souvenirs littéraires*, I, 3rd edition, 1906. p. 849.

17. *Le Monde illustré*, March 22, 1884; *La Vie moderne*, 1880, p. 227; BLANCHE, *Propos de peintre*, 1919, pp. 15–16.

18. ZOLA, *L'oeuvre*, Leblond edition, p. 308.

19. TAINE in *Paris-Guide*, A. Lacroix, 1867, I, p. 849.

20. BENOIT, *L'art français sous la Révolution et l'Empire*, p. 133, n. 1.

21. LANDON, *Salon de 1810*, p. 11; *Le prisme*, c. 1840, pp. 98–101 and 116–20.

22. *Journal des Artistes*, December 16, 1827 and March 14, 1841.

23. *Journal des Artistes*, 1845, p. 248; DUSEIGNEUR, *Les expositions particulières aux XVIIIe and XIXe siècles* in *L'Artiste*, 1882, I, p. 540–56.

24. LAGRANGE, *Des Société des Amis des arts en France*, J. Claye, 1861.

25. BAUDELAIRE in *Le Corsaire-satan*, January 21, 1846. For the Société Taylor see: *Bulletin de l'Alliance des arts*, January 30, 1845, pp. 225–6; MAINGOT, *Le Baron Taylor*, 1963, p. 86 seq.

26. HAUTECOEUR, *L. David*, 1954. p. 181 seq.

27. RIAT, *Courbet*, 1906, p. 131 seq.

28. MITTERAND, *Zola journaliste*, Colin, 1962, p. 59 seq.; LETHEVE, *Impressionistes et symbolistes devant la presse*, Colin, 1959, p. 35 seq. For the 'salons comiques' see: CHADEFAUX, *Le Salon caricatural de 1846* . . . in *GBA*, March 1968.

29. VIRMAITRE, *Paris-Médaillé*, p. iv and the same author's *Paris-Palette*.

CHAPTER EIGHT

COMMISSIONS AND MARKETS

1. NATANSON, *Peints à leur tour*, A. Michel, 1848, p. 40.

2. MALO, *Thiers et les artistes de son temps* in *Revue de Paris*, July 1, 1924.

3. Quoted by LELIEVRE, *Vivant-Denon*, 1942, p. 42.

4. *Dubosc modèle*, p. 72.

5. MONTALIVET, *Le roi Louis-Philippe et la Liste Civile*, 1851, p. 115.

6. JOUIN, *Lettres inédites d'artistes français du XIXe siècle*, p. 224.

7. For Soitoux see: LETHEVE, *La République de Soitoux* in *GBA*, October 1963. Artists were not generally very appreciative of Haussman, cf. HAUTECOEUR, *Histoire de l'architecture classique*, VII, p. 75.

8. CHENNEVIERES, *Souvenirs d'un Directeur des Beaux-Arts*, 2nd part, p. 3 seq.

9. BOUCHOT, *Le Salon de 1893* in *GBA*, 1893, I, p. 445.

10. STRYIENSKI, *Landelle*, p. 62–3.

11. *Journal des Artistes*, December 2, 1827 and September 7, 1828; BURTY, *Croquis d'après nature*, 2nd series, p. 13.
12. VIEL-CASTEL, *Des beaux-arts* in *L'Artiste*, I, 1831, p. 289.
13. DELACROIX, *Correspondance générale*, I. p. 290.
14. FOURCAUD, *Rude*, p. 160.
15. DELACROIX, letter in *L'Artiste*, 1831, I, p. 49.
16. *Bulletin des Arts*, June 10, 1846.
17. DELACROIX, *Journal*, April 3, 1847.
18. BALZAC, *Les paysans*, Conard, 1844, p. 12.
19. ETEX, *Pradier*, 1859, p. 37.
20. Quoted by LUC-BENOIST, *La sculpture romantique*, p. 30.
21. LAURENS, *La légende des ateliers*, p. 310.
22. VIRMAITRE, *Paris-Palette*, p. 57.
23. *Ibid.*, p. 114.
24. VOLLARD, *En écoutant Cézanne*, pp. 180 and 257.
25. JAL, *Causeries du Louvre*, 1833, p. 99.
26. SOUBIES, *Les Membres de l'Académie des Beaux-Arts*, II, p. 28.
27. STRYIENSKI, *Landelle*, p. 79.
28. BURTY, in *Paris-Guide*, Lacroix, 1867, II, p. 261 (which gives valuable information on the art trade).
29. For picture hire see: TABARANT, *La vie artistique au temps de Baudelaire*, p. 13.
30. ROSENTHAL in *GBA*, 1910, I, p. 59.
31. STRYIENSKI, *op. cit.*, p. 14.
32. *Bulletin de l'Alliance des Arts*, July 10, 1844.
33. GAUTIER, in *L'Artiste*, January 3, 1858; HENRIET, *L'Artiste*, November 15, 1854 and February 1, 1860.
35. MOREAU-NELATON, *Millet*, II, p. 71 seq.
36. VENTURI, *Les archives de l'impressionisme*, I, p. 14; the Memoirs of DURAND-RUEL, *ibid.*, II.
37. ZOLA in his notes for *L'oeuvre*, Leblond edition, pp. 410–22.
38. Though Durand-Ruel often had a difficult role to play one cannot be unaware of the fact that pictures which he bought from Manet for 35,000 francs were later sold by him to American collectors and museums for more than 800,000 francs (WHITE *Canvases and careers*, p. 126).

CHAPTER NINE

MONEY MATTERS: EARNINGS AND EXPENDITURE

1. MOREAU-VAUTHIER, *Gérôme*, p. 33.
2. POULAIN, *Bazille et ses amis*, p. 23.
3. Courbet papers (BN Estampes).
4. Letters from Zola to Cézanne quoted in VOLLARD, *En écoutant Cézanne*, p. 12.
5. ROUSSEL and DUBOIS, *De quoi vivait V. Hugo*, Ed. des Deux-Rives, 1952, p. 115–16.
6. *La Vie Moderne*, 1880, p. 258; AVENEL, *Les riches depuis 300 ans*, 1909.
7. BERGERET, *Lettre d'un artiste sur l'état des arts en France*, 1848, quoted by NAEF, *Parmi les gravures de la collection Ingres* in *Bulletin Musée Ingres*, December 1965.
8. ZOLA in his notes for *L'oeuvre*, Leblond edition, p. 423.
9. TOMEL, *Petits métiers parisiens*, Charpentier, 1898.
10. *Journal des Artistes*, June 27, 1841.
11. Cavé, who was Director of Fine Arts, could only offer 4,000 francs, though he considered that the picture was worth 20,000 francs. But Delacroix accepted

the offer, which corresponded to his own valuation (BLANC, *Les artistes de mon temps*, p. 85).

12. LARROUMET, *Meissonier*, p. 127.
13. LELIEVRE, *Vivant-Denon*, 1942, p. 89.
14. GIGOUX, *Causeries sur les artistes de mon temps*, p. 88. Ingres' 'poverty' in Florence has been questioned by his more reliable biographers (cf. LAPAUZE, *Ingres*, I, p. 212) but in any case it was perfectly genuine in Rome between 1815 and 1818.
15. JOUIN, *Lettres inédites d'artistes français du XIXe siècle*, p. 168.
16. *Ibid.*, pp. 314–17.
17. COURTHION, *Autour de l'impressionisme*, N.E.F., 1964, p. 12.
18. Letter from Monet to Bazille August 8, 1969 in POULAIN, *Bazille et ses amis*, p. 157.
19. Pissarro's earnings are analysed by WHITE, *Canvases and Careers*, pp. 134–8.
20. DAYOT, *Les Vernet*, 1898, pp. 189–236.
21. VIRMAITRE, *Paris-Palette*, p. 210.
22. STRYIENSKI, *Landelle*, p. 103–4.

CHAPTER TEN

ENGRAVING AND OTHER SIDELINES

1. GIGOUX, *Causeries sur les artistes de mon temps*, pp. 184–6.
2. GONCOURT, *Manette Salomon*, p. 380.
3. BLANC, *Les artistes de mon temps*, p. 101 seq.
4. WELLISZ, *Jasinski*, Van Oest, 1934.
5. JOUIN, *Lettres inédites d'artistes français du XIXe siècle*, p. 194.
6. PLANET, *Souvenirs de travaux de peinture avec Monsieur Delacroix*, edited by Joubin, 1929, p. 107.
7. GERARD, *Correspondance de F. Gérard*, Lainé et Havard, 1867, p. 171.
8. MOREAU-NELATON, *Manet*, II, p. 51.
9. SAUNIER, *Auguste Lepère*, Le Garrec, 1934.
10. CHAMPFLEURY, *Les aventures de Mademoiselle Mariette*, 1856, p. 196.
11. VALMY-BAYSSE, *G. Doré*, M. Scheur, 1930, pp. 57–9.
12. *Le Courrier français*, February 16, 1902; LETHEVE, *Caricature et presse sous la IIIe République*, 1959, p. 49.
13. GONCOURT, *Journal*, January 5, 1893.
14. *GBA*, 1862, I, p. 293.
15. AMAURY-DUVAL, *L'atelier d'Ingres*, p. 161.
16. JULLIEN, *Fantin-Latour*, Laveur, 1909, p. 11 seq.; LOSTALOT, *Les copistes au Musée du Louvre* in *L'Illustration*, August 23, 1890; REFF, *Copyists in the Louvre* in *The Art Bulletin*, December 1964, pp. 552–8.
17. GONCOURT, *Manette Salomon*, p. 56.
18. LANOE, *Histoire de la peinture de paysage*, Nantes, 1903, p. 49.
19. Viel-Castel's reminiscences quoted by GUILLERME, *L'atelier du temps*, Hermann, 1964, p. 168.
20. BESSIS, *Les éleves de Delacroix* (unpublished dissertation for the Ecole du Louvre).
21. DELECLUZE, *L. David*, p. 284.
22. FIDIERE, *Chapu*, p. 51; FAURE-FREMIET, *Frémiet*, 1934, p. 27; MOREAU-VAUTHIER, *Gérôme*, p. 51.
23. *Paris-vivant*, 1858.
24. BANVILLE, *Mes souvenirs*, Charpentier, 1882, pp. 384–5; AMAURY-DUVAL *op. cit.*, p. 29.
25. *La Caricature*, March 5, 1843.

CHAPTER ELEVEN
ARTISTS AND SOCIETY

1. On the artistic Bohemia see: DELVAU, H. *Murger et la Bohème*, 1866; GOU DEAU *Dix ans de bohème*, 1888; WARNOD, *La vraie Bohème de Henri Murger*, P. Dupont, 1947.

2. GAUTIER, *Histoire du romantisme*, 1874, pp. 32 and 219; MAIGRON, *Le romantisme et la mode*, Champion, 1911. For Pradier see: DU CAMP, *Souvenirs littéraires*, I, 3rd edition, 1906, p. 246.

3. SILVESTRE, *Histoire des artistes vivants*, p. 305. For the sculptor Dumont's difficulties in gaining admittance to the Institut on account of his beard see: VATTIER, *Augustin Dumont*, p. 83.

4. Letter from Duranty to Zola quoted in REWALD, *Histoire de l'impressionisme*, p. 256; BLANCHE, *Propos de peintre*, 1919, p. 142.

5. *GBA*, 1869, I, p. 512 seq.; *JAL, Les soirées d'artistes* in *Le livre des 101*, I, 1831.

6. CHESNEAU, *Peintres et statuaires romantiques*, p. 65.

7. GONCOURT, *Gavarni*, 1873, pp. 169-70.

8. On the cafés: DELVAU, *Histoire anecdotique des cafés et cabarets de Paris*, 1862; VIRMAITRE, *Paris-Palette*, pp. 54-7; CHAMPFLEURY, *Souvenirs et portraits de jeunesse*, p. 186; RIVIERE, *Renoir et ses amis*, pp. 28-32.

9. For the Café Guerbois: JULLIEN, *Fantin-Latour*, Laveur, 1909, p. 158; CLEMENT-JANIN, *La curieuse vie de Marcellin Desboutin*, p. 90; SILVESTRE, *Au pays des souvenirs*, 1892, Chapter 13.

10. JOURDAIN, *L'atelier Chantorel*, pp. 118-19.

11. FIDIERE, *Chapu*, pp. 63-4; SILVESTRE, *Histoire des artistes vivants*, p. 196; CHENNE-VIERES, *Lettre sur l'art français en 1850*, 1851.

12. On Fradelle: BERGERET, *Lettre d'un artiste sur l'état des arts en France*, 1848, quoted by NAEF. 'Parmi les gravures de la collection Ingres, in *Bulletin Musée Ingres*, December 1965. For the Société Taylor, *Bulletin de l'Alliance des arts*, pp. 225-6; MAINGOT, *Le Baron Taylor*, 1963, p. 86 seq.

13. *L'Avenir national*, May 5, 1873.

14. VAN GOGH, *Lettres à Theo*. p. 194; ANGRAND, *Naissance des artistes indépendents (1884)*, Debresse, 1965.

15. CHAMPFLEURY, *Souvenirs et portraits de jeunesse*, p. 183.

16. MOREAU-NELATON, *Corot*, II, p. 163.

17. *Dubosc modèle*, p. 146.

18. DAUDET, *Les femmes d'artistes*, 1874, p. 5.

19. On the National Guard: AMAURY-DUVAL, *L'atelier d'Ingres*, p. 159; *Journal des Artistes*, 1840, II, pp. 71-3; TEXIER, *Tableau de Paris*, I, Paulin et Lechevallier, 1852, p. 189.

20. SILVESTRE, *Histoire des artistes vivants*, p. 7.

21. REYBAUD, J. *Paturot à la recherche de la meilleure des républiques*, 1848, p. 48.

22. SOUBIES, *Les membres de l'Académie des Beaux-Arts*, II, p. 171.

23. *Bulletin des Arts* (under the heading *République des lettres et des arts*), March 10, 1848, p. 305.

24. HERBERT, *The Artist and Social Reform*, Yale University Press, 1961.

25. VACHON, *Pour devenir un artiste*, p. 259.

26. MOREAU-NELATON, *Daubigny*, p. 113.

27. Quoted by BENOIT, *L'art français sous la Revolution et l'Empire*, p. 251.

28. *Victor Hugo raconté par ceux qui l'ont vu*, 1931, Chapter XLIX.

29. CLEMENT-JANIN, *La curieuse vie de Marcellin Desboutin*, p. 157.

30. Letter by Courbet quoted by D'IDEVILLE, *Courbet 1878*, pp. 35-6.

31. REWALD, *Histoire de l'impressionisme*, p. 255; CHAMPFLEURY, *Souvenirs et portraits de jeunesse*, p. 229.
32. JOUIN, *Lettres inédites d'artistes français du XIXe siècle*, pp. 45 and 90.
33. *L'Artiste*, 1841, VII, p. 277.
34. DELABORDE, *L'Académie des Beaux-Arts*, 1891.

CHAPTER TWELVE

FIN DE SIECLE

1. BERTALL, *La comédie de notre temps*, I, 1873, pp. 480-3.
2. JOURDAIN, *L'atelier Chantorel*, p. 74.
3. DU SEIGNEUR, *Paris, voici Paris*, 1889, pp. 212-13.
4. *L'Artiste*, 1882, I, p. 548.
5. GONCOURT, *Journal*, May 1, 1882.
6. *Le Courrier français*, June 2, 1883.
7. For women artists at the end of the nineteenth century see: UZANNE, *La femme à Paris*, 1894, Chapter II; LA FAYE, *La Princesse Mathilde*, 1929.
8. FLAMENT, *Le Bal du Pré-Catelan*, 1946, p. 155.
9. LETHEVE, *Un personnage typique de la fin du XIXe siècle : l'esthète* in GBA, May 1965; JULLIAN, *R. de Montesquiou*, Perrin, 1965.
10. COLETTE, *Mes apprentissages*, p. 195.
11. LORRAIN, *Pelléastres*, 1903, pp. 75-6; and the same author's *M. de Phocas*, 1901, pp. 124-5.
12. MIRBEAU, *Des artistes*, First series. Flammarion, 1922, p. 17 seq.
13. LETHEVE, *Les Salons de la Rose-Croix* in GBA, December 1960.
14. Van Gogh to E. Bernard, quoted by REWALD, *Leso st-impressionisme*, p. 123.
15. BALDICK, *La vie de J.-K. Huysmans*, 1958, p. 320.
16. On Montmartre and the legends surrounding it see: EMILE-BAYARD, *Montmartre hier et aujord'hui*, 1925; 'Montmartre' in *Le Crapouillot*, July 1959.
17. For the cabarets: *Revue encyclopédique*, 1896, pp. 251-5.
18. On the ball given by Alexandre Dumas: *L'Artiste*, 1833, V, p. 120; DUMAS, *Mes mémoires*, Chapter XXXVIII.
19. MONTORGUEIL, *Paris-dansant*, 1898, p. 121 seq.; ROQUES, in *Le Courrier français*, February 12, March 19, June 25 and July 9, 1893.
20. EMILE-BAYARD, *op. cit.*, pp. 90-1 and 288.
21. VERLAINE, *Les poètes maudits*, Vanier, 1884.

INDEX OF PROPER NAMES